ALDOUS HUXLEY:
SATIRE AND STRUCTURE

ALDOUS HUXLEY

Satire and Structure

By

JEROME MECKIER

BARNES & NOBLE, Inc.
NEW YORK
PUBLISHERS & BOOKSELLERS SINCE 1873

79-8451

823.912

c1

Published by
Chatto & Windus Ltd
40 William IV Street
London W.C.2.

Clarke, Irwin & Co. Ltd
Toronto

c - 1969.

First published in the United States, 1971
by Barnes & Noble, Inc.

ISBN 389 01031 6

Printed in Great Britain

Contents

The Novels of Aldous Huxley

Crome Yellow 1921

Antic Hay 1923

Those Barren Leaves 1925

Point Counter Point 1928

Brave New World 1932

Eyeless in Gaza 1936

After Many a Summer Dies the Swan 1939

Time Must Have a Stop 1944

Ape and Essence 1949

The Genius and the Goddess 1955

Island 1962

Preface

'No other writer of our time,' Edwin Muir once wrote, 'has built up a serious reputation so rapidly and so surely; compared with his rise to acceptance that of Mr. Lawrence or Mr. Eliot has been gradual, almost painful.'[1] Forty-three years later, the subject of this eulogy would be difficult to identify if the remarks were quoted anywhere but in a preface to a study of Aldous Huxley. Huxley did receive the Academy of Arts and Letters Award of Merit for the Novel in 1959, but the previous year, James Sutherland forecast that although Huxley's novels were 'still being reprinted, read, and enjoyed', they had little chance to 'survive the century'.[2]

If one talks with intellectuals who began their romance with serious literature in the mid-1920s, they will recall eagerly reading Huxley's poems, novels, and essays as they appeared. The Gospel according to Huxley generated as much excitement among twentieth-century intellectuals[3] as each new instalment of Dickens' *Old Curiosity Shop* did with the general reading public a century before. Within a decade after Huxley's first books arrived, Grant Overton remarked that 'the first (London) editions of all of them are held at a premium by dealers and collectors'. The asking price per volume was ten to fifteen pounds in London and as high as seventy-five dollars in New York.[4] Yet in 1960, when he revised *The Novel and the Modern World* (1939), David Daiches deleted his sharply critical essay on Huxley. The chapter was removed because to Daiches, Huxley no longer seemed relevant to the genre or the area covered by his title.

Of all the unfortunate praise that can descend on a novelist, two types seem to stand out: the insistence that he personifies his times, and the reception of his works as a liberating influence. Almost every critical notice about Huxley contained one or the other (sometimes both) of these statements. For Muir in 1926, Huxley is 'so completely of the period' that he can 'say unerringly what nine out of ten literate people wish to be said'. In the memorial volume dedicated to Huxley, Kenneth Clark remembers that 'When one was young one read his books for their bright conversations, in which people said things that would have shocked one's school-masters. They were liberating books.'[5] Clark's comments and those of Stephen Spender in the same volume are a curious echo of judgments that sounded more like praise in 1932. A history of the English novel published in that year concluded that no young writer was 'more representative of his generation' than Huxley.[6]

In the 1920s, critics referred to Huxley as though he, and not the husband of Molly D'Exergillod in *Point Counter Point* (VII), 'had won the distinction' of being mentioned in Proust's *Sodome and Gomorrhe*. Carl and Mark Van Doren called him a 'brilliant, perverse young man'.[7] Critics spoke of his 'engaging licentiousness of intellect', of the diabolical operations of his mind. Whether referring to an individual work (the 'genial blasphemy' of *Antic Hay*) or to Huxley's overall tone ('that accent, half scientific, half obscene'), Huxley's advocates attributed to him two distinctions he could not possibly have kept. He could not always be the bright young modern, the bad boy of literature. Nor could he continue as the mocking spokesman of the generation he supposedly liberated once he began stipulating the direction society should take. In an ambiguous letter to Huxley following the publication of *Point Counter Point*, Lawrence wrote: 'You've shown the truth, perhaps the last truth, about you and your generation . . .' In fact, Lawrence went on, 'it would take ten times the courage to write *P. Counter P.* that it took me to write *Lady C.*'[8] Even if Lawrence was really more embarrassed than pleased by the book, especially with his own appearance in it as Mark Rampion, he resorts to the two tributes of representativeness and outspokenness which virtually constitute a critical epitaph.

By stereotyping Huxley as the voice of the 1920s, critics put themselves in an awkward position to evaluate the future endeavours of a writer who was to produce continuously until 1962. Though the false impression that Huxley did all his writing between 1920 and 1930 can still be gathered from some critics, many of Huxley's subsequent interpreters took one or the other of two equally unsatisfactory courses: they either pointed out what they considered sharp changes in Huxley and bemoaned them, or they adopted a pose similar to the early Huxley's and began to debunk his accomplishments and the popularity he had attained. An occasional critic, such as M. M. Kirkwood, hailed, in 1937, Huxley's move from a so-called scientific scepticism to a new faith.[9] But in general, where Huxley was formerly hailed as an artist while often charged with immorality and irreverence, he was now blamed for permitting his moral vision to interfere with his art. William York Tindall concluded, in 1942, that Huxley's piety hurts his fiction[10] and though there was much perceptiveness in this remark, it soon became an excuse for not reading the later works.

The debunking began in the late 1930s with the work of David Daiches. In the *New Republic* as well as in *The Novel and the Modern World* (1939), Daiches reviewed Huxley's novels and questioned his right to a place among the major novelists of the century. Most of all, he challenged the validity of Huxley's technical innovations, referring to the 'essential inorganic quality of his technical apparatus'.[11] He suggested, and numerous critics followed suit, that the real Huxley should be sought in the essays rather than the novels. The uncritically accepted repetitions of Daiches' judgments are too numerous to catalogue. Probably the extreme example of the trend started by Daiches is R. C. Bald's condemnation of Huxley as a borrower or plagiarist. Though he begins midly by rebuking Huxley for his 'too acute literary awareness', he soon has Huxley alluding not only to the words and phrases of other writers, but to their characters and techniques in an indebtedness that Bald feels goes beyond decency.[12] The Huxley who in the 1920s seemed a literary revolutionary and a subverter of values is labelled almost totally derivative in the 1950s. Many of the more recent summations of Huxley's work, such as Sutherland's, are merely extensions of the reaction to the earlier stereotyped praise, a reaction that began as early as 1939 and that has largely repeated itself ever since.

Huxley has recently found several admirers willing to examine his work at book length. But John Atkins, in *Aldous Huxley: A Literary Study* (London, 1956), is primarily concerned with Huxley's ideas and chiefly confronts Huxley's non-fiction prose. As an oriental, Sisirkumar Ghose, although he discusses the novels intelligently in *Aldous Huxley: A Cynical Salvationist* (London, 1962), focuses too strongly on Huxley's religious evolution and his adoption of the Vedantic philosophy. Finally, Alexander Henderson, though full of warmth towards his subject in *Aldous Huxley* (New York, 1964), seems to follow no particular approach while still falling short of a total picture. The date of this book is deceptive and its scope is further limited by the fact that, despite its reissue in the year after Huxley's death, it was first written in 1935.

In the following pages, two general principles have been observed. First, it is of little benefit to Huxley to base the case for him on his appeal to his original audience of the 1920s and 30s. To point out the innumerable ways in which any Huxley novel is a virtual index to the ideas, trends, and fads of the years surrounding its composition might make fascinating reading but would inevitably reduce Huxley to literary history, perhaps even to sociology. And second, none of Huxley's many interrelated aspects can be neglected. All must receive some attention within a framework that only a treatment of Huxley primarily as a novelist can provide.

Admittedly, *Point Counter Point*, with its elaborate structure that is a tribute in words to the musical compositions of Bach and Beethoven, appeared one year after the centenary of Beethoven's death had been celebrated all over Europe. Also undeniable is the fact that *Point Counter Point* critically examines marriage in all its variant forms and does so in the very year when the rising divorce rate of the 1920s reached its graphical peak. But surely it is the elaborate structure itself that the well-meaning critic must examine. And surely Huxley's phenomenal sensitivity to his times, a sensitivity that gained him his first hearing, must not blind one to the relevance his novels have for any decade of the present century one cares to specify. Thus the following chapters seek to isolate Huxley's major satiric themes and to insist on their perennial nature. The governing purpose is to trace the relationship between these themes and the novelistic formats Huxley uses to present them. At his finest, Huxley manages to fuse satire and structure so that the form (or design) of his novels becomes part of his attack on modern life and exposes his characters as thoroughly as he does himself when talking about them directly. It is the evolution of this fusion of satire and structure and an examination of the reasons behind Huxley's weakening ability to maintain it in some of the later novels that serve as the backbone of this book.

Throughout the following pages, the focus is on Huxley's eleven novels in the hope of rehabilitating his reputation as a novelist. The novel is clearly the common denominator in the Huxley canon from 1921 through 1962. And it is in the novels, such as *Point Counter Point, Brave New World, Eyeless in Gaza*, and *Island*, that Huxley himself attempts to bring together and resolve his artistic, social, and moral concerns. As the outline that follows illustrates, a discussion of Huxley's novels requires an examination of nearly all of this author's many sides. It requires the multiplicity Huxley himself recommended as a prerequisite for any grasp of the unity upon which life's surface diversity (and an author's) may actually be based.

The period from 1921 to 1936, from *Crome Yellow* through *Antic*

Hay, Those Barren Leaves, Point Counter Point, and *Brave New World* to *Eyeless in Gaza,* can be described as Huxley's great decade and a half of increasing mastery of the novel. While most of the first five chapters centre on this period, they never do so without references to the later works which themselves provide the basis for major portions of the last two chapters. The first two introductory chapters discuss Huxley's main satiric themes and the structure he devises to embody them. Huxley's satire against egoistic and eccentric characters, his stress on wholeness and completeness as antidotes to the fragmentary, compartmentalized life his characters lead, must be measured against the discussion-novel-of-ideas he invents as his satiric vehicle. These chapters also offer a brief sketch of Huxley's development, in the course of which he comes, at times knowingly, to personify many of his former targets. The brash young novelist who laughs at Mr. Barbacue-Smith's *Pipe-Lines to the Infinite* (*Crome Yellow,* VI) later attends Swami Prabhavananda's readings from Hindu Scripture[13] and takes mescalin in the hope of having a mystical experience.

The third chapter examines Huxley's first three novels as a natural trilogy, a reworking of similar themes in terms of recurrent characters, and thus a fitting prelude for counterpoint in Huxley's masterpiece, *Point Counter Point.* Because Huxley, in *Point Counter Point,* abandons the mystical tendencies of Calamy in *Those Barren Leaves* for the full life advocated by Mark Rampion, who is based on D. H. Lawrence, the fourth chapter contains a lengthy discussion of the relationship between Huxley and Lawrence. It provides a new slant on this famous friendship-antagonism by attempting to uncover the full extent to which Lawrence influenced Huxley as well as the reasons behind their eventual disenchantment with one another. The role of Lawrence as a satiric target in Huxley's novels also receives some attention. In his efforts to come to terms with Lawrence the person and the artist, much of Huxley's subsequent career is foreshadowed. It is possible to argue that Lawrence was the key event in Huxley's life, although the period of strong Lawrencian influence (1926–1932) forms no more than an interlude in Huxley's literary career of nearly half a century.

The remaining chapters deal with Huxley's structural technique and his growing utopian concerns. The fifth chapter is written in defence of counterpoint. It tries to show that Huxley's musical metaphor is indeed appropriate to the novel's satiric themes and overall design. Part of the purpose of these essays is to establish counterpoint as one of Huxley's perennial interests and as possibly the ultimate factor in his success as a novelist. As a serious literary craftsman, Huxley has done something new and original with the novel and one cannot explain this away by pointing to his antecedents. In addition to examining the use of counterpoint in *Eyeless in Gaza* and *Time Must Have a Stop*, the sixth chapter suggests several ways in which Huxley's eventual religious beliefs are clearly foreshadowed in many of his earlier artistic and technical concerns. The chapter also returns to the question of viewpoint originally broached in the introductory essays and stresses that Huxley's obsession with sight, viewpoint, and epiphanic vision is always as much moral as it is technical. Though Huxley shares the interest of Virginia Woolf and James Joyce in subjective views of reality, he is more fascinated by the satiric possibilities inherent in contrasts between a character's personal outlook and a more objective view.

The concluding chapter treats Huxley's three utopias (*Brave New World*, *Ape and Essence*, and *Island*) as a final exercise in counterpoint with *Island* as the correct and Vedantic answer to the other two. Huxley's last novel is also analysed as his endeavour to achieve a final synthesis, to create a life-style in which science, sex, and religion – which rarely co-exist in Huxley's work – each have an undisputed place. At one point, this book suggests that Huxley was a Lawrencian life-worshipper whose mistrust of the physical was almost as great as his suspicions of art. At another, it contends that Huxley is a student of mysticism rather than an experienced mystic. But the Huxley canon is always seen as a unified whole and the fact that Huxley always recommended what he wished himself and his readers to attain is never in doubt.

Though not one of the essays that follow will argue that Huxley's interest in mysticism improves his novels, the fact that the often-mentioned fusion of Huxley the essayist-moralist and Huxley the novelist is fairly complete only in Huxley's final novel is worth noting. The essayist-moralist in Huxley was not an Edward Hyde who gained control over Dr. Jekyll the novelist in order to make him produce essays disguised as novels. Even if some of the later novels do not repay re-reading, *Time Must Have a Stop* (1944) is a considerable accomplishment. A major purpose of this book on Huxley's novels is to suggest that he was always engaged in a conscious struggle with the form of the novel. He was continually trying to stretch its confines, to make it do new things: either to control and render the formlessness of English society in the 1920s, to undercut Wellsian scientific utopias, or to communicate the essentially non-dramatic and incommunicable religious experiences that mystics claim to have had.

An intellectual with a mistrust of mind and language, an artist who prefers unpopular truth to artistic effect and whose search in art for standards to live by is accompanied by a mistrust of art, a life-worshipper who feels the physical will always let you down, Huxley is an alleged mystic who is always clear and rational, and a knowledgeable scientist who has written the century's severest critiques of science. He supports individuality but opposes egotistic individualism and eccentricity; he advocates centricity but is careful to distinguish this from regimentation. He responds with fervour to *The Cloud of Unknowing* and with gusto to Felix the Cat, whom he once termed his 'favourite dramatic hero'. Although hampered by temperamental and artistic limitations, Huxley often seems the personification of the multiplicity sought by Philip Quarles.

With the possible exception of Evelyn Waugh, Huxley is the great prose satirist of the century. Among the re-readable passages from his novels, surely the saga of Hercules the Dwarf in *Crome Yellow* (XIII) is unforgettable for its blend of satire and pathos. Nor should one overlook Mr. Scogan in his disguise as a fortune teller (XXVII). He predicts to an attractive customer that next Sunday if she lingers by a certain stile along the footpath she will meet and make love with a fascinating man named, of course, Scogan. In *Those Barren Leaves*, the naive Irene offers the observation that contraception has rendered chastity superfluous (Part 3, IV). The same novel also contains pointed criticism of Dickens and two fine spoofs of Dickensian situations: the boarding house scenes at Miss Carruthers's (Part 2, III) and the wooing of Miss Elver by the designing Mr. Cardan (Part 3, VIII).[14]

In the bizarre world of Huxley's novels, Swiftian ironies and Dickensian zaniness alternate with more terrifying prospects. There are Neo-Pavlovian Conditioning Rooms in *Brave New World*, but these are balanced against the confrontation scene in which the Director of Hatcheries learns he has a natural son by a wife who is an old-fashioned mother (X). In *Point Counter Point*, Lord Edward can be telephoned in the lab by his crippled brother who insists he has 'just this moment discovered a most extraordinary mathematical proof of the existence of God . . .' (XI). Or consider the scene in *Ape and Essence* where the Arch-Vicar offers the already outraged Dr.

Poole a pair of binoculars so he can see the annual orgy more clearly.[15]

These scenes, and others much more savage in tone, rest on Huxley's conviction of the importance of satire for the twentieth-century novel. Though capable of skilful use of such modern techniques as stream of consciousness – especially in *Eyeless in Gaza* (IV) where he keeps switching from the mind of the newly widowed John Beavis to the reflections of James and Young Anthony – Huxley's primary concern is with satire. Even the essay-like *Island* can be seen as an attempt to re-emphasize the satire *Brave New World* directed against the society of Mustapha Mond. Pete Boone, in *After Many a Summer Dies the Swan*, underlines Huxley's main concern when he recalls Mr. Propter's opinion of satire. 'A good satire,' Propter stated, 'was more deeply truthful and, of course, much more profitable than a good tragedy.' And yet, Propter continued, few satires have been effective 'because so few satirists were prepared to carry their criticism of human values far enough' (Part 2, V). Huxley, however, never hesitates. He questions twentieth-century ideas of the individual and national ego, of sexual ethics, and of religious practice and belief. In both *Point Counter Point* and *Eyeless in Gaza*, as chapters six and seven will show, the structural technique (the arrangement of chapters and the method by which discussion scenes proceed) is itself part of Huxley's satire against his characters.

If Beavis, in *Eyeless in Gaza* (XXXVI), dreams of travelling in the East, Huxley says Anthony 'did a slight Joseph Conrad in the East Indies'. *Beyond the Mexique Bay*, a travel book, compares the officials at Copan to the Second Murderers of Elizabethan plays. An essay in *Texts and Pretexts* coins the phrase 'intellectual Cupid', an accurate epithet for Philip Quarles and, occasionally, for Huxley himself. Of Philip's father Huxley observes in *Point Counter Point*: 'Brought up in an epoch when ladies apparently rolled along on wheels, Mr. Quarles was peculiarly susceptible to calves' (XX). The susceptibility is not only comic, but Huxley's image for nineteenth-century feminine motion seems particularly accurate. These are only a few examples of the amusing, often cutting phrases Huxley's wit continually supplies, but which an analysis of his perennial themes and structural concerns must often pass by.

Huxley's vocabulary, in accord with Philip Quarles' advice to the novelist in *Point Counter Point* (XIX), draws to its advantage on many disciplines, scientific as well as humanistic. At times, especially in a novel that satirizes Dickens, the style strives towards Dickensian figures. The doctor in *Those Barren Leaves* sweats so heavily he looks 'as though he had been buttered' (Part 2, VI). In the same novel, the Italian grocer that Cardan does business with emits 'a blast of garlicky breath that smelt so powerfully like acetylene that one was tempted to put a match to his mouth in the hope that he would break out into a bright, white flame' (Part 3, V). Frequently it is an encyclopedic style, one in which a single sentence may seem the product of weeks of research: the organ that pipes in music to the women's changing room in *Brave New World* (XI) 'effortlessly passed from Gaspard Forster's low record on the very frontiers of musical tone to a trilled bat-note high above the highest C to which (in 1770, at the Ducal opera of Parma, and to the astonishment of Mozart) Lucrezia Ajugari, alone of all the singers in history, once piercingly gave utterance'. The purposely exaggerated erudition helps to emphasize the fact that the effortless but inhuman technology of brave new world society has rendered traditions and human achievements meaningless.

Huxley revitalizes Swiftian irony in the section of *Those Barren Leaves* dealing with Francis Chelifer (with which the first chapter of this book will begin) and in, among other places, those two modest proposals for the future, *Brave New World* and *Ape and Essence*. He also reactivates the Butlerian misquotation as Henry Wimbush, who cannot cope with other people, proclaims in *Crome Yellow* (XXVIII) that the 'proper study of mankind is books'. Huxley is repeatedly astonished at the ease with which his characters twist words and their meaning, thereby revealing the manifold distortions within their own minds and personal lives. The District Hatchery Commissioner spouts a parody of Browning's optimism and becomes a caricature of his society's scientific egotism when he declares, in *Brave New World*, 'Ford's in his fliver, all's right with the world' (III). Speaking in his own voice in *Tomorrow and Tomorrow and Tomorrow*, Huxley, altering Pope for satiric purposes, observes that 'hope springs eternal in the male breast in regard to the female breast'. In *Those Barren Leaves*, he notes, in a more Miltonic vein, that on the 270 thousand pounds of Mrs. Aldwinkle's income, 'the sun never set. People worked; Mrs. Aldwinkle led the higher life. She for art only, they – albeit unconscious of the privilege – for art in her' (Part 1, VI).

In *Cakes and Ale* (1930), William Ashenden, who is Somerset Maugham himself, wonders 'who could possibly succeed Edward Driffield (Thomas Hardy) as the Grand Old Man of English Letters' (XI). To which Alroy Kear, a novelist, replies: 'Of course there's

Aldous; he's a good deal younger than me, but he's not very strong and I don't believe he takes great care of himself.' At age thirty-six and when author of only four novels, Huxley had achieved such tremendous early popularity that he could be considered, even if half-jokingly, one of Hardy's heirs apparent. The neglect Huxley subsequently suffered becomes quite clear when one realizes that he lived for thirty-three years beyond Kear's statement and never came an inch closer to the position Maugham casually marked out for him in 1930. Yet whatever else the following pages may accomplish, this book on Huxley should show that he would never have made a satisfactory Grand Old Man. In *Island* (1962) as in *Crome Yellow* (1921), he remained intellectually young and adventurous. Huxley's thought deepens, the syntheses attempted become more complex, but an exploratory openness to life is always evident.

It is thus easy enough to fabricate a great tradition without Huxley (indeed without almost everybody); but a complete picture of twentieth-century British fiction, a discussion of the novel and the contemporary world, is impossible without him. This is, of course, more of a contention than a literary judgment, but the succeeding pages may provide some of the needed support.

Among the many people who were kind to me while I thought about or actually wrote this book, the first place in time, if not also in importance, belongs to Dr. Terence F. Dewsnap, now at Bard College. As my advisor at Le Moyne College in 1963, he spurred my interest in Huxley and in satire so that my evaluation of Huxley goes back through my article – 'Aldous Huxley: Satire and Structure' in *Wisconsin Studies in Contemporary Literature*, VII (Autumn, 1966), 284–294 – to the essay I wrote under Dr. Dewsnap's direction.

I would also like to thank Dr. Monroe Engel and Dr. Reuben Brower, both of Harvard University, for reading my manuscript chapter by chapter as I was writing it. Dr. Engel's critical vigilance, especially in the chapter on Huxley and Lawrence, was more than I had a right to expect. I must also say a word of thanks to Master Alwin Pappenheimer of Harvard's Dunster House for accepting me as resident tutor in English. It was while filling this appointment (1965–67), and with the encouragement of the other tutors (Philip Weinstein, Maurice de Grasse Ford, Richard Stevenson, and Lee Huebner) that I wrote the major portion of this book.

Also, a word of thanks to Robert Kern and Paul Green, teaching fellows at Harvard, for reading parts of the manuscript and allowing me to practice my ideas in front of them; and to my colleagues at the University of Massachusetts, particularly Dr. Everett Emerson, Dr. Robert Keefe, Dr. Thomas Lombardi, and Dr. Ernest Hofer; and one final word of gratitude to Mr. C. Day Lewis of Chatto and Windus for his invaluable editorial assistance.

CHAPTER I

Satire

I. ECCENTRICITY AND PHARAOH'S DREAM

The unique existence led by Francis Chelifer in *Those Barren Leaves* (1925)[1] best illustrates the extent to which Aldous Huxley satirizes the majority of his characters for being escapists and eccentrics. The section entitled 'The Autobiography of Francis Chelifer' reveals that the young poet has abandoned verse to edit *The Rabbit Fanciers' Gazette* with which was incorporated *The Mouse Breeders' Record*. Avoiding the house he was born in lest it bind his days each to each, Chelifer lives in an unsavoury place called Gog's Court and praises the unintelligent babbling of his fellow boarders at Miss Carruthers's. On the surface, Chelifer resembles the eccentrics who abound in Huxley's novels. He is apparently like Henry Wimbush in *Crome Yellow* (1921), an amateur historian who, in writing the history of his ancestors, has had to devote himself to such things as research on lavatory sanitation in early Renaissance England. Yet Chelifer's eccentricity is conscious. After the war, he sought a job 'at the heart' of modern life, but declined his college's offer of a fellowship because of the position's 'illusory nature'. In Gog's Court, he contends, he inhabits 'the navel of reality'.

Chelifer has seen, as did Huxley, the breakup of communal society into a collection of tangential egoists each of whom inhabits his own private world. This breakup is such an actuality for Chelifer that to live anywhere except among eccentrics and as an eccentric would constitute escapism. Through Chelifer, Huxley shows eccentricity and unreality so firmly established that the artist can only deal with life by becoming unreal himself. Chelifer insists that normality, centricity, and all who speak of such things

> are the odd exceptions, they are irrelevant to the great reality, they are lies like the ideal of love, like dreams of the future, like belief in justice. To live among their works is to live in a world of bright falsehoods, apart from the real world; it is to escape. Escape is cowardly; to be comforted by what is untrue or what is irrelevant to the world in which we live is stupid (Part 2, v).

Since the deepest of modern realities is stupidity and the centre of reality has slipped from heart to navel, the truly representative artist cultivates unawareness. Like Chelifer, he regards his talent as something antediluvian.

The world in which we live, Huxley contends, belongs to men such as Lord Edward Tantamount and Sidney Quarles, both in *Point Counter Point* (1928). The first is one of Huxley's many caricatures of scientists and is trying to graft a tail onto the leg of a newt in order to demonstrate the natural harmony of life; the second is the eccentric father of the novelist Philip Quarles and wants to do the biggest book ever written on democracy. Whereas Tantamount puts his whole self into his absurd experiments and is grotesquely asexual, the only part of his daughter, Lucy, that has not welcomed repeated violation is her mind. Quarles, on the other hand, though intellectually a failure, enjoys cheap sexual escapades that his son, Philip, imprisoned in an analytical mind, badly needs. In their futile pursuits, both men, Sidney and Lord Edward, have become personifications of what, for Huxley, is a principal nemesis: one-pointedness. 'I have known men,' Huxley insisted in *Proper Studies* (1927), 'whose religion was homeopathy, others whose whole life was constellated round the faith that is anti-vivisection.'

The egoist-eccentric in Huxley's world is consistent to extremes. By reducing his own and the world's diversity to a single factor, he runs always on the same track. In *Point Counter Point* by contrast, Elinor Quarles sees in her son, little Phil, a symbol of life's complexities as she detects in him Philip (his father), Walter Bidlake (his uncle), and Mr. Quarles (his grandfather). 'Phil', she realizes, is just a name given 'to a collection, never long the same, of many individuals who were born, lived, and died within him, as the inhabitants of a country appear and disappear, but keep alive in their passage the identity of the nation to which they belong' (XIX). Unlike the eccentric, the individual, Huxley feels, must keep the many selves within him alive and allied.

The individual and society, Huxley suggests, should be analogous in that each can maintain an underlying unity despite a diversity of surface. Little Phil, Mr. Quarles, Walter Bidlake – each is composed of 'a colony of separate individuals'.[2] But if the intellect is permitted to distort and simplify its intuitions of the world, the individual destroys all the members of the colony of himself save one. He attains, through reduction of multiplicity, an artificial, crippling unity that traps him in a private world of his own making. Chelifer, taking his cue from an eccentric society, kills the part of himself that writes poetry, the parts that idealize love and dream of the future. What Wimbush does with his *History of Crome*, Chelifer does with *The Rabbit Fanciers' Gazette*: he narrows the world to proportions he feels he can manage. Chelifer's predecessor as editor, a Mr. Parfitt, becomes the perfect example of the one-pointed eccentric when he points out that no Mouse Breeder desired the war. If Kaiser William had devoted himself to avocations like ours, Parfitt argues, no danger of modern warfare would ever have arisen. (Part 2, II).

Each character in a Huxley novel is thus his own vested interest. Huxley asks us to 'Imagine Pharaoh's dream interpreted successively by Joseph, by the Egyptian soothsayers, by Freud, by Rivers, by Adler, by Jung, by Wohlgemuth',[3] or by Gumbril Sr. of *Antic Hay*, Mark Rampion of *Point Counter Point*, Mrs. Thwale of *Time Must Have a Stop*, and Col. Dipa of *Island*. Huxley realizes 'it would "say" a great many different things' to each of these people, depending on the preoccupation of each, but whether it means any or all of these things is the question every Huxley novel asks. Coleman, the diabolist, summarizes the peculiarly hellish, yet comic modern situation that all Huxley novels deal with when he realizes in *Antic Hay* (1923) that walking through London puts him in 'the midst of seven million distinct and separate individuals, each with distinct and separate lives and all completely indifferent to our existence' (v).

Coleman's observations recall the satiric parable of Hercules the Dwarf that appeared in *Crome Yellow*, Huxley's first novel (XIII). Only three feet, four inches tall – a height he attained by his fifteenth year – Hercules suffers humiliation when the first woman he asks to marry him picks him up and shakes him for his impertinence. Unable to cope with reality, Hercules is forced to 'abandon all ambitions in the great world ... to retire absolutely from it, and to create, as it were, at Crome a private world of his own, in which all should be proportionable to himself'. He marries a dwarf-sized wife named Filomena, lives in a dwarf-sized house, and hires no servant more than four feet tall. In this world built to his own dimensions, he becomes increasingly fond of his limitations and even writes verses exalting the small and condemning height as abnormality. A sample poem refers to 'obscene giants' who once trod the earth before 'Art grew great as Humankind grew small'. Hercules egotistically consecrates himself one of 'The rare precursors of the nobler breed'.

His hopes of peopling the world with persons his own size collapse when Filomena gives birth to a normal son. As a youth, Hercules had been stretched on the rack in an attempt to make him conform to his parents' notion of desirable stature. Now, at eighteen months, his son 'was almost as tall as their smallest jockey, who was a man of thirty-six'. When the son returns from the Grand Tour with friends his own size, the youths make Simon the butler dance a jig on the table top while pelting him with walnuts. A similar fate befalls Gulliver in chapter two of his 'Voyage to Brobdingnag'. After Hercules overhears his son promise to stage 'a concerted ballet of the whole household', he joins his wife upstairs and together they commit suicide. As he slices open his veins and allows the blood to flow into the warm water of his tub, Hercules personifies the futility of eccentric escapism.

The story of Hercules, which Henry Wimbush reads aloud from the history of Crome he is writing, does not lack pathos. As the dwarf's veins surrender their blood, 'the whole bath was tinged with pink'. His death comes quickly for there 'was not much blood in his small body'. But the note of satire predominates and Hercules furnishes the key to our interpretation of the countless eccentrics in Huxley's world. Their Herculean efforts to make life suit their expectations rarely succeed and they seldom perceive how vulnerable their reading of Pharaoh's dream becomes when endangered by other interpretations.

That the eccentrics in Huxley's world are countless is easily demonstrated. Crome's founder, a Sir Ferdinando, was 'preoccupied by only one thought – the proper placing of his privies. Sanitation was the one great interest in his life' (xi). However, the pun in the title of his treatise (*Certaine Priuy Counsels by One of Her Maiestie's Priuy Counsels*) does not rival for badness the one etymologically extracted from 'where is my pencil' by John Beavis in *Eyeless in Gaza* (1936), (xxx). Ferdinando puts his privies in the room nearest heaven and lines the walls with great books in order to counteract man's brutish aspects and emphasize his nobility. Beavis is a philologist writing 'an exhaustive essay on Jacobean slang'. As is true of many Dickens characters, everything Beavis writes or says is influenced by his occupation. He spends only part of his waking life on slang but it usurps a place in everything he does until the hobbyhorse rides the man.

Even relatively minor characters display remarkable eccentricities despite brief appearances. *After Many a Summer Dies the Swan* (1939) contains the legendary Charlie Habakkuk, 'who had first clearly formulated the policy of injecting sex appeal into death' (Part 2, III). A certain Tim in *Point Counter Point* sets fire to newspapers and lets the hot ashes fall on his wife's naked body (xxv). As 'her bit of war work', Mrs. Budge of *Crome Yellow* eats over 10,000 peaches in three years to supply the army with the needed pits (xxvii). Socially useless, morally perverse, and spiritually blind, Huxley's eccentrics choose the exclusiveness of self over anything expansive or inclusive. Huxley's satire aims at turning them back towards the demands of society. It tries to open their egos to a vision of wholeness on levels both personal and divine.

By reducing things to their own limitations, Huxley's characters suggest an orchestra gone haywire. In *Point Counter Point*, the instruments Huxley feels are meant for harmony emit cacophony:

> The parts [of the orchestra] live their separate lives; they touch, their paths cross, they combine for a moment to create a seemingly final and perfected harmony, only to break apart again. Each is always alone and separate and individual. 'I am I,' asserts the violin; 'the world revolves around me.' 'Round me,' calls the cello. 'Round me,' the flute insists. And all are equally right and equally wrong; and none of them will listen to the others (II).[4]

In the human fugue, Huxley realizes, there are millions of instruments and each member of the human orchestra is trying to establish himself and his private world as the *cantus firmus* or main melody of the universe by mere quantity of sound. Instead of striving for unity, each remains by choice separate and alone. The very name of Shearwater, the scientist in *Antic Hay*, accentuates his insistence that life revolves around kidney research: for him, life is sheer water.[5]

The quintet at a concert in *Antic Hay* amazes Gumbril Jr. with the oddness of its individual members and the beauty of their combined exertions (XII). The momentary coming together of diverse musicians playing different instruments fascinates both Huxley and Gumbril. The different instruments are a manifestation of the players' diverse temperaments while the music becomes the symbol for the type of harmony men should produce. The quintet's harmony amounts to a virtual Wordsworthian spot in time or moment of illumination for Gumbril Jr. In it the unity connecting incongruous individuals is suddenly revealed. For a brief Keatsian moment, the quintet's harmony transfigures each of its players into something that is larger and more impersonal than any one of them. Temporarily, the various readings of Pharaoh's dream are not conflicting but complementary. As chapters two and five will show, *Point Counter Point* is, in one sense, Gumbril Jr.'s spot in time writ large, an attempt to suggest some potential harmony underlying the cacophonous surface of modern life.

In short, Huxley agrees with William Hazlitt, as opposed to Henry Fielding, that 'the proper object of ridicule is egotism', not affectation. He wishes 'to persuade people to overcome their egotism and their personal cravings, in the interest either of a supernatural order, or of their own higher selves, or of society'.[6] As Huxley develops, his satire assails the eccentric for his incompleteness, then widens to attack the less than fully developed society, and finally narrows again to challenge the spiritual eccentric before offering a final plea and blueprint for a perfect society. From Henry Wimbush to *Brave New World* (1932) to Eustace Barnack and Jo Stoyte to Pala in *Island* – a pattern of development that will be examined in the next chapter.

The point to be emphasized here is that Huxley radically departs from the tradition of the English novel by satirizing his egotistic eccentrics while exploiting their comic appeal. His characters have their ancestry in the novels of Laurence Sterne, Charles Dickens, and Sir Walter Scott, but Huxley's attitude towards them is more severe than George Meredith's. The satirical come-uppance Micawber and perhaps even Pickwick occasionally receive in Dickens would be their constant fare in Huxley, for in one sense, all of Huxley's novels are a satire directed against Dickens and his apparent fondness for eccentric characters. The alleged vulgarity of Dickens' characters, Huxley seems to feel, involves not only their babyishness but also an egotism that is all-absorbing.[7] Consider Dickens' description of Tony Weller in *Pickwick Papers* and Huxley's account of Mr. Boldero in *Antic Hay*. Stephen Marcus calls attention to the elder Weller's 'power o' suction', his infantile desire to absorb food and drink.[8] Mr. Boldero has become a successful businessman because he can absorb other people: 'Other people's ideas, other people's knowledge – they were his food. He devoured them and they were at once his own. All that belonged to other people he annexed without a scruple or a second thought, quite naturally, as though it were already his own' (x). By immediately repeating other people's comments back to them, he enables his private world to swallow theirs. Huxley's egoists, like many of Dickens' comic characters, are still in the phase of childhood that assumes the world exists solely for their benefit. Even Wordsworth, who had to collide with trees to prove they were other than himself, knew it was necessary to grow up. Neither sublime nor introspective, the egotism of Huxley's characters rarely permits more than a minority of them to grow up as they grow old. Some, particularly Anthony Beavis of *Eyeless in Gaza* and Sebastian Barnack in *Time Must Have a Stop*, do overcome their egos and grow up as they grow old. But the majority, such as the Rev. Mr. Bodiham in *Crome Yellow* (IX), who sees every event as a confirmation of his theory that the Second Coming is imminent, are satiric versions of characters like Captain Cuttle (*Dombey and Son*), whose every thought and motion is controlled by his past experiences at sea.

The one-sided egotists whom Dickens laughed at, Huxley finds extremely dangerous. A world wherein they abound seems destined to end with socially planned eccentricity. In *Brave New World* (I–III), Bokanovsky's Process and the rooms for bottling and decanting combine to manufacture incompletes and eccentrics. By a process known as 'Podsnap's Technique',[9] forty-eight sets of identical twins can be produced more quickly than ever before from every artificially fertilized or 'bokanovskified' egg. The sets of twins from each egg all look exactly alike and thus experience some solidarity, but each caste is also convinced that its particular form of incompleteness, its particular degree of intellectual development and job capability, is better than any other. Deltas, for example, are conditioned to associate books with loud noises and flowers with electric shocks. Their book-less, flower-less lives will never concern them afterwards, for, as the District Hatchery Commissioner observes in a Butlerian reversal, 'what man has joined, nature is powerless to put asunder' (II). The attitudes of a self-satisfied Delta, of many Dickens characters, and of Huxley's eccentrics do not greatly differ.

Hypnopaedia (sleep-teaching) completes the Bokanovsky process. Pillow microphones teach Betas to prefer themselves to Alphas and Deltas, to those above them as well as those below: Deltas have to wear khaki and Epsilons cannot read or write. Alphas are cleverer but work harder than Betas. Thus nothing is pleasanter than life as a Beta. Mustapha Mond, the World Controller, and his assistants create an artificial social stability by making each automaton think his caste is the foremost, the centre of the universe. It is the realization on a national scale of the consistency Parfitt and other Huxley eccentrics attained individually by channelling their whole lives into one useless direction. Surely it is a fine irony that the 'perfect' society keeps all its citizens from flying off in different directions by assigning each member of an artificially created group the brand of socially useful eccentricity and egotistical superiority he is to practice. Those who will spend their lives upside down repairing the undersides of vehicles in space, for example, are conditioned to experience happiness only when standing on their heads. On the Fordian assembly line, a worker does the same task over and over again. Similarly, the eccentric excludes all activity that is not connected with his particular obsession. In *Brave New World*, each individual's place on the assembly line (or, if you prefer, his obsession) is built into him from birth. As Alpha, Beta, and Delta, violin, cello, and flute still refuse to listen to each other, but each is now so convinced it is the main melody and so conditioned to an occupation, that it works peacefully and feels no desire to prove it is paramount. The World-Controllers co-ordinate the efforts of each caste so that overall results are achieved even if Alpha, Beta, Delta and Epsilon never really meet. The national pastime of *Brave New World* is 'centrifugal Bumble-puppy', a game in which all the motion is presumably away from the centre. It is the game Huxley characters play every day of their lives.

In addition to the recurrent orchestra metaphor, Huxley continually envisions society as a collection of parallel lines that never cross. The widowed and essentially heartless Mrs. Viveash, in *Antic Hay*, summarizes the eccentric's position when she suggests managing life 'on the principle of the railways' through the use of 'Parallel tracks' (VI). If you meet someone, 'For a few miles you'd be running at the same speed. There'd be delightful conversation out of the windows.' And when you have said all you wish, 'away you'd go, forging ahead along the smooth polished rails'. Denis, the young poet in *Crome Yellow*, who resembles Huxley physically and, moreover, is extremely shy, sits next to Jenny at breakfast:

'I hope you slept well,' he said.
'Yes, isn't it lovely?' Jenny replied, giving two rapid little nods. 'But we had such awful thunderstorms last week.'
Parallel straight lines, Denis reflected, meet only at infinity. He might talk for ever of care-charmer sleep and she of meteorology till the end of time. Did one ever establish contact with anyone? We are all parallel straight lines. Jenny was only a little more parallel than most (IV).

Although one must remember that Jenny is considerably deaf, her deafness here takes on symbolic significance. This brief conversation seems typical of so many others in Huxley's so-called discussion novels, where so much gets said and so little is ever understood.

Denis himself becomes the target of Huxley's satire as he attempts once again to make contact. He tries to confide in Mary Bracegirdle, who is simultaneously trying to confide in him. He longs to explain the shock he experienced at finding in Jenny's notebook – Jenny whom he considered too deaf to have a viewpoint of her own – a vicious but true caricature of himself, while Mary wants to relate her disappointment over Ivor Lombard's departure the morning after sleeping with her:

> It was Denis who first broke the silence. 'The individual,' he began in a soft and sadly philosophical tone, 'is not a self-supporting universe. There are times when he comes into contact with other individuals, when he is forced to take cognisance of the existence of other universes besides himself.'
>
> He had contrived this highly abstract generalization as a preliminary to a personal confidence. It was the first gambit in a conversation that was to lead up to Jenny's caricatures.
>
> 'True,' said Mary; and, generalizing for herself, she added, 'When one individual comes into intimate contact with another, she – or he, of course, as the case may be – must almost inevitably receive or inflict suffering.
>
> 'One is apt,' Denis went on, 'to be so spellbound by the spectacle of one's own personality that one forgets that the spectacle presents itself to other people as well as to oneself.'
>
> Mary was not listening. 'The difficulty,' she said, 'makes itself acutely felt in matters of sex . . .'
>
> 'When I think of my own case,' said Denis, making a more decided move in the desired direction, 'I am amazed how ignorant I am of other people's mentality in general and, above all and in particular, of their opinions about myself . . .'
>
> '. . . This very morning, for example . . .' he began, but his confidences were cut short. The deep voice of the gong, tempered by distance to a pleasant booming, floated down from the house. It was lunch time (XXIV).

The speakers move on parallel lines, each talking only about himself. How clearly Denis, in speaking of the individual as a dependent

universe, has seen with Huxley's eyes and stated the theme this whole
first chapter has stressed. The ego's refusal to recognize other
universes besides its own – Denis puts it all perfectly. How clearly,
too, he states his own problem: ignorance of other people's opinions
and mentality. Unfortunately, he personifies this problem at the
very moment he is formulating it.

Both speakers move their arguments inward, towards the self.
When Mary generalizes, she does so 'for herself'. She presents the
problem she wishes to discuss in terms of 'she' and adds 'or he, of
course' as an afterthought. Both have come from unsuccessful encounters with other people, but ironically, their previous failures
cause the present disaster. Neither seems to have learned anything
since only the wordless gong means the same thing to them both.
Spellbound by the spectacle of their own personalities, each insists on
being the confider. Samuel Beckett inserts his characters in ash cans,
but Huxley, drawing on the novels of Thomas Love Peacock (1785–
1866), puts his, such as Denis and Mary, around a dinner table or in
a garden of some country house and shows their mutual isolation
just as effectively.

Of all the parallel lines that never meet, Lord Edward Tantamount's
case in *Point Counter Point* is unique in its compounding of irony and
satire and is only one of many possible examples of a recurrent Huxley
theme: the bungled epiphany. Affluent but bored, Edward stumbles
across a quotation from Claude Bernard in an 1887 magazine:

> The living being does not form an exception to the great natural harmony
> which makes things adapt themselves to one another; it breaks no
> concord; it is neither in contradiction to, nor struggling against, general
> cosmic forces. Far from that, it is a member of the universal concert of
> things, and the life of the animal, for example, is only a fragment of the
> total life of the universe (III).

Bernard's sentiments may be described as philosophy tinged with
mysticism. They contradict the conclusions Denis drew from his
abortive conversation with Jenny. In fact, they resemble Huxley's
views. Fragmentation, Huxley feels, should be seen as an appearance
and the aware person should be able to detect how innumerable parts
come together to form a concord, a total life. Tantamount hovers on
the verge of epiphany. 'It was all obvious, but to Lord Edward an
apocalypse. Suddenly and for the first time he realized his solidarity
with the world.'

Unfortunately, Lord Edward interprets the passage as straight science. He rephrases Bernard's thoughts into the following parody: 'What was one day a sheep's hind leg and leaves of spinach was the next part of the hand that wrote, the brain that conceived the slow movement of the Jupiter Symphony.' For Lord Edward, the possibility of brotherhood, of fusion with others, is apparent only in a digestive and biological way. The life of the animal nourishes the man whose corpse nourishes the soil whose crops nourish the animal. 'It comes down to chemistry in the end . . . all chemistry,' Edward concludes, taking a one-pointed approach. What he has learned is not incorrect, but it is only the smallest part of the total truth, the overall view. Tantamount mishandles his apocalypse because he cannot see it from more than one aspect. By reducing the many to one, he becomes living proof of Huxley's contention that science, because it brings unity out of multiplicity at all costs, is an eccentric discipline.

To Everard Webley, a sort of Sir Oswald Mosley, whose British Freemen support a policy vaguely defined as progress, Lord Edward exclaims: 'Progress, indeed! What do you propose to do about phosphorus for example.' Given Lord Edward's theory, phosphorus contained in dead bodies must be used to nurture the soil. 'Parallel straight lines never meet,' Webley replies (v), 'so I'll bid you goodnight.' The ludicrous history of Lord Edward may be summarized as the evolution of a parallel line. He would no doubt be glad to learn that in *Brave New World* his advice has been taken and that more than a kilo and a half of phosphorus is recovered from every adult corpse (v). But that does not change the fact of his eccentricity nor the irony contained in his name. His experience was tantamount to genuine illumination, but not quite.

Huxley's novels, then, are full of eccentrics whose egoism is continually satirized. But in the Chelifer section with which this chapter began, Huxley achieves an irony almost Swiftian in its convolutions, as reality and unreality, the normal and the deviant, the rule and the exception, all change places. The writing of poetry is a normal pursuit and hence to indulge in it in an eccentric society would be eccentric. Chelifer would like to be Shelley, but must be Keats instead. In Shelley's day, Chelifer writes, a man could forget the real nature of things by retreating to Italy, where Chelifer himself is vacationing. But to 'escape, whether in space or time, you must run a great deal further now,' Chelifer reflects, 'than there was any need to do a hundred years ago when Shelley boated on the Tyrrhenian and conjured up millennial visions' (Part 2, 1) in an actual world almost identical with the world of imagination.

Like Keats, Chelifer exercises negative capability, but his capacity for sympathetic projection leaves him worse off than Descartes. To annihilate himself and become all that others are means he must become, like those around him, an egoist and an eccentric. By identifying with others, as Huxley so often recommends and so few of his characters ever do, Chelifer becomes imprisoned in himself. His refusal to 'run away from the reality of human life' leads him to subscribe to the main tenet of the eccentric's code: 'Let each party stick to his own opinion. The most successful men are those who never admit the validity of other people's opinions, who even deny their existence' (Part 4, VII).[10]

Huxley's concern with escapism and eccentricity, and with the egotism he claims is their cause, is so pervasive that even a chapter cannot trace all its manifestations. Lord Edward re-enacts in 'real life' what Hercules did in the parable. The possible consequences of the courses taken by these two and others like them are spelled out in *Brave New World*. The disaster that awaits any individual, artist or otherwise, who tries to identify with his fellows in an eccentric society is exemplified by Chelifer. The predominance of one-pointed personages in Huxley's novels leaves him even more vulnerable than Dickens to the charge that he creates few three-dimensional figures. It is a character's one-pointedness, even more than the fact that he may be the mouthpiece for an idea, that makes him seem mechanical. Lord Edward reappears, but is no rounder than Miss Budge, who performs in only one paragraph. Nevertheless, eccentrics provide Huxley with most of his finest moments as a satirist and it is society's lack of three-dimensional figures that Huxley wishes to stress.

The images Huxley fashions for society (orchestra of discord but with a capacity for harmony, conflicting readings of Pharaoh's dream, parallel lines) have been examined at some length because in *Point Counter Point* Huxley attempts to demonstrate structurally what his first three novels state metaphorically. Indeed, these images illustrate in Huxley what, according to some critics, is perhaps characteristic of all modern literature, namely an anti-utopian, almost satirical strain in which the artist realizes his values only through images of their violation. In *Point Counter Point*, Huxley tries to dramatize his satire; one might almost say he attempts to make it visible. *Point*

Counter Point (1928), *Eyeless in Gaza* (1936), and, as a sort of after-glow, *Time Must Have a Stop* (1944) constitute the three novels in which thematic concerns and the structural technique of counter-point combine successfully for excellent satiric effect, an effect that the earliest novels anticipate and the late ones fail to equal. For the time being, however, it is sufficient to note that the world of the Huxley novels is without a centre and the characters in it fragmentary. Each flies off from the norm and sets up a world of his own. The odd-ball characters once confined in Swift's Academy of Lagado – men who devoted their whole lives to such projects as extracting sun rays from cucumbers – cover the earth.

Anyone who reads the few recollections of the 1920s currently available often suspects that Huxley's novels did not draw on that decade but instead created it. A. C. Ward, for example, summarizes what he calls the creed of the twenties: 'I believe in the uncertainty of all things. I believe that all things are possible, nothing incredible. I believe in myself as the closest manifestation – however irrational, imperfect, unsatisfactory – of reality . . .'[11] Most of Huxley's charac-ters have even fewer scruples about equating reality with their own viewpoint and pursuits. The remarks about uncertainty, as the next segment of this chapter will show, seem taken from Calamy's con-versation with Mr. Cardan in *Those Barren Leaves* (Part I, III). Most critics have noted how Huxley reflects the decade's mood of despair, its intellectual snobbery, its disrespect for elders, dogmas, and taboos, but the degree to which Huxley portrayed all these things, particu-larly the decade's exaggerated individualism, as a loss of freedom, as causes of isolation within the self, is rarely stressed sufficiently. Huxley may have helped liberate the members of his own generation, but, unlike them, he never seems, in retrospect, to have considered liberation an end in itself. Edward Sackville-West has recalled that the period of the 1920s lacked not ethics but religion, a realization Huxley was coming to during the period itself.

Though his chapter on Huxley and Waugh is thin and incomplete, Sean O'Faolain, in his prefatory remarks on the 'fervent twenties', contends that 'the men and women of literary talent who came to their majorities between 1920 and 1930 were no longer able to write or think or live as socially integrated citizens, but, rather, as more or less isolated receptivities'.[12] The observation may be intended to include all the writers O'Faolain discusses, but Huxley's novels, with their copious supply of eccentric artists (*Crome Yellow* presents the painters Gombauld and Tschuplitski, Wimbush the amateur historian, the poet Denis Stone, and Mr. Barbacue-Smith, the writer of pseudo-religious inspirational prose), seem the basis for O'Faolain's remark rather than one of its targets. The failings of the society of the decade are evident in the self-enclosed, eccentric artists who make Huxley's early novels the *locus classicus* for the 'modern temper', a temper that Frank Swinnerton decides makes the individual 'impatient, imperious, little tolerant of other methods and other sorrows'.[13]

Alan Pryce-Jones lists *Those Barren Leaves* and Evelyn Waugh's *Vile Bodies* as the two most realistic pictures of the 1920s and underlines the 'conversational air' of the decade, its eagerness to approximate 'all art to conversation'. V. S. Pritchett defines the twenties as a time of talk, reliance on personal judgment, and the pursuit of conversation as disinterested enquiry as well as for its own sake.[14] In devising the discussion-novel-of-ideas as his satiric medium, Huxley patterns his novels and manipulates his discussion scenes to imitate a major practice of the period. When he exposes the search for truth through conversation as a process in which the personalities involved merely exhibit their egotism, his early novels become, among other things, a satiric microcosm of the decade in which they were written. Shaw had tried to express ethical concepts in dramatic form and what Shaw did on the stage Huxley attempted in the novel.

It would be hard to believe that either egotism or eccentricity are exclusively twentieth-century creations, although some of the writers just quoted appear to believe they are. In the closing years of the nineteenth and the opening decades of the present century, however, egotism did have political and philosophical implications which it currently preserves mainly in the more nationalistic societies. In 1898, when Huxley was four years old and Hitler nine, a British journal called *The Eagle and the Serpent* (the two animals that combine in 1926 to form Quetzacoatl in D. H. Lawrence's *The Plumed Serpent*) declared its intention to uphold 'the egoistic philosophy',[15] apparently Nietzsche's. One of the periodical's maxims, 'A Race of Freemen is necessarily a Race of Egoists,' could take its place in any of the Fascist Webley's speeches to the British Freemen in *Point Counter Point*.

Where Ibsen supported the individual ego rather than mankind as the highest ideal and Nietzsche saw man as the bridge between animal and superman, Huxley advocates the re-integration of each individual's animality and rationality as a prelude to the building of bridges between men currently divided even within themselves. Huxley's satire against egoist-eccentrics is a response aimed simultaneously at his times and at a perennial obstacle to a unified society. The national egotism that united but eventually destroyed the Germany of the 1930s and 1940s was a new form of an old foe, and in *Ends and Means* (1937) and *Beyond the Mexique Bay* (1934) Huxley recognized it as such. Anthony Beavis' attempts to surmount his own egotism in *Eyeless in Gaza* (1936) are the prelude to his realization that nations must do the same with theirs. Thus the extent to which Huxley captured the period of his youth in print never ceases to impress, but most of the preceding pages have emphasized the humour and relevancy that still survive in Huxley's satiric treatment of perennial impediments to a less frustrating existence.

II. SPLIT-MEN AND THE QUEST FOR WHOLENESS

Huxley satirizes his characters not only for being divided from one another, but for being split within themselves. His painters, poets, and scientists – whom we may call 'artists' in the broad sense since they determine how we shall live – comprise, as the epigraph to *Point Counter Point* suggests, so many dichotomies of mind against body. The idea of counterpoint, of one person's limited viewpoint or preoccupation in opposition to other viewpoints, must thus be extended to include the opposition within the individual of his mental and physical natures. In a disintegrated society, the artists, who should see life steadily and whole, are, Huxley complains, almost incurably split inasmuch as each is either Houyhnhnm or Yahoo, all intellect or all genitals. Nineteenth-century ideals have broken down, and except for a spokesman Huxley inserts into some of his novels, no one calls for the creation of new standards.

The First World War, in Huxley's opinion, was the final step in the gradual breakdown of nineteenth-century ideals. His essays refer to it as 'the appalling catastrophe'.[16] In the novels, characters such as Mr. Cardan in *Those Barren Leaves*, who functions the way Mr. Hillary does in Thomas Love Peacock's *Nightmare Abbey*, lament the loss of the nineteenth-century milieu. Young Calamy has just observed that he cannot imagine 'a more exciting age' than the present when social institutions and the most sacred scientific truths are 'perfectly provisional and temporary', when 'nothing, from the Treaty of Versailles to the rationally explicable universe, is really safe'. He finds 'the intimate conviction that anything may happen . . . infinitely exhilarating' (Part I, III). But Cardan replies that he prefers the 'simple faith of nineteenth-century materialism' on which he was brought up. 'We were all wonderfully optimistic then,' he recalls, 'believed in progress and the ultimate explicability of everything in terms of physics and chemistry, believed in Mr. Gladstone and our own moral and intellectual superiority over every other age.'

As in Peacock, contrasting opinions are presented by speakers both of whom believe in what they say, but the spokesman's opinion, the viewpoint Huxley prefers (here it is Cardan's), emerges as the more desirable one. In this very simple example of something that becomes quite complex in *Point Counter Point*, a topic is discussed by two characters of dissimilar outlook and temperament and each addresses himself to it according to the sort of background he represents. Of the two resultant opinions, one seems more reasonable and becomes more acceptable by contrast with the other. Huxley does not take the outlook of Cardan's epoch as an ideal. He has no sympathy for materialism and considers progress a myth, since an advance in any one area is paid for by a sacrifice in another. Cardan himself admits most of his era's ideas were wrong or absurd. What makes the world the old man so fondly recalls superior to Calamy's is its possession of standards, self-esteem, and optimism, to all of which, in Cardan's opinion, his era as a whole subscribed.

Contrasted with Cardan's comments, the continual precariousness Calamy finds so exciting becomes little more than encouragement for egotists to set up secure private worlds. The 'intimate conviction' that anything may occur makes for minimal intimacy among Huxley's characters. Calamy was born shortly before World War I, whereas Cardan entered as 'a twin to *The Origin of Species*'. Yet in Cardan's case, the event that destroyed the old framework was itself a new one. Cardan's era as a whole believed everything would be explained in terms of chemistry and physics. It was not a case of Shearwater, in *Antic Hay*, explaining all in terms of the kidneys or of the disgruntled schoolteacher, Gumbril Jr., concentrating on pneumatic trousers with built-in cushions for humanity's posteriors. Cardan's age as a whole felt superior to its ancestors. Each individual's ego did not raise him above his contemporaries. What is needed, Huxley believes, is not another Victoria, but a new set of standards that can invest society with the same centric quality Huxley ascribes to the past.

The Cardan-Calamy exchange shows that even the bright young modern (as Huxley was called) is always more than just a debunker, much as his treatment of Gumbril Jr. in *Antic Hay* (I) and Calamy in *Those Barren Leaves* (Part 3, XIII) makes him an agnostic with decisive mystic leanings. Here, in his third novel, long before the sociological-political essays of *Ends and Means*, he argues for communal standards. He reveals a good deal of nostalgia for certain aspects of the past along with some pronounced utopian longings. Both *Brave New World* (1932) and *Island* (1962), in looking forward, will also look backward to a time when all lived by a code held in common.

Where is centricity to come from? Huxley looks in the early novels to the artists. He believes nations are not only influenced but in fact 'invented' by their poets and novelists.[17] Where the artist does not form and guide society, intellectuals pursue their specialities in increasing isolation until the eccentric artist breeds eccentric intellectuals and an eccentric society. Such a society – the one that envelops Chelifer for example – plays its part in the vicious circle by producing more eccentric artists. St. Paul and the Psalmist have gone the way of Virgil and Horace, Huxley writes,[18] and no single set of authoritative books now provides common ground for Western culture.

Whereas in the past, Huxley notes, minds moulded by the same religion and literature could understand one another readily, moderns have only science and information in common. We are, Huxley writes, a 'shattered Humpty Dumpty'. Though the Cardan-Calamy exchange idealizes the past century, the ideal situation was probably that of the sixteenth century. Then, Huxley argues in *The Olive Tree*, the Frenchman who peered inside himself saw something similar to what his introspective counterpart in England or Germany would see. Huxley satirizes his introspective, introverted characters because, owing to a lack of standards, introspection – a practice Huxley bears no animus towards *per se* – now means isolation. It was once outgoing, a method of perceiving the inner reality of others while scrutinizing oneself. Part of Vedanta's appeal for the later Huxley has to be its contention that it teaches a person to put himself in the presence of God by the same contemplative method mystics have used throughout the ages. Thus by proper self-discipline, Anthony Beavis in *Eyeless in Gaza* or Sebastian Barnack in *Time Must Have a Stop* can look

28

within themselves and experience the same vision enjoyed by St. Teresa in the sixteenth century.

If life copies art, even the bad variety, then the importance of good art cannot be sufficiently stressed. Much of Huxley's criticism of the arts in his novels and essays can be seen as an attempt to furnish the needed stress. Huxley feels the artist has failed society. A thorough search of his novels turns up one eccentric artist after another. Huxley satirizes the eccentric in general and the eccentric artist in particular. In *Crome Yellow*, Mary Bracegirdle discusses Tschuplitski, an artist who has already given up the third dimension and is preparing to give up the second: 'Painting's finished,' she says, 'he's finishing it' (XII). Casmir Lypiatt, the would-be da Vinci of *Antic Hay*, Helmholtz Watson, the unfortunate slogan-writer in *Brave New World*, the young poet, Sebastian Barnack, in *Time Must Have a Stop* – these are only a handful of the characters who are artistically as far off the main track as Eupompus and the Philarithmics in Huxley's parable 'Eupompus Gave Splendour to Art by Numbers' from the collection of short stories entitled *Limbo* (1932).

To the famous portrait-painter, Eupompus, number suddenly appeared to be 'the sole reality'. He filled a canvas with 33,000 swans, each 'distinctly limned' as in a Pre-raphaelite masterpiece. His disciples counted and recounted the birds by a process they called contemplation. Before finishing his picture of 'Pure Number', however, Eupompus killed two of his followers with a hammer and exited through a window to his death. Huxley concludes the painter killed himself and his disciples in a fit of temporary sanity. In the novels after this selection from his first book of short stories, Huxley wields the hammer against the eccentric artist.

Philip Quarles virtually quotes D. H. Lawrence when he asserts, in *Point Counter Point*, that there is 'less specialization, less one-sided development' in the artist. Consequently, he should be 'sounder right through than the lop-sided man of science; he oughtn't to have the blind spots and the imbecilities of the philosophers and saints' (XXVI). Huxley agrees, yet Quarles' own novels consist almost entirely of intellect and his wife must go to the dynamic Everard Webley for sexual satisfaction. Quarles has some of Keats' power, but in a perverted form. He can become almost anyone 'theoretically and with his intelligence' (XIV), but in Keats' sensuality and feeling, he is completely lacking. The marriage of Philip and Elinor constitutes a diagram of mind against body, with Quarles imprisoned in the former. Elinor exercises her feelings and he theorizes from her experiences. He can sympathize with his intelligence in a way Elinor says, with more viciousness than she intends, 'is all but human'. Though a dedicated author, Philip is a split-man who has made an entire world out of only half of himself. He and the tonsured Burlap are different sides of the same coin since each caters to only half of his total self. Burlap may write about St. Francis, but he uses his position as a magazine editor and his Christ-child physique to further his sexual designs. He attains his idea of happiness by taking baths with women. When the woman in question is named Beatrice, Burlap's conception of the Beatific vision is grossly rendered. In Huxley, the artist, even more so than society, exists in a state of mind against body, point counter point. 'Passion and reason,' the Fulke-Greville poem Huxley uses as an epigraph complains, 'are self-division's cause.'

The Huxley novels are full of Richard Greenow's progeny. In 'The Farcical History of Richard Greenow', the opening story of *Limbo*, Dick is, metaphorically, an hermaphrodite, a man who has not fused his mind and his emotions, his male and his female characteristics. His neglected emotions revenge themselves, as Huxley insists any neglected part of the whole man always does; and Dick has, as it were, attacks of feeling during which he becomes Pearl Bellairs and writes syrupy popular novels. Dick does not complain as long as 'the two parts of him' remain separate. But Pearl begins to take permanent control, and Dick, an intellectual and the supporter of a pacifist journal at the start of World War I, eventually succumbs to her desire to write recruiting songs. When Dick's repressed emotional life asserts itself, it turns out to be incredibly vulgar, or, as Huxley would say, Pickwickian.

Like all the Huxley characters who follow the Greenow pattern, the author, Hugh Ledwidge, in *Eyeless in Gaza*, and Jo Stoyte, a millionaire in *After Many a Summer Dies the Swan*, combine professional or artistic acumen with an emotional life less developed than Little Nell's. Again Dickens is one of the targets as Huxley satirizes mind-body eccentrics, split-men who force all their energy into exclusively mental or purely physical outlets. One cannot envision Ledwidge or Stoyte performing the act of love any more than one can believe Micawber has fathered children, or that Pickwick could marry Mrs. Bardell. Situations and characters that Huxley feels pleased Dickens or provided material for one of Robert Louis Stevenson's best-known stories become occasions for satire. From characters who rule out other people, it is a short step to those who rule out part of themselves. The hero of Huxley's stories and novels is thus either physically Pickwickian or a sort of Jekyll and Hyde who must be mental and then physical by turns.

Ledwidge's successful novel, *The Invisible Lover*, idealizes (i.e. spiritualizes) his wife, Helen. But the book cannot compensate for Hugh's failure as a husband. A reviewer termed Hugh's novel the story of Dante and Beatrice as told by Hans Christian Andersen (XXI). In terms of physical signs through which love finds its expression, Hugh is the invisible lover who cannot cope with flesh and blood. Helen, as her name suggests, prefers to be carried off occasionally, yet Hugh is as incapable as Quarles of a give-and-take relationship. He has an emotional life, but it is of the sickly green variety.

Even less attractive, however, is Jo Stoyte's obsession for Virginia. Her given name is a misnomer, her nickname is 'Baby'. Stoyte owns several companies, yet his temper tantrums suggest that the nurses in the children's hospital he has endowed are right in regarding him as 'a great big kid' resembling 'something in Dickens' (Part I, III). Like Chawdron in the story named after him in *Brief Candles* (1930), he is a sort of Pickwick-Babbitt, emotional child and professional Philistine. He remains 'a demi-god who had to have a nanny to change his diapers' (Part I, X). Virginia seems barely at the age of consent, and the 'perverse contrast' between her apparent childishness and her actual experiences intoxicates Stoyte. He and Virginia are both mixtures of the child and the adult. Emotionally, their lives are less developed than the children's who play sexual games in the shrubbery of *Brave New World*. Huxley's Pickwickian males corroborate D. H. Lawrence's charge that the twentieth-century is physically retarded.

Jude Fawley, Thomas Hardy's split-man, could not stabilize the desires of his mind and the demands of his body. He oscillated in *Jude the Obscure* (1895) from one to the other, from Arabella to Sue and back again. In Lawrence, the oscillation is over and, except in the Lawrencian hero, the mind has triumphed over the atrophied body. Many of Huxley's split-men are also static, having declared their allegiance either to the mental or the emotional. But Huxley castigates both forms of disproportion since he never permits the awareness that he is redressing a balance to exalt the physical over the mental. Hardy was sympathetic towards the victimized Jude, but

Lawrence vehemently attacked Europe's devitalized society. To him Arabella almost becomes a heroine by comparison with Sue. Huxley, however, prefers to make his split-men as grotesque and ludicrous as possible. Where Joseph Conrad's Kurtz, in 'Heart of Darkness' (1902), discovers an irrational primitivism in the darker recesses of his own character, Greenow uncovers Pearl Bellairs. While Jude fluctuates between the heroines of Hardy's novel, Stoyte moves from big business to infantile sex. The division within Jude that Hardy externalized by means of two women becomes an imbalance that Huxley renders physically in a grotesque sketch of Professor Cacciaguida that makes him, in *Time Must Have a Stop*, a caricature of evolution: a 'commanding head', but with 'the narrow chest and shoulders of a boy', the belly and hips 'of a middle-aged woman', and a 'pair of thin little legs . . . the front end of the organism fully adult and the rest hardly more than a tadpole' (III).

Perverse contrasts between childishness and maturity permeate Huxley's novels. Eustace Barnack in *Time Must Have a Stop* grips the 'wet brown teat' (V) of his cigar in 'unweaned' lips (X). Sebastian is Mrs. Ockham's 'gigolo baby' (XXII). These instances testify to Huxley's interest in the theme of age and help to explain the *bildungsroman* element in many of his novels. If characters such as Lord Edward Tantamount are mentally adults and physically children, how is a man's age to be figured: in years, in terms of completeness, or according to spiritual maturity? At the time of *Point Counter Point*, Huxley takes completeness as the standard. Mark and Mary Rampion are supposed to be the only adults in the novel, and those whose bodies and minds have not developed equally are stripped of their claims to maturity by Huxley's satire.[19] Though as old as science itself when he is in lab, Tantamount draws his notion of how lovers should act from Pickwick and Micawber. His wife, Hilda, makes him propose by behaving like a Dickens heroine. She discovers her body, as do the wives of most Huxley intellectuals, with another man, in her case with the complete sensualist, John Bidlake. In Tantamount plus Bidlake, she finds the equivalent of one real lover.

Huxley is as engrossed in studies of children as Dickens was, but Huxley's Little Nells, Paul Dombeys, and Amy Dorrits are people one would ordinarily have taken for adults. Dickens often inverted father-son relationships and showed the child as father of the man. Nevertheless, Huxley seems to hold Dickens' Pickwickian males at least partially responsible for the twentieth-century's emotional vulgarity, just as Mark Twain blamed the South's chivalry on Sir Walter Scott.

D. H. Lawrence once remarked that Huxley's novels were written by a talented adolescent.[20] In the novels after *Point Counter Point*, however, it is Rampion, a character based on Lawrence, who is demoted to childhood and replaced by men like Bruno Rontini. For Huxley then makes maturity synonymous with spiritual awareness. One's adult life begins with the first perception of the beatific vision or Divine Ground. Though not advanced in years, Rontini dies a very old man while none of the other characters who perish in *Time Must Have a Stop* – Eustace Barnack, Jim Poulshot, Mrs. Weyl – are any older than the day they were born.[21] Adulthood is a phenomenon in Huxley, more of a rarity than childhood in Jane Austen. It can be passed on, it seems, only from the possessor of it to his spiritual heir. Mr. Propter's intended beneficiary in *After Many A Summer Dies the Swan* is Pete Boone, but Jo Stoyte, the man who wants to live forever, shoots him by mistake. Ironically, the man who would remain a child even if he survived to the Last Judgment destroys the potential adult.

Rontini has better luck with Sebastian. Young Barnack, conscious of his poetic skills, is embarrassed by the contrast between his precocious mind and his baby-face. However, his claims to adulthood become valid only after he attains Rontini's wisdom. In Huxley's split-men, the struggle between body and mind (and in the later split-men, the struggle of the temporal against the eternal) is presented as a contest between child and adult with the character's chances for maturity as the stake. Huxley takes the fact of imbalance literally – as Swift did in *A Modest Proposal* with the contention that a country's population is its foremost natural resource. If the mind has developed more than the body, the physique must be shown as an evolutionary throwback and the thoughts must be those of a man while the feelings remain those of a child.

Of several Huxley spokesmen who war against the split-men, Mark Rampion of *Point Counter Point* and Mr. Propter of *After Many A Summer Dies the Swan* deserve particular mention. Propter, whose name means 'because', cites egocentricity as the cause of man's predicament. Ironically domiciled near Hollywood, a city built on personalities, Propter calls on the individual to realize his ego is 'a fiction' whose frenzy can be replaced by 'a God conceived . . . as a more than personal consciousness'. Without this conception, man is 'doomed to perpetual imprisonment in the ego' (Part I, VIII–IX), and Hollywood remains the symbol of modern society. Without it, Huxley foresees a brave new world where regimentation triumphs and characters seeking to get out of themselves participate in fruitless solidarity exercises. In *Brave New World*, an atmosphere of sham mysticism predominates as Bernard Marx and eleven others finish a Solidarity hymn:

> The group was now complete, the solidarity circle perfect and without flaw . . . Twelve of them ready to be made one, waiting to come together, to be fused, to lose their twelve separate identities in a larger being (V).

Someone shouts 'the feet of the Greater Being are on the stairs', but the Being, perhaps the Great Ford himself, never comes. Morgana Rothschild's displeasing eyebrows, Bernard notes, are all that come together. With a shout of 'Orgy-porgy' (for 'Georgy-porgy') the exercise degenerates into a debauch. Instead of fusion into a larger reality, each settles for the intensely personal satisfaction of copulation.

Mark Rampion, whose qualified resemblance to D. H. Lawrence will be examined in the fifth chapter, calls for a re-uniting of flesh and spirit that will permit man to join his animal with his rational functions. The complete man, Rampion insists, must know what the beast knows as well as what the mind knows. For Rampion and Huxley, man is both Houyhnhnm and Yahoo and exists completely only when these two elements are balanced; when, instead of being point against point, they are in the true counterpoint of equilibrium. The caricatures Rampion draws of humanity's parade towards its goals show every marcher with either oversized head or oversized genitals (XVI) and Huxley's characters are often similarly grotesque. All of the characters in *Point Counter Point* could easily be placed in Rampion's drawing depending on whether it is their body or their mind that they accentuate. The early lizards died of too much body. Like theirs, the existence of Old Bidlake, painter and sensualist, is oriented towards the flesh and never towards the mind. By contrast, Philip Quarles sacrifices the physical and affective life to the intellectual with equally disastrous results. Their respective arts mirror their personal inadequacies, as Bidlake's paintings of women present mindless flesh and Quarles' novels do not seem to be the products of flesh and blood.

The social mores of twenty-second-century America, in *Ape and*

Essence (1949), illustrate the Bidlake-Quarles dichotomy on a community scale. Huxley always shows the national consequences of what he condemns and of what he suggests as alternatives. Except for a two-week mating period of uninterrupted orgy, sex is prohibited in post-World-War-III California and females wear signs saying 'NO' on their breasts and buttocks. All are Bidlake for two weeks a year and Quarles the rest of the time, but always they are incomplete. 'You mustn't think,' Loola tells the hesitating Alfred Poole as the orgy commences. 'If you think, it stops being fun.'[22]

Shearwater, the kidney expert in *Antic Hay*, finally learns that one must 'render therefore unto Caesar the things which are Caesar's', that body and mind must be 'in proportion' (XI). For him, proportion has magical powers. Although he learns his lesson late and then misapplies it so that he, like Tantamount, bungles his epiphany, Shearwater's moment of insight is valid, for Huxley initially defines salvation as 'a state of mind' in which 'the various elements of our being are in harmony among themselves and with the world which surrounds us'.[23]

In the most amusing episode of *Antic Hay*, Gumbril Jr. transforms himself into Toto, a re-incarnation of the Rabelaisian or Complete Man. He grows a beard, pads his overcoat, brandishes a cane. He becomes a 'great eater, deep thinker, stout fighter, prodigious lover; clear thinker, creator of beauty, seeker of truth and prophet of heroic grandeurs' (IX). By engaging himself in all directions, instead of channelling his energies into one, Gumbril Jr. remains perfectly balanced at the centre. The incident is farcical, but Gumbril Jr. does attain what Rampion insists the ancient Greek enjoyed: the benefits of his animality as well as his humanity. The sane, harmonious Greek, Rampion exclaims in *Point Counter Point*, does not 'want to kill part of himself'. Instead, he 'strikes a balance' (X). The intrinsically hostile forces of his conscious soul and his unconscious, instinctive energies hold each other in check. Contraries, as Blake, whom Rampion calls the last complete man knew (IX), are necessary for progression. The 'revolt in favour of life and wholeness' that Rampion cries for is realized fleetingly in Gumbril's transformation, as Gumbril refuses to kill any part of himself and recaptures in his person the many-sidedness Elinor Quarles sees in little Phil. Unlike Chelifer, Gumbril Jr. manages to keep the whole collection of his present and potential selves in a state of balanced equilibrium. Instead of being exclusively himself, he opens outward in all directions. Of course it cannot last. Only if Gumbril Jr. lived in Pala, a society where, as Dr. MacPhail points out in *Island* (IX), 'our ambition is to be fully human', would it perhaps have been permanent.

Satire against split-men is thus a constant element in all of Huxley's novels, even after the split-man changes from one whose body and mind fail to balance to one who, in the later novels, cannot balance the claims of time and craving against those of eternity. However, Huxley seems less successful with his satire against walking counterpoints than he is in his attacks on egoists. Both of his major targets have been hit by previous satirists, but the number of characters Huxley can create, each with body and mind in different proportions, cannot match in quantity or humorous quality the variations that can be made on the egoist-eccentric. Some of his characters personify both of his targets and Huxley insists that eccentricity and imbalance are related. Nevertheless, the saga of Hercules is a more memorable episode than the story of Richard Greenow or Gumbril's masquerade as Toto. The later Huxley abandons his talent for short satiric parable altogether (unless one wishes to consider *Brave New World* and *Ape and Essence* satiric parables of extended length).

Huxley's treatment of the body-mind dichotomy is further complicated by Lawrencian borrowings and by his awareness that his own personality is a case in point. Lawrence and Huxley were not close friends until 1926, so the desires of Gumbril Jr. and Shearwater for completeness may be an indication of their author's dissatisfaction with a predominantly mental constitution. Huxley's awareness of his own similarities with Gumbril Jr., Denis Stone, and Philip Quarles prepared him for Lawrence's 'blood philosophy'. Charles Rolo is partially correct in sensing that Huxley's intellectual virtuosity tried 'from the start' to 'puncture . . . the values of the intellect as opposed to the animal sense and the spirit'.[24] Yet Huxley's endorsement of the 'phallic consciousness' is always a bit humorous in itself, for it is an intellectual acceptance. 'But do do a book of the grand orthodox perverts,' Lawrence writes in March of 1928,[25] and *Do What You Will* (1929), a book of essays really written by Mark Rampion, is the result. Despite some fine criticism, Huxley's rationalism is apparent throughout it as Swift, Pascal, Baudelaire, and numerous others are virtually thrust into a scale and their lack of balance mathematically registered. The difference between Lawrence's attack on split-men and Huxley's is that the latter is also intentionally satirizing himself. In ridiculing the sexual failures of

Philip Quarles or Sebastian Barnack, Huxley makes the same desperate effort to become Rampion instead of Quarles that he makes to separate himself from his characters' contempt for other people. His failure on the first count still warrants some commendation, since the effort made is heroic and sincere. Unlike Lawrence, Huxley never lionizes himself.

Huxley thus satirizes his characters for being exclusively mental creatures whose sex life is sickly and childish or for being predominantly physical with abortive mentalities. Although often contemptuous of intellect and at times, one suspects, abnormally adverse to the physical side of man, Huxley remains committed to the ideal of balance and one cannot permit his attacks on either the intellectual or particularly the physical aspects of human nature to destroy the sense of commitment to that ideal. Those who find themselves at times disconcerted by Huxley's Swiftian disgust for physical functions – that is, with the rational animal's capacity to make love as well as with his need to excrete – generally fail to recognize how complex Huxley's disgust actually is. For one thing Huxley is as hard on the Houyhnhnm within man and within himself as he is on the Yahoo and as a satirist he is prone to exaggerate his wrath. His anti-physical feelings never reach the extreme they attain in Swift nor do they thrust themselves at the reader as frequently. Huxley's report of Virginia's comment about the copulating baboons in *After Many a Summer Dies the Swan* (Part 1, VII): 'Aren't they cute! Aren't they *human!*' not only exposes her shallow notion of love but has to go alongside Huxley's equally severe contempt for the barrenness of the purely mental life as lived by any of his own prototypes such as Philip Quarles. Nor can one overlook Huxley's easily justified disdain for characters, like Jeremy Pordage, also in *After Many a Summer Dies the Swan* (Part 2, I), whose preoccupation with themselves makes their sexual life 'simultaneously infantile and corrupt'. Corrupt because it involves furtive fornication, and infantile because the feelings for another that are necessary in love remain stifled or malformed.

In short, the satire Huxley directs against the Yahoos in his fiction or against the Yahoo element in all men stands out strongly for the same reason that Swift's aversion to these bestial creatures is more obvious than his at times unfavourable opinion of the rational horses: the physical offers greater possibilities for repulsive presentation.

Undoubtedly, Huxley's personal shortcomings must be taken into account. Shy, mainly intellectual, impressive in physique but delicate despite his height, a breaker of taboos in prose but probably quite fastidious in his personal life, Huxley always remained an idealist trying to live with reality. Thus love is a fine ideal but quite ludicrous when the necessity of sitting in blissful calm with the loved one and 'Quietly sweating palm to palm' is recognized.[26] The ideal of love, Francis Chelifer insisted earlier in this chapter, is one of those 'bright falsehoods' to be avoided in a post-war world. Huxley certainly made the physical element in love as ridiculously unattractive as he could either because he felt, as Lawrence often did, that it boiled down to another form of egotism, or because, like Swift, he was fascinated by his own attraction-aversion to it, or, finally and most likely, because his satiric sense recognized a viable method of undercutting his less likeable 'modern' characters, even the autobiographical ones. Thus the hygienically controlled promiscuity of *Brave New World* becomes Huxley's reduction to absurdity of what he considers the modern desire for a perpetual good time.

Huxley's women, even more so than Evelyn Waugh's villainesses, are virtual nymphomaniacs whose minds have never attained puberty. Virginia Maunciple in *After Many a Summer Dies the Swan* is one example and Barbara, an ignorant Cynthia to Chelifer's would-be Endymion in *Those Barren Leaves*, is another. Or else, like Myra Viveash in *Antic Hay* or Veronica Thwale in *Time Must Have a Stop*, they are not only promiscuous and heartless, but possibly capable of devouring their males (both women are widows). Gumbril Jr.'s pursuit of Myra, like Walter Bidlake's passion for Lucy Tantamount in *Point Counter Point*, exposes the failure of the sexually Prufrockian twentieth-century man at the same time that the destruction latent in the modern female practically makes her a symbol of modern life's recurrent disillusionments.

But unlike Swift, Huxley, who seems to have disliked, or at least distrusted, the physical all his life, never stopped searching for an answer to that dislike. His period of discipleship under D. H. Lawrence (to be discussed in chapter four) is one long attempt to feel with his whole being the attractions his mind assured him should be found in the physical half of his nature. His subsequent belief that the physical life constitutes an impediment to spiritual progress – or so Anthony Beavis concludes in *Eyeless in Gaza* – does not prevent him from seeking a final synthesis of body, mind, and soul in *Island*, his last novel.

Rather than denigrate Huxley along with Swift, one should

remember that the severest indictment of Swift comes from Huxley himself in *Do What You Will* (1929). When Huxley underlines Swift's need to seek out what nauseates him for the sake of the pleasure in overcoming his own repulsion and scoffs at the Dean's 'refusal . . . to accept the physical reality of the world', it is difficult not to hear Quarles-Huxley exorcising himself. And when Huxley proposes Rabelais as an antidote to Swift, one feels Huxley, like Gumbril Jr., wants to play Toto, the Complete Man.

Nevertheless, it would be a mistake to conclude that Huxley's personal difficulties cripple his art. In a rationally oriented age, Swift slashed away at man's pride in his reason. Huxley, in a scientific age, can be equally ruthless when dealing with man's major egotistic assumption in this century, namely, that he is the triumphant product of biological evolution and a living proof that life is naturally progressive. Much of Huxley's preoccupation with physical functions, and indeed the entire plot of *After Many a Summer Dies the Swan*, is a healthy satiric assault on the idea of progressive evolution revealed by Aldous' grandfather, T. H. Huxley, and taken as a modern apostolate by Aldous' brother, Julian. There is even the possibility that Lord Edward Tantamount, with his foolish theories about the interconnection of all forms of life, is at least partially based on Julian. Huxley later came to value the possibility that man would eventually evolve on the mental-spiritual plane until he could acquire with ease what the would-be mystic now struggles to attain. But the anti-physical element in Huxley's satire abides as an effective refutation of the unrealistic attitude towards human nature that he symbolized in the construction of Sir Ferdinando's privies at Crome. Like Swift's excremental vision, Huxley's anti-physical satire often serves as a forceful satiric weapon, and is always a complement to his anti-intellectual satire, both satires stemming from dedication to the ideal of balance.

The need for whole men and the longing for a society integrated by tenets held in common are therefore related matters for Huxley and each variety of wholeness is contingent upon the other. His characters are cut off from one another and split within themselves, and neither division can be overcome if the other is ignored. Though not the only novelist to present egoistic characters who rule out other people, nor the first to fictionalize the split-man, Huxley convincingly connects the theme of isolation within the self with that of mental and emotional imbalance. Whereas James Joyce in *Ulysses* and William

Faulkner in *Absalom, Absalom!* may be said to impose patterns on their material, the structure for Huxley's fourth novel appears to emerge out of the themes and metaphors of his first three. The modern novel, as written by Conrad, Virginia Woolf, and Joyce, often seems concerned with technique as an end in itself, with the unmodified objectivism of Conrad opposing the unrelieved subjectivism of Mrs. Woolf. But Huxley believes his technical advances must serve the purposes of his satire. Some discussion of the structure Huxley devised to expose eccentricity and incompleteness and imply the possibility of a return to wholeness is now in order.

Structure and Development: Procrustes Makes His Bed

Huxley's major achievement, especially when compared with that of previous discussion novelists such as Thomas Love Peacock and W. H. Mallock, consists in the development of a structure for his novels that in itself carries out and supports his satire. The structural technique he perfects continually exposes the egotism of his characters. It satirizes their fragmentary existence while also suggesting they are parts of a recoverable whole. By structure this essay means the planned framework of a novel, the overall arrangement of the entire work or of a particular scene and, finally, the technical method by which the structure is attained. In *Point Counter Point*, the format is supposedly a musical one but the characters or instruments that come together in the discussion scenes fail to produce anything but discord.

At a dinner party in *Point Counter Point*, for example, Spandrell, Philip Quarles, Walter Bidlake, and Illidge, who is Lord Edward Tantamount's laboratory assistant, discuss distortion (XXI). Spandrell contends everything that happens is like the man it happens to, but Quarles insists men distort events in order to make them like themselves. Quarles makes the ego responsible for the distortion and the diabolist Spandrell, a repetition of Coleman who appeared in *Antic Hay*, is unmasked. If he belongs to the devil's party, he does so not as a victim of his character but as a self-made man. Yet Spandrell's version is better fitted to Quarles. Philip is a victim of his temperament, though he prefers a definition of distortion that would make his emotional sterility the result of his own rational decisions. Illidge, whose presence at the better social gatherings is due to brains and not birth, accuses Spandrell and Quarles of considering the question as gentlemen of leisure. One of the very few characters in all of Huxley's novels to betray Cockney origins, Illidge may have a right to feel out of his element in the predominantly upper class atmosphere of the Huxley world, but he transforms that right into an obsession that warps his character. As the discussion proceeds, the speakers become more and more like Hercules in the parable from *Crome Yellow*: each tailors the topic under discussion to his own limitations. Spandrell's comments are distorted by his diseased philosophy, Philip's by his temperament, and Illidge's by class consciousness. Each speaker sees through his fellows but never through himself. Quarles, who is 'naturally cold', finds it easy to be reasonable and can dismiss as 'avoidable evils' the whores and alcohol Spandrell cannot resist. A bit of Quarles' intellect added to some of Spandrell's sensuality plus a tincture of Illidge's social consciousness, and something resembling the Complete Man might emerge.

In effect, theme has become structure. What is being satirized and what makes the novel go are one and the same: the eccentricity of its characters. What the novel is about and the way it is put together have merged. Quarles, himself a novelist, writes in his craftsman's notebook: 'A theme is stated, then developed, pushed out of shape, imperceptibly deformed until, though still recognizably the same, it has become different' (XXII). Each character in a Huxley discussion sequence bends each theme to suit his own deformity. He makes it fit into his personal rendering of Pharaoh's dream. The novelist makes each new character or situation an occasion for pushing an already stated theme into a new shape that looks back to the original formulation while adding to it by means of a variation. *Point Counter Point* insists on man's egotism and continually shows it in operation. Structure and theme expose the characters as uncrossing parallel lines. The image of self-centred speakers as parallel lines is made visible, is, in fact, rendered dramatically, until the discussion scene just mentioned could almost be diagrammed with four uncrossing lines standing respectively for each of the egoistic speakers.

Huxley referred to this structure a bit grandiosely as 'musicalization', a device similar to counterpoint in music. Actually, musicalization is a metaphor for variation, a technique most novelists employ. However, Huxley does fashion variation into a complex satiric weapon almost ideally suited to his needs. Counterpoint occurs in music when a melody is added to a given tune until plurality results; that is, a melody not single but attended by one or more related but independent melodies. As a group of Huxley eccentrics discuss a topic, a series of variations develops because each eccentric bends the topic to suit himself. Even when the characters discuss distortion, each distorts his definition of that phenomenon to make it suitable to his own way of life. Spandrell insists people are victims of their characters because he would like to think he is. If, as Quarles charges, people are wrongly brought up on *Romeo and Juliet* rather than on reality, then his own preference for art over life is less culpable.

In the society represented by the discussion group, there is no communal theme. The spokesman, when one is present, provides the main melody; but each eccentric plays a variation of it that is stubbornly off centre. Where Mark Rampion speaks for a balance of body and mind (xxxiv), the other characters pervert his statement to favour either mind or body, since each character is incomplete and caters to one more than the other. The discussion scenes in *Point Counter Point* become dramatized versions of the orchestra image wherein violin, cello, and flute compete for supremacy in the uncontrolled counterpoint of pure competition. The novel takes its title from a form of musical composition in which, despite opposing voices or instruments, a definite harmony is engendered, but the characters in *Point Counter Point* cannot measure up to the demands of the form and it becomes part of the satire directed against their willingness to remain militant, egotistic separatists.

Thomas Love Peacock also accumulates oddball characters at country houses and around dinner tables, but Huxley's ultimate predecessor is probably Ben Jonson. In *Every Man Out of His Humour*, Jonson defined a humour character as one whose spirits and powers all run one way. Huxley praised 'Ben's reduction of human beings to unpleasant Humours' as a process both 'sound and medicinal'.[1] Counterpoint is employed in many Huxley novels, but in *Point Counter Point* and *Eyeless in Gaza* it reaches a state of technical perfection that Peacock scarcely foreshadows.

The typical Peacock novel contains, as does *Point Counter Point*, some fine caricatures. Mr. Chainmail of *Crotchet Castle* (1831) is a possible take-off on Sir Walter Scott or Horace Walpole, since he wishes to live in the twelfth century. Cythrop of *Nightmare Abbey* (1818) amused his model, Shelley, more than Huxley's Burlap pleased John Middleton Murry. When the question arises in *Crotchet Castle* as to what constitutes the *summum bonum* for society, each character unhesitatingly proposes his own crotchet. MacQuedy the Utilitarian suggests universal schooling in political economy. Skionar, who is probably modelled on Coleridge, wants everyone to study transcendentalism. When Dr. Gaster sprains an ankle in *Headlong Hall* (1816), a deteriorationist interprets it as another sign of the general decay. The perfectabilitarian says Gaster now has the prospect of rest and a good breakfast, so that everything is really improving. But a status-quo-ite explains that the pain and the good breakfast balance out, leaving Dr. Gaster the same as before. Characters in Huxley continually reveal themselves as Peacockians who look at the world through the narrow chink of some one theory or intellectual discipline: each of the New Zealand scientists who inspect the ruins of post-World-War-III America in *Ape and Essence* insists his field of science accomplished the most destruction.[2]

Peacock also anticipates Huxley by setting a voice of reason – such as Mr. Hilary of *Nightmare Abbey* or Dr. Folliott in *Crotchet Castle* – in the midst of his crotcheteers. But neither Peacock nor Mallock seem to have Huxley's strong interest in ideas. Of these three 'discussion' novelists, Huxley alone seems deeply committed to the exposure of fallacious theory and the inculcation of positive alternatives. This is not to say, however, that Huxley is more interested in ideas than in people since his interest in the former is his way of being concerned with the latter. But unlike Huxley, neither Peacock nor Mallock consider the diversity of opinions their characters present a sign of society's most serious predicament. Nor should they, since the crotchets they laugh at never run so deep as to prevent their characters from meeting on neutral ground.

The discussion device that functions so amusingly in *Crotchet Castle* and elsewhere becomes the mainspring of Huxley's novels. *Crome Yellow* is the novel most imitative of Peacock, but Huxley's experiments eventually produce a *Point Counter Point*. Shelley's friend, though his books have always been underrated, never markedly developed from one novel to the next and the Peacockian format lay dormant throughout the late nineteenth century. W. H. Mallock's *The New Republic* (1878) contained no new breakthroughs, although it offered excellent caricatures of Matthew Arnold (Mr. Luke) and John Ruskin (Mr. Rose), and a less successful jibe at Huxley's grandfather in the person of Mr. Storks.

What Peacock seems to find most interesting, as his granddaughter noted,[3] is not the isolation each character's theory imposes on him but the absurdity of having opinions at all. His target is always the alleged 'march of intellect'. The theories many people rigidly hold, he insinuates, do not improve the well-being of mankind. Obviously he prefers Hilary's congenial outlook to the black-bile philosophy of Cythrop-Shelley, Flosky-Coleridge, and other representatives of the so-called morbid side of romanticism. But if he does not laugh at all opinions, he does so at most. As a novelist mainly interested in poking fun at the leading opinions and movements of his day, his manner is his means of discrediting his matter.

At the climax of *Point Counter Point*, however, Rampion glances around the table at Spiza's and labels the eccentricity of each character: Spandrell is a morality-philosophy pervert, Quarles an intellectual-aesthetic pervert, and Burlap a pure-little-Jesus pervert (xxxiv). One sees everything in terms of morals and tries to be as immoral as possible, another transforms everything into mind and art in order to avoid the claims of emotion, a third makes love under the guise of religion. Every subject that arises is twisted by each pervert until it fits his scheme of things. The subjects that arise, however, are the main themes of the novel: the relation of art to life, mind to body, man to society. These themes all involve relationship, and that, perhaps, is the novel's broadest concern. Huxley develops the Peacockian format into a vehicle for his own themes and there is a continual connection between these themes and the way they are discussed. The problems that Huxley feels confront his society are the matters his characters discuss, and they discuss them in such a manner that they personify the problems they examine. The failings Huxley perceives in twentieth-century society and the discussion novel he resuscitates and expands seem to demand one another.

What Huxley also does is to find a means of exposing the distortions constantly made by his characters without having to confine them to one spot. The novelist thus follows Walter Bidlake, who is one of many self-portraits in Huxley, in his movement away from Illidge, Spandrell, and Quarles (in the scene this chapter began with) towards a situation in which Walter, hopelessly in pursuit of Lucy Tantamount, demonstrates how a man makes an event fit his character. The egoistic eccentricity the characters display when together is also seen in their private lives. Events involving different eccentrics build to scenes in which some of the characters confront Mark Rampion. They approach the centre he represents and their lives seem incomplete by comparison with his. They then fly off into situations wherein they pervert or ignore his teachings. The motion of the novel is thus roughly analogous to that of its characters. It moves towards or away from Rampion, who remains balanced at the centre. Chapters I through VII move towards the discussion of VIII through X. After that, Rampion returns to develop his views in Chapters XVI, XXIII, and XXXIV. The discussion in VIII and X brings

Spandrell into confrontation with Rampion. In XVI, Burlap and Rampion meet, while in XXIII Webley speaks on power and Rampion's views of progress and machines form a contrast. The climax discussion in XXXIV pits Rampion against Quarles, Spandrell, and Burlap and has a summary quality as Rampion confronts in a group the perverts he previously dealt with individually.

Abrupt transitions (five or six a chapter) from one set of characters to another in a series of short, cinematic scenes present all the parallels simultaneously, even when they are in different places. Though the eccentrics cannot penetrate each other's private world effectively enough to make genuine contacts, Huxley's technique can. Huxley uses what Quarles' notebook calls 'multiplicity' (XIV) to expose eccentricity. 'Multiplicity of eyes and multiplicity of aspects seen,' is what Quarles calls for in his notebook. 'For instance,' he continues, 'one person interprets events in terms of bishops; another in terms of the price of flannel camisoles. . . . And then there's the biologist, the chemist, the physicist, the historian. Each sees, professionally, a different aspect of the event, a different layer of reality. What I want to do, Quarles concludes, 'is to look with all those eyes at once.' Some of the scenes should thus be seen stacked one above the other as though taking place simultaneously. By looking 'through all those eyes at once', Huxley exhibits numerous layers of unsatisfactory love and inadequate wholeness and the absurdity of each layer (or individual) that sets itself up as a totality is underlined. The more layers that can be shown, Huxley might argue, the queerer the total picture, and, perhaps, the more salutary the effect on self-centred lives. Huxley often seems prepared, perhaps too prepared, to attach the same magical powers to 'multiplicity' and inclusiveness that Shearwater, the kidney expert, found in 'proportion'.

The Rampions, Mark and Mary, personify the theme of integral living. In them, and through the variations on them, Huxley attains another kind of wholeness: he treats his themes and events from all aspects; that is, in every possible form he can think of. Elinor and Philip, Burlap and Beatrice, and Walter and Lucy are contrasted with the Rampions; and, within the same family circle, Philip's excessive intellectualism is displayed with the cheap sexual escapades of his father, Sidney, and the blatant sensuality of his father-in-law, John Bidlake, as the background. Though dealing with only a small segment of one country's society, Huxley tries to get everything into the novel, by making each scene a modulation in mood and situation of the scenes surrounding it and each character and the plot he is involved in a variation of other characters and plots in the novel. Huxley strives for inclusiveness through intensity and depth rather than scope. 'The whole story of the universe is implicit in any part of it,' writes Quarles (XIX), and thus to take any event and begin to examine its different shades and variations is to make that event 'a window' to the entire cosmos. If the cosmos consists entirely of interconnected phenomena, as Huxley contends, then any part of it should be 'diaphonous' and, by dealing with the variant forms and associations that part suggests, the novelist could, by 'spinning the work out interminably' encompass the universe. The characters must be, Quarles insists, 'diaphonous' so that, as was the case with Blake's grain of sand, infinity can be seen in them. Huxley's characters reveal significant vistas behind their familiar selves. In fact, they are an animated version of Rampion's drawing of 'Fossils of the Past and Fossils of the Future' (XVI).

Huxley perfects in *Point Counter Point* a technique suited to the presentation of life's diversity and his own insistence that nothing short of everything will ever do. He seems to feel he cannot talk about completeness unless he can offer some sort of total picture. His response to the exclusive point of view through which each of his characters looks at the world is an attempt to demonstrate how many points of view there are. Where each of them sees all events from one angle or aspect, Huxley tries to see each theme or event from all aspects. To see even a part of the world, namely that of London's socialite intelligentsia, in as many of its dimensions as possible requires the same Herculean effort Huxley's characters waste in reducing reality to their own limitations.

One of the insights Anthony Beavis finds most satisfying in *Eyeless in Gaza* is his perception of the unity beneath diversity, of the fact that each organism is unique, but only above sub-stratums of physical and mental identity (LIV). For Huxley, perceptions of the individual's diversity and that of the outside world are balanced by an awareness of a person's oneness and of 'the whole universe as a single individual mysteriously fused with ourselves'.[4] The eccentric may turn his life into a refutation of this Blakean vision, but the structure of *Point Counter Point* embodies both realizations, that of oneness as well as that of diversity. The novel's broadest counterpoint consists in its implication of a unity underlying the complexities of existence. The divergent melodies, even if considerably off beat, are clearly related to the central melody. Huxley suggests no course of action that his characters seem likely to accept and Rampion converts no one, but Huxley wishes to intimate that harmony is not hopelessly lost, that Gumbril Jr.'s Wordsworthian spot in time at the concert in *Antic Hay* can be made permanent. The vision of the universe as a single person fused with oneself receives some tenuous support from the fact that the split-men in the novel, added together, might form one man.[5]

'It is conceivable,' Huxley once wrote, 'that the moment of world existence, of which we are each aware during a human life-time, may be an essential part in a musical whole that is yet to be unfolded.'[6] In an attempt to anticipate that musical whole, Huxley always challenged a limited viewpoint, no matter how sincerely held. To the scientists he often spoke as a humanist, yet to D. H. Lawrence, who felt man was atrophying, he would point out the inescapable scientific fact of evolution. Like the Vedantists he eventually joined, Huxley castigates the West for its lack of spiritual values but finds Henry Ford's *My Life and Work* refreshing after a dose of India's spirituality.[7] The problem for Huxley is to find a large enough synthesis, one that can hold his own vast erudition as well as all the things he has yet to see, for he feels that anything short of total vision is a move towards the subjective and incomplete. In the novel, his problem as an artist is similar: how to find a form which will satirize incompleteness and hold life's multiplicity while implying its unity, but do so without cutting life down, as did Procrustes, to make it fit a mould.

How each individual in *Point Counter Point* is to become organically related to society's central melody (to keep Huxley's metaphor) is, however, never precisely clear. The artificial stability of *Brave New World* is not the answer, nor does Huxley mean all men must become Rampion. On Huxley's utopian Pala, however, people of different temperaments are taught to take one another into account. Each individual in *Island* performs a series of jobs from scientific research to woodcutting to exercise some of the different selves he contains. Each person strives for as much awareness and as complete a mental and physical life as his capabilities permit. When the individual adopts a speciality, he does so with a knowledge of other pursuits and other people as a background. He is, as it were, conditioned towards wholeness, whereas the Deltas and Epsilons of *Brave New World* are trained to be incomplete.

The total meaning of Pharaoh's dream, Huxley appears to believe, can only be approximated by the individual (or novelist) who tries to comprehend as many readings of it as possible. Webley and Lord Edward look at the same things from different angles. Because neither can put himself into the other's point of view, they fail to see their outlooks are complementary. Through his structural technique, Huxley attempts to become the reintegrating artist incarnate, the man who is without blind spots because he can view life from the vantage point of innumerable personalities ('With religious eyes, scientific eyes, economic eyes, *homme moyen sensuel* eyes'). By giving a multiplicity of viewpoints, he is not escaping the responsibility of interpreting life; instead, he imparts a sense of his own wonder not at the fact that men should be so unlike, but that they should be as similar as they are.[8] The cutting remark that ends the novel ('Of such is the Kingdom of Heaven') contains its modicum of truth. Seen from a sufficiently lofty and impartial vantage point, the world of *Point Counter Point* retains traces of a former unity.

Huxley's achievement is considerable, but certain reservations must be expressed. In the novel of ideas, writes Quarles, 'the character of each personage must be implied, as far as possible, in the ideas of which he is the mouthpiece' (XXII). Consequently, Huxley's personages often seem little more than a series of ideas covered with skin. As Quarles confesses, it is a case of characters rattling off 'neatly formulated notions'. Frederic Hoffman's suggestion that Huxley's ideas are his characters is a good one,[9] and one can argue that Huxley's reduction of characters to their ideas is echoed by Faulkner's reduction of them to their conscious and subconscious thought patterns in a novel such as *As I Lay Dying*. But Huxley wishes at times to present Rampion as a person rather than an idea. In most of his appearances, however, except for the idyllic courtship of Mark and Mary in IX, Rampion is not a rounded character but is, in fact, the boring gasbag Lawrence found him.

Quarles' role in the novel also presents problems. By inserting a novelist into a novel, Huxley and Quarles contend, the musicalization is increased. If Quarles tells part of the story as he works on a novel within Huxley's novel, the result is an additional variation. The characters are seen as Quarles describes them and as Huxley presents them and an additional point of view is built into the novel. The widely-separated chapters in which Quarles discusses the novelist's art become in themselves a recurrent minor melody within the overall composition. In writing about the other characters, Quarles exhibits his own limitations. Even Philip's critical notions, despite Huxley's adoption of them, expose his liabilities, since the multiplicity he strives for appears to leave his feelings as undeveloped as ever. Quarles himself confesses he can deal with 'complications', such as those of counterpoint, but not with 'simplicities' since they demand a talent 'which is of the heart, no less than of the head' (XIV). It is significant that on the list of eyes – religious, scientific, economic – Quarles compiles, no mention of 'Loving eyes' is made until his wife reminds him. However, the insertion of Quarles and his notebook also serves, and at times seems primarily intended to serve, as a means whereby Huxley can control the criticism of his own work by telling his readers, as though in a Fielding preface, how the novel should be read.

It is possible that Huxley may have intended Quarles' attempt to attain purely intellectual sympathy with a variety of different viewpoints to be taken favourably as a reasonable approximation of Keatsian negative capability, even though D. H. Lawrence found it 'disgusting'.[10] The novel itself seems to imply, however, that the inclusion of Philip is Huxley's attempt to transcend through technique his own limitations. The sense of humanity's oneness rises out of the novel because there is an Olympian point of view at work. Quarles is clearly a version of Huxley himself and thus by thrusting Quarles into the novel, Huxley tries, with only partial success, to stand outside himself and his own temperament, to sympathize with the whole of which his fictionalized self is only a limited part. It is Huxley, not Quarles, who achieves multiplicity of viewpoint. Huxley thus wants to get inside his novel and exert additional control over it at the same time that he desires to remain outside it and obtain a god-like viewpoint. ('For a being who can take the god's-eye view of things, certain diversities display an underlying identity.')[11] These conflicting aims often seem unresolved since the gap between Quarles and Huxley is wider at some points in the novel than at others.

Though the structure of *Eyeless in Gaza* remains to be discussed in chapter six, *Point Counter Point* stands as Huxley's major accomplishment in the novel. In it, he manages to present structurally what the egoist heroes of his earlier novels painfully discover: the fact that reality, including one's self, is perceived at every moment in different but related forms by dozens of other people. The novel's structure refutes each character's contention that he is the centre, that the world revolves around him. It pits one interpretation of Pharaoh's dream against another, and this struggle between contrapuntal viewpoints is seconded by the turmoil within each character where body and mind compete for ascendancy.

The force behind all the novels up through *Point Counter Point* is Huxley's search for new images to express the separation caused by egotism. If the earlier novels sometimes seem fresher and less pretentious than *Point Counter Point*, it may be because Huxley's ideas have remained stationary, while his technique has become more sophisticated. Perhaps, under Lawrence's influence, Huxley desires to be more of a social prophet than is healthy for a satiric novelist. *Point Counter Point* is frequently less funny than *Crome Yellow* or *Antic Hay* and it is tempting to explain this by arguing that Huxley now takes himself too seriously, that he is less entertaining and more caustically satiric because he finds the situations he formerly described less amusing. The difference in tone between Denis' humorous conversation with Jenny and Rampion's caustic dismissal of Quarles, Spandrell, and Burlap is quite noticeable, though the ultimate import of the two scenes does not differ that drastically.

Even in *Point Counter Point*, despite an attempt at self-transcendence, Huxley never leaves his rationalism behind. Denis Stone in *Crome Yellow* and Gumbril Jr. in *Antic Hay* were satiric treatments of himself, but they were still done from his own viewpoint. By putting Quarles' outlook into the novel, Huxley tries to rise above his own way of seeing things. Indeed, his satiric indictment of Quarles is probably the most penetrating as well as the severest of the many self-portraits in his fiction. But musicalization, whether described by Quarles or practiced by Huxley, is ultimately more mathematical than musical and the novel as counterpoint is an anology that is intellectually but not audibly verifiable. The notion that body and mind, as if in two adjoining scales, can be made to balance is similarly mathematical. Though it begins with Bach and ends with Beethoven, *Point Counter Point* is most susceptible to diagram.

'Perhaps,' writes Huxley in *Texts and Pretexts*, 'separation is really an illusion, perhaps there is, after all, some mysterious unity . . . the best way to be happy is to try to live out of personal separateness in the all – to try to share, in Byron's words, "the immortal lot" of the spirit of things, to form, in Keats's "a fellowship with essence." '[12] Chelifer adapted to the spirit of things in *Those Barren Leaves*, but only to the earthly spirit, and became, disastrously, a fellow of essence.

In most of the novels following *Point Counter Point*, Huxley takes his own advice. He tries to share the immortal lot of the spirit of things. This is not, as some critics have suggested, an evasion of the problems his own novels have raised. *Point Counter Point* does imply the existence of a mysterious unity, but the novel's structure, like Spandrell's suicidal note to the British Freemen, is Huxley's final card. Implication, a not overly positive process to begin with, can go no further. The structure of *Eyeless in Gaza* refutes Anthony's contention that his life is not a process of growth in the Words-worthian manner, but Miller, doctor, pacifist, anthropologist and mystic, brings Anthony all he needs to know, just as the leech-gatherer in *Resolution and Independence* resolved Wordsworth's doubts. Like Pascal, whom he disparages in *Do What You Will*, Huxley decides to bet on the existence of what he cannot prove exists. With oriental scripture and the writings of Eastern and Western mystics as his authority, he assumes there is a mysterious unity, instead of implying it exists or satirizing society for its absence. The underlying unity he perceives among men Huxley takes as a sign of an equally possible union with God. His shift from the social to the religious level in his search for unifiers becomes a calculated jump towards what he believes is man's final end. Whatever steps seem to be skipped or fallacies involved, whatever the favourable and un-favourable consequences for Huxley as a novelist, his subsequent development does not amount to irresponsible escapism.

II

Huxley's development, his movement from exaltation of the artist and the complete life towards mystical heroes who attain union with the Divine Ground, has been dealt with by other critics. What has not been noted about this process – one which has firmly begun in *Eyeless in Gaza* and seems to have happened by *After Many A Summer Dies the Swan* – is the way Huxley reverses himself on several points and approves of attitudes and actions he formerly satirized. In fact, he becomes several of his former targets.

The dividing line between early and later Huxley is a bit arbitrary, but *Eyeless in Gaza* (1936) seems a good choice. Though there are indications of Anthony Beavis' mystical outlook in Gumbril Jr. of *Antic Hay* and in Calamy of *Those Barren Leaves*, *Eyeless in Gaza* contains Huxley's first fully-realized mystic-hero. As the sixth of Huxley's eleven novels, it continues the technical experimentations of *Point Counter Point* while formulating its author's burgeoning religious concerns.

Unlike most satirists, Huxley offers solutions to the problems he poses. In the later novels, he seeks permanent alternatives to the egotism of the possessive Mrs. Aldwinkle, who virtually kidnaps Chelifer in *Those Barren Leaves*, and the selfish cravings of the millionaire, Jo Stoyte, in *After Many a Summer Dies the Swan*. Huxley insists everyone is potentially a mystic trying to identify with something larger than himself. Mr. Propter, an old school friend of Stoyte's but his opposite in outlook, seems to be talking when Huxley describes the need 'to forget one's own, old, wearisome identity' as a desire to 'escape' (Part 2, II). Huxley comes full circle: he began by satirizing escapists but now finds the impulse to be one commendable, provided it leads to escape from the egoistic self. In *The Perennial Philosophy* (1945) (v), an answer to Cardan's desire, in *Those Barren Leaves*, for a viewpoint all can subscribe to, Huxley considers escape from the self a justifiable prison break.

Theological eccentricity becomes the new target in *Time Must Have a Stop*, as Huxley attacks Eustace Barnack for choosing his own ego over an escape into the divine equanimity (XIII). Every two or three chapters after Eustace's fatal coronary, Huxley records a new episode in Barnack's struggle to preserve his egoistic self from absorption into the white radiance of eternity. As a sort of anti-Dante, Eustace shuns rather than embraces, the Beatific vision. Mr. Propter equates life with time and craving, evils in themselves and in what they cause. Thus Huxley feels one must 'escape from history'[13] into contemplation of the Divine Spirit. Drugs that confirm the titular assertion of *Time Must Have a Stop* by diminishing our interest in time and craving may be a means to self-transcendence. Huxley's own experience with mescalin, as recounted in *The Doors of Perception* (1954) and *Heaven and Hell* (1963), allegedly helped him achieve, as so few of his characters do, a genuine Keatsian experience: union with the 'thisness' of things, plus the mystic's conviction of the world's oneness. Breaking down the barriers between men, the paramount concern of the early novels, yields to destroying those between man and God. 'I am I' must be replaced, Huxley insists, by 'Thou art That'.[14] The particle of the divine substance in man (Thou) can lead, via meditation, to knowledge of God (That), followed by an experience of union with him. This is the basis of the perennial philosophy, Huxley's name for the basic tenets of mysticism. He sees this fundamental creed, especially when it is distilled into what he calls the Minimum Working Hypothesis, as the bridge or common denominator between religions. Those who ignore the perennial philosophy discovered in the novels by Anthony Beavis and Sebastian Barnack are not only subjected to a satire that is more bitter and sarcastic than that of the earlier novels but are also declared anathema: 'In the sphere of ethical thought they are eccentrics'.[15]

As Huxley moves towards mysticism, one-pointedness no longer draws his satire as frequently as before. The ideal man, Huxley maintains in *Ends and Means*, is non-attached. He places no responsibility to things in this world in the way of his devotion to God. Mark Rampion may resemble D. H. Lawrence, but Huxley's final preference is for mystics such as William Law and St. Teresa. Mr. Propter, Bruno Rontini of *Time Must Have a Stop*, and the mature Sebastian from the same novel seem even less geared to their time and place than the architect Gumbril Sr., in *Antic Hay*, with his miniature reconstruction of London according to the plans of Christopher Wren. Huxley insists the attainment of mystical union with God does not exclude social concern and his own essays deal with birth control, propaganda, and modern warfare, while also explaining mystics and mysticism. Anthony Beavis is an active pacifist as well as a mystic. But the mystic hero remains essentially one-pointed in that all his acts and thoughts are channelled in one direction: towards the attainment and maintenance of union with the Divine Ground.

This is not, Huxley argues, in *The Perennial Philosophy* (III), 'any of those evil one-pointednesses of ambition or covetousness, or . . . [the] all too human one-pointednesses of art, scholarship and science, regarded as ends in themselves'. It is, instead, 'the supreme, more than human one-pointedness' of 'man's final end'. But while Rampion and, momentarily, Gumbril Jr. as Toto refused to kill any part of themselves, the mystic entertains no such refusal. Propter, Sebastian Barnack, and Bruno Rontini combine lack of desire for things of this world with self-imposed sexual continence. Huxley's *Island* is full of satisfied lovers, but marriage and sexual relations there come under the heading of religious experience.

With the shift from D. H. Lawrence to St. Teresa, the counterpoint of mind and body diminishes as a theme. Huxley puts less faith in the ideal of completeness. The new duality is that of time and eternity, and this is a counterpoint only the mystic can manage.

Rampion balanced the mental and the physical, but only the mystic can live both in time and, through contemplation, in the presence of God. Rampion's contempt for those who try to be more or less than fully human yields to Propter's search for good in *After Many a Summer Dies the Swan* on the levels below and above the human, on the animal and spiritual planes (Part 1, IX). Motion up or down will take man out of his ego; but the human plane we all live on, the one Rampion recommends, is irredeemably evil.

The all-important artist, the man whom Quarles said should be without blind spots, is no longer raised above the philosophers and saints. Since, to Huxley, art and religion seem to influence one another less than art and life do, 'art can never be completely redemptive. It can only point in the direction from which redemption comes'.[16] Once the artist, if he be mystic as well, reaches 'the primordial and ineffable Fact' in his own experience, he finds it pointless to go on writing about it or anything else. In the final chapter of *Time Must Have a Stop*, Sebastian Barnack has not written a play in five years.

The artists the later Huxley praises are those with a mystical bent. To strive for maximum achievement, Huxley decides, the artist must practise mortifications similar to the mystic's. From that he can proceed to the self-effacement that leads to 'unitive knowledge' of the Divine Ground. Art loses its terminal value and becomes a stepping stone, for to be centric, Huxley feels, one must be theocentric as well. Thus in an essay on El Greco in *Themes and Variations*, Huxley celebrates that painter's aspiring figures for asserting the soul's capacity to reach an ecstatic union with the divine Spirit.

Chelifer's vision of life, as recorded in *Those Barren Leaves*, becomes more insistent in the later novels. Huxley, the ardent supporter of centricity, must finally concede that the centre cannot hold, that reformation cannot begin at the wheel's axis and move outward along the spokes. The estimate of Pala's ideal society offered in *Island* by Bahu, the ambassador of the neighbouring dictator, Col. Dipa, echoes Chelifer's views about the irrelevance of normality and those who support it. Bahu finds Pala's goals admirable, but 'unfortunately they're out of context, they've become completely irrelevant to the present situation of the world in general' (v). Faced with a choice of identifying with the present situation (as did Chelifer) or flying off on his own (as do Huxley eccentrics), Huxley opts for the centrifugal. The satirist of fugitives from the norm puts his faith for the future of civilization in a series of splinter groups who flee an incurable society of possessors and militarists.

A scriptwriter in *Ape and Essence* (1949) advises us that the saint cannot cure 'our regimented insanity', as Gandhi tried to do, 'at the centre'. He can only work 'from without, at the periphery'.[17] The novel concludes with Alfred Poole and Loola making their way to a community of 'Hots', an isolated settlement where normal sex relationships survive. In *Brave New World* Helmholtz Watson is deported to an island where he joins the unorthodox individuals that even Mustapha Mond terms the most interesting set of people in the world (XVI). Huxley becomes interested in theocentric and marginal groups, such as the Benedictines, the Oneida Community, and the Society of Friends, groups that would very likely have been treated with levity in *Crome Yellow*. The ideal society, as Bahu observes, can stay viable only so long as it remains out of touch with the rest of the world, only so long as it preserves its centricity by an eccentric flight away from a centre that is thoroughly corrupt. Unlike the unsatisfactory retreats of Denis Stone and Gumbril Jr. at the ends of their novels, Pala's isolation is her one slim hope for survival. Despite a number of social essays and a final utopian novel, the Huxley of the 1950s and 60s is as deliberately out of step with his times as Evelyn Waugh was. He places his trust either in some Pala the future may create or in the next world.

As he shifts from the theme of balanced excesses to that of unitive knowledge of God, religious terminology replaces sexual metaphor in Huxley's vocabulary. The builders of private worlds seek 'onanistic satisfactions',[18] but Virginia Maunciple learns, in *After Many a Summer Dies the Swan*, that every attempt to die to self through alcohol or sex is followed by 'a little resurrection' back to the self and separation (Part 2, II). In *The Genius and the Goddess* (1955) Rivers insists 'the only vocabulary is the theologian's'. Sleeping in his youth with Katy Maartens may have been an immoral act, but it made Rivers aware of something larger than himself; in retrospect, he can only describe the incident as an act of grace, an initial step towards God. The sexual act itself is put in religious terms and evaluated in light of man's final end.

The relentless assault against egotism, however, and the position that good and bad depend on whether an action takes one towards or away from the Divine Ground bring Huxley, as an artist, dangerously close to the one-noted eccentricity he continually satirized. As he moves towards mysticism, although he displays knowledge in so many fields, Huxley becomes as much of a pedagogue-pervert as Mark Rampion confessed himself to be (xxxiv). In parts of *Point Counter Point* and throughout the later novels, he preaches at his readers, often with the same unfortunate effect the Rev. Pelvey had on Gumbril Jr. in *Antic Hay* (I). Despite multilateral concerns, Huxley increasingly subverts diverse material to one or two ends.

In as much as Huxley's perpetual enemies are egotism, eccentricity, and the separateness both engender, his favourite image by far is, appropriately, that of 'the introvert Procrustes',[19] who would chop and trim the objective world to make it fit the bed prepared for it in his mind. By contrast with the egoist Procrustes, who is the legendary model for most of his characters, Huxley supports inclusiveness, the building of bridges, and the closing of gaps. His reiterated theme in *Music at Night* and elsewhere is that we must say 'not only, but also'. He fights the cravings of the ego wherever they appear, but he begins to find them everywhere. Huxley's standards of completeness rule out tragedy as an acceptable art form. 'To make a tragedy,' Huxley contends that an artist must do what the eccentric does, he 'must isolate a single element out of the totality of human experience and use that exclusively as his material.'[20] The homogeneity being forced on a [German] people who were enjoying the blessings of variety makes Hitler, Huxley complains in *Beyond the Mexique Bay* (1934), an eccentric who does to a nation what the one-pointed character does to all but one of his many selves.

The root that means 'two', *duo* or *bis*, Huxley observes in *The Perennial Philosophy* (I), connotes badness in Indo-European languages and serves as linguistic proof of 'the essential badness of division'. Rivers even calls for a new set of words to 'express the natural togetherness of things'.[21] In *The Art of Seeing* (II), Huxley blames the conscious 'I' with preparing the body for disease. Personalities, Mr. Propter argues in *After Many a Summer Dies the Swan*, are 'illusory figments' of self-will that obscure the 'more-than-personal consciousness' that can be reached through self-transcendence (Part I, VIII). This consciousness is not only more than any person is individually, but impersonal in itself, since belief in a personal God, Huxley feels, leads to 'overvaluation of the individual ego'.[22] In *Grey Eminence* (1941) (III) sin becomes 'the manifestation of self'; and in *The Perennial Philosophy* (VI) holiness becomes 'the total denial of the separate self'. The real Satan, Huxley decides in *Grey Eminence* (VI), is what keeps men from dying to themselves. The ego, the untranscended personality, is unhealthy, ungodly, sinful, and even Satan himself.

III

What brings the preceding account of Huxley's development more in line with the structural concerns of the present chapter is simply this: as Huxley moves from satire of one-pointedness to acceptance of one form of it, the structure of his novels becomes one-pointed as well. The counterpoint technique that can be seen moving towards maturity throughout Huxley's first three novels disappears almost entirely after *Eyeless in Gaza*. That novel contains some of Huxley's finest writing along with the seeds of his dissolution as a novelist. Only *Time Must Have a Stop* constitutes something of a return to earlier, more dramatic procedures and it is, not surprisingly, the best of Huxley's last four novels.

Where Laurence Sterne challenged the formalism and selectivity of the novel, Huxley questions the modern novel's use of point of view. It is the partiality and egotism contained in the individual's point of view that Huxley wishes to expose. To tell a novel from one character's point of view, even from Rampion's in *Point Counter Point*, would thus cater to egotism. Point of view is possibly the modern novel's major experimental concern, but Huxley is the only modern novelist interested not only in showing, as realistically as possible, how his characters perceive reality, but also in calling them to account for the fallacies in their method. In *Mrs. Dalloway* (1925), for example, Virginia Woolf presents reality as it strikes the individual mind from one instant to another, but the novel remains bound up at any given moment in the mind of one of its protagonists. This is presumably what Robert Humphries means when he refers to Virginia Woolf's 'subjective fictions', or terms *The Waves* (1931) an 'incommunicative' novel.[23] As Humphries notes, Mrs. Woolf herself contended that 'the important thing for the artist to express is his private vision of reality, of what life subjectively is'. Huxley's vision of life is that it is an amorphous collection of irreconcilable subjective views and needs some valid objective standards.

The conflicting versions of Sutpen's rise and fall in William Faulkner's *Absalom, Absalom!* (1936), more so than the different viewpoints through which the decline of the Compson family is seen in *The Sound and the Fury* (1929), are never forced to take each other into consideration, are never resolved. The four versions of Sutpen, like the differing opinions Huxley characters express in a discussion scene, are equally valid subjectively. Only in *As I Lay Dying* (1930), a work that is actually more of a Huxley novel than is *Mosquitoes* (1927), does Faulkner, like Huxley, strive for a kind of synthesis. In James Joyce's *Ulysses* (1922), Molly and Leopold Bloom, despite what they reveal to the reader in interior monologues, remain even further apart in their views of marriage and sex than Lord Edward and Webley in their conceptions of progress. Even Mrs. Woolf has reservations as she feels, when reading Joyce, a sense of being 'confined' or 'shut in' a 'bright but narrow room'. 'Is it due to the method', she asks, 'that we feel neither jovial nor magnanimous, but centred in a self which, in spite of its susceptibility, never embraces or creates what is outside itself and beyond?'[24]

The methods used by Joyce and Mrs. Woolf seem primarily to depict – in Mrs. Woolf's case to support – a way of seeing things that Huxley opposes. Humphries' statement: 'The unifying subject, as it is in almost all stream-of-consciousness passages, is the character's egocentric consciousness'[25] could have come, as a complaint, from Huxley himself. His novels satirize characters for being trapped in their own minds, for not taking other viewpoints into account when formulating their own. Discussion scenes and abrupt changes of scene bring Lord Edward's version of Pharaoh's dream into collision with Webley's.

On the other hand, Huxley criticized Joseph Conrad for not knowing what goes on in the minds of his characters. Although of considerable length, the comments on Conrad must be quoted virtually in full:

> The mysterious thrilling charm of his [Conrad's] characters . . . is due to the fact that he knows nothing at all about them . . . The God's-eye view of those novelists who really know, or pretend they know, exactly what is going on in the minds of their characters, is exchanged for the traveller's-eye view, the view of the stranger who starts with no knowledge whatever of the actors' personalities and can only infer from their gestures what is happening in their minds. Conrad, it must be admitted, manages to infer very little . . . His bewilderment is infectious . . . Mystery is delightful and exciting; but it is foolish to admire it too highly . . . There will always be mysteries . . . But it is best to know what is knowable . . . If Conrad's characters are mysterious, it is not because they are complicated, difficult or subtle characters, but simply

because he does not understand them . . . Conrad only looks on from a distance, without understanding them, without even making up plausible hypotheses about them out of his imagination.[26]

To Huxley, Conrad is part of the modern predicament: he is no better off in regard to Lord Jim or Mr. Kurtz than Denis Stone is in his encounters with Jenny. It seems plausible to argue that Huxley wishes the God's-eye view and the traveller's-eye view to supplement one another. The artist who sacrifices either of these two ways of looking at the world lets society down. Thus Philip Quarles functions within the context of *Point Counter Point* while an omniscent Huxley remains outside and above. Though Huxley never puts it in so many words, he appears to regard the cultivation in the modern novel of interior monologue or stream of consciousness as a surrender to the subjective self, a willingness on the novelist's part to tolerate, or at least not challenge, a character's equation of reality with his own perceptions of it. Conrad cannot penetrate his characters and Mrs. Woolf's cannot break out of themselves. Admittedly, the foregoing would be crude grounds indeed on which to base any complete evaluation of either Conrad or Mrs. Woolf's achievement, yet Huxley's point is well-taken and his exposure of limited viewpoints in *Point Counter Point* is in keeping with his search for some strongly desired but as yet, in 1928, vaguely defined universal standard of judgment and behaviour.

Huxley thus feels Conrad knows as little about other people as the typical Huxley character does and that Mrs. Woolf's novels celebrate individuals who are as content with their own impressions as the typical Huxley eccentric. Far from being, as some critics have charged, an attempt simply to seem as modern as some of his contemporaries, Huxley's experimental method is something of a satire on theirs. His structural technique and intent stress the futility and disaster of resting content with one's own point of view, for the multiplication of viewpoints satirizes those who equate their subjective opinion with objective reality. On some approximation of multiple point of view, of sympathetic projection into the viewpoints of other people, the salvation of Denis Stone, Gumbril Jr., Calamy and numerous other Huxley characters clearly depends. As a proponent of as broad a prospective as possible, Huxley refuses to rule out either the 'God's-eye view' or the 'traveller's-eye view'. He is quite willing to enter a character's mind and unveil that individual's subjective interpretation of reality, but he seldom forgoes the comedy to be derived from contrasting that subjective interpretation with his own traveller's-eye view of the character or with the traveller's-eye view of the character taken by other personages in the novel.

Reality, for Huxley, remains something larger than any individual viewpoint. As a novelist, Huxley tries to do what his characters fail to accomplish on even a minimal level: to supplement each aspect of an event with as many other aspects as possible. The method of perception he utilizes as a novelist in *Point Counter Point* is the one he recommends to his characters and readers. Whether the novelists mentioned in the preceding paragraphs wrote better novels than *Point Counter Point* is not at issue. The point to be stressed is that for Huxley, more so than for these novelists, point of view is the main moral as well as a primary technical problem. The contrast between the way Huxley's characters perceive events and the way Huxley feels they *ought* to perceive them is a primary concern of *Point Counter Point* and is one of the reasons why the novel is still re-readable.

Sterne lived 364 times faster than he could write. Similarly, there are more points of view than even Argus could take and Huxley's desire to see an event or a relationship in all its aspects, to say 'not only, but also', is ultimately self-defeating, an impossibility. *Eyeless in Gaza*, as chapter six will show, is less ambitious from the outset since it settles for Anthony Beavis's final conception of all the different events of his life as an interrelated whole.

Through the use of image, satiric parable, Swiftian irony, and 'musicalization', Huxley exposes eccentricity and traces it to the egotism he believes is its source. In *Point Counter Point*, he fuses satire and structure. After that novel, however, he begins to do what he satirizes his characters for doing: he often takes one point of view, the mystic's. *Point Counter Point* hints at a physical and mental unity underlying diverse people and situations and *The Perennial Philosophy* examines the spiritual unity that Huxley contends underlies different religions and separate consciousnesses. Huxley's pursuits in both these works appear similar. In both he seeks unifiers and attempts to avoid isolation within the self. Yet the novel seems intensive and expansive, as more potential connections are suggested with each introduction of new characters and events, while the essays are reductive, resulting in a Minimum Working Hypothesis.[27] Synthesis is replaced by distillation. Thus, although Huxley claims to be writing from the viewpoint held in common by many of the great religious thinkers, he sometimes gives the impression of having too readily sacrificed openness of mind to a desire for an absolute standard. The mystic's viewpoint leads him to praise, in *Tomorrow and Tomorrow and Tomorrow* (1956), such works as *Zen and the Art of Archery* and to endorse, in *Island*, the absurd play called *Oedipus in Pala* (XIV). Huxley becomes a bit eccentric, just as he always was an illustration of body-mind imbalance. Ultimately, he, too, is a bit like Procrustes.

CHAPTER III

The Counterpoint of Flight

Despite the fact that their tone perceptively darkens, Aldous Huxley's first three novels – and for freshness and exuberance they may be his finest comic achievement – seem at first glance much too similar. The same characters appear from one novel to the next under different names that one tends to regard as aliases; and the situations, though never repetitious, seem ultimately to support a basic repertoire of themes. Thus an examination of *Crome Yellow* (1921) leaves one as thrilled with Huxley's first novel as his original audience was. But if a perusal of *Antic Hay* (1923) and *Those Barren Leaves* (1925) follows immediately, one may conclude that Huxley has written the same novel three times. This is not a thoroughly misguided judgment, but rather an imprecise one and therefore it states negatively what is actually a positive accomplishment.

What Huxley has done, however, is to go over and over the same themes but never from precisely the same angle and never with the same results. The heroes of the first two novels are defeated in different ways by similar problems whereas the third protagonist enjoys a tentative, modified, perhaps only temporary success. Each time his hero confronts the central problems and fails, Huxley has someone similar to him, but also different, try over again from a slightly different approach.

When these three novels are looked at as a sort of trilogy, they remain infinitely readable in themselves but also take on an added significance in that the thematic alterations they catalogue reveal in microcosm the direction in which Huxley will develop in terms of ideas as well as craftsmanship. The changes the three novels exhibit in their handling of the same set of themes show Huxley doing between 1921 and 1925 what he would only permanently accomplish and accept by 1934 with the appearance, in *Eyeless in Gaza*, of his first full-fledged mystic-hero. At the same time, the increasing mastery of structure and technique from novel to novel and the sense one has that all three novels are really one book with three complementary, perhaps even contrapuntal, sets of characters and events make the many-layered complexity of *Point Counter Point* (1928) inevitable.

63

I

Crome Yellow, Huxley's first novel, is the love song of its hero, Denis Stone. The young poet has come to Crome[1] to tell Anne Wimbush he loves her. What the novel's thirty chapters actually record, however, is his failure to deliver the message. The theme of ineffectual communication spans the novel while permeating the majority of scenes. The direction of these scenes is towards a sort of awakening wherein Denis, who has concluded that people are uncrossing parallel lines, is suddenly forced to look at himself as he appears to others.

Hercules the Dwarf is a grotesque figure in a satiric parable that Henry Wimbush presents as a piece of straight history from the book he is writing on Crome (XIII). Denis, on the other hand, appears as the hero of a supposedly realistic story. Yet the pair actually belong to the same species of eccentric in trying to make reality conform to their expectations. Like the dwarf, who reduced life to his own proportions, Denis has a fund of patterns to impose on events but is seldom prepared for experience itself. To him, life is a rehearsable play. He blocks out scenes with himself in the central role and attempts to stage them. The missed cues and unexpected replies that follow as the interpretation of Pharaoh's dream that is written and directed by Denis Stone falls apart provide excellent comedy. Denis plans, for example, to tell Anne how adorable she is, but the scene collapses when she comments on the attractiveness of his white flannel trousers. The conversation takes 'a preposterous and unexpected turn' (IV) in which the heroine usurps the hero's opening line and addresses him as though he were a little boy and not a contender for her love.

Language, a perennial problem for Huxley characters and even, as chapter seven will show, for the artificially stabilized society of *Brave New World*, stands between Denis and reality the way Keats' sensuous richness threatened his involvement with society. Denis regards words as though they were things. They become his substitute for reality and his conversation deteriorates into one long fallacy of misplaced concreteness. As a Procrustean, Denis wants the meaning of *carminative* to correspond with its beautiful sound. Although he feels it should illustrate his theory that the artist creates something out of nothing through the power of words, *carminative* nevertheless means *windtreibend*. Denis' mind, Huxley notes, 'wandered down echoing corridors of assonance and alliteration ever further and further from the point' (I). Denis' centrifugal use of language takes him away from reality and into a private world.

Whenever Denis supplies the literary touch, it is simultaneously the embalmer's. His neatly-turned observations transform an object into a frozen scene for some Grecian Urn. Anne looks at the sunflowers and finds them magnificent, but Denis must observe that their dark faces and golden crowns make them 'kings in Ethiopia' (IV), an apt description but ultimately a substitute for seeing things as they are. If he lacks a fine phrase of his own, Denis quotes another poet, for an object becomes 'more real' to him if he can employ 'somebody else's ready made phrase' (IV). In Denis' propensity for quotes and for the continual transformation of life into art, Huxley satirizes his own tendency to be too precious, overly multisyllabic, and, at times, esoterically erudite. Rehearsed scenes, ready-made phrases, words instead of things – these are the barriers Denis imposes between himself and life. He is the first in a series of Huxley characters who personify a paradoxical union of egotism and shyness. Jeremy Pordage of *After Many a Summer Dies the Swan* (1939) is an example of Denis in middle-age. He has the young poet's penchant for apt quotation and for books over experience. In the scene in which Anne comments on his trousers, Denis had hoped to work up to the old romantic stand-by, the pregnant silence. But he fails to impregnate the silence, just as the boxes containing the unedited Hauberk papers Pordage must sort out are 'Twenty-seven crates of still unravished brides of quietness' (Part I, v) and the only brides the ineffectual Pordage will ever know. Denis is also a forerunner of Philip Quarles. He agrees with Quarles that one should live first and then make one's philosophy fit life, but Denis says this with arms outstretched 'in an attitude of crucifixion'. He is once again playing a role, whereas Anne says she has 'always taken things as they come' (IV). Thus if Denis and Anne married, they would become Philip and Elinor Quarles. In the course of the novel, Denis discovers he is a split-man. His responses are purely mental, for although he shouts his love for Anne 'mentally', 'not a sound issues from his lips' (IV). His emotions, like Quarles', remain 'theoretical' (XVII).

Denis is basically an escapist. But the barriers he puts up are also moulds that re-shape the world of experience into forms his ego can manage. He has elected himself life's playwright and he expects the portion of life treated in the novel to be handled from his point of view. In choosing art over life and translating the latter into the former, he also personifies Huxley's suspicion that the entire process by which life becomes art makes the artist as much of a theme-bending egotist as any of the speakers in a *Point Counter Point* discussion scene. The artist who imposes patterns on experience, Huxley fears, produces works that embody his own limitations. Philip Quarles' novels provide an all-too-obvious example. Denis, Gumbril Jr. of *Antic Hay*, and Calamy in *Those Barren Leaves*, the heroes of Huxley's first three novels, are three of the author's fictional versions of himself and his own limitations. The first two heroes fail to get out of themselves. They do not achieve a viewpoint broad enough to protect them from their egos. Calamy, however, is a potential success; and it is Calamy's method Huxley tries, first as a novelist in *Point Counter Point*, and later as a mystic in both novels and non-fiction prose.

Jenny Mullion, whose deafness stands between her and the other characters in the novel, is, ironically, the person who penetrates Denis' barriers. All through the novel she functions as a comical sphinx whose riddle Denis tries to read. Her 'enigmatic remoteness' unsettles him as she periodically emerges from her interior world 'like a cuckoo from a clock'. It is after an abortive conversation with her that Denis decides the world consists of parallel lines (IV). This is a quasi-philosophical theory made from his own vantage point and with the tacit assumption that he, at least, is striving for contacts. An accidental glance into Jenny's notebook, however, confronts Denis with his own egotism: he discovers a cutting caricature sketch of himself (XXIV). The phenomenon of other people, the existence of points of view different from and unsympathetic to his own is made plain to him. He finds it 'inconceivable that he should appear to other people as they appeared to him'.

Denis' egotism is threatened, his way of looking at himself and the world comically overturned. The validity of one's personal viewpoint – to be questioned technically and structurally in *Point Counter Point* and politically but perhaps more naively in *Ends and Means*[2] – is effectively challenged. In Denis, Keats' way with language exists without Keats' ability to become the people and things he described. The red notebook forces Denis to see himself with Jenny's eyes. Cast as a nonentity in Denis's play, Jenny suddenly appears in the role of Max Beerbohm.

The possibility of realizing the intricateness of other people to the same extent one is aware of complexity in oneself frightens Denis and intrigues Huxley. Denis must come to terms with 'the vast conscious world outside himself'. In so doing, he can no longer imagine himself the world's sole intelligent being, nor ignore the fact that others are 'in their way as elaborate and complete as he is in his . . .' (XXIV).[3] He must live with the fact that he seems as ridiculous and secondary to others as they do to him. His first move, however, is a retreat as he contrives his immediate departure from Crome. Jenny's cartoon has exploded his barriers, but the phony telegram he sends himself provides him with a new means of escape. He plays his leave-taking as a funeral scene and makes the reader wonder if his epiphany has taught him anything. His bad habits continue as he aptly quotes Landor (XXX), but so does his ineffectualness, since nobody notices. Henry Wimbush and Crome's other inhabitants remain self-absorbed. Despite his epiphanic experience with Jenny's notebook, Denis' departure constitutes escapism, a flight *from* rather than *to*. The confrontation of a Huxley hero with the phenomenon of other people must be tried again in the author's next novel.

II

Huxley's second novel, *Antic Hay*, is organized around images of futility. It ends with Myra Viveash and Theodore Gumbril Jr. taxiing back and forth across London while Shearwater, scientist and kidney expert, pedals a stationary bicycle. The essayist Mercaptan's 'delicious middles' (essays meant for publication neither at the start nor end of a journal) are thus the perfect art form for a novel of futility whose characters have little sense of their origins and no ends to pursue. Though Gumbril Jr. is practically Denis Stone and Prufrock all over again, the novel draws its atmosphere from T. S. Eliot's *The Waste Land*. Myra Viveash, who resembles Ernest Hemingway's Brett Ashley in *The Sun Also Rises* and Evelyn Waugh's Margot Beste-Chetwynd in *Decline and Fall*,[4] epitomizes the ennui of modern life when she insists 'tomorrow will be as awful as today' (XXIII). In a novel full of tag names, Mrs. Viveash's suggests light without heat. She kindles love for herself in every male in the novel, but can offer no answering warmth of her own. Her voice, the articulation of society, seems to come from a deathbed and is 'always on the point of expiring' (V).

The influence of T. S. Eliot's poetry on satiric novels of the 1920s and 30s has never been sufficiently stressed. In Waugh's *A Handful of Dust* (1934), the title of which comes from *The Waste Land*, F. Scott Fitzgerald's *The Great Gatsby* (1925), and in *Antic Hay*

(1923), past and present are ludicrously contrasted and characters are dwarfed by roles their ancestors played with ease. Gumbril Sr. seems a weak version of Christopher Wren, as is Gumbril Jr. of the Rabelaisian man, and Coleman makes a ridiculous Satan. Casmir Lypiatt wishes to fill Michelangelo's shoes, but is clearly patterned on the bragging, unsuccessful Romantic painter, Benjamin Haydon.[5] In art, in life, even in their capacity for evil, Huxley's characters in *Antic Hay* are a shrivelled lot. Like Denis Stone, they all play roles; they are all escapists trying to be something they are not. The extent to which each inhabits a private world is further emphasized by the different role each chooses in an attempt to increase his stature. What Christopher Wren, Satan, the Complete Man, and a bombastic Romantic painter could say to each other is hard to determine.

In conversation with the diabolist, Coleman, Shearwater confesses that the kidneys are his only interest in life. 'You hold the key to everything,' Coleman mockingly replies, 'The key, I tell you, the key' (IV). Coleman has read T. S. Eliot: 'We think of the key,' T. S. Eliot wrote in *The Waste Land* (414–415), 'each in his prison. Thinking of the key, each confirms a prison.' Shearwater has made kidneys into an imprisoning private world on the assumption that they are talismanic. The old roles absurdly revived by Gumbril Jr. and Lypiatt no longer work, nor does the new science, as personified by Shearwater, seem any more successful. Yet Shearwater holds the key to everything in a real sense, inasmuch as what he has done, like the saga of Hercules and the autobiography of Chelifer, explains the eccentricity of many of Huxley's characters.

Between Denis and Gumbril Jr., however, one important difference exists. Gumbril seems more aware both of his own inadequacy and of egos other than his own. He even has a dream-self in which he succeeds where Denis failed. Like Gaveston in Marlowe's *Edward II* (I, i, 59–60), he prefers 'men, like satyrs [who] . . . with their goat-feet dance an antic hay'. In his dream, chance encounters and plotted opportunities occur and recur as they never did for Denis. Reality fulfills Gumbril's expectations and, in his dream life, he combines Keatsian power with breadth of vision comparable to Huxley's in *Point Counter Point*: he can 'understand all points of view' and is able to 'identify himself' with such unfamiliar types as mill girls and engine drivers (I).

Unfortunately, Gumbril is really the victim of a plot full of more outrageous coincidences than any Waugh or Dickens novel contains.

He masquerades as Toto, the Rabelaisian man, but the first woman he conquers is Rosie Shearwater, his wife's friend. The theme of missed opportunity, so prevalent in *Crome Yellow*, recurs as a co-incidental meeting with Myra Viveash prevents Gumbril from joining Emily. His disguise as Toto, an attempt at actualizing his dream-self, has led to Emily and a happiness Gumbril can only fatalistically describe as 'unreal, impossible' (xɪɪ). Emily scarcely functions in the novel as a developed character, but she symbolizes the possibility of mystical union with the mysterious presence the sleepless Gumbril often feels approaching but never dares to face. She not only represents Gumbril's final opportunity to transcend himself but is also an intimation of the fusion of the sexual and the mystical (in which the first leads to the second) that Huxley will return to in *The Genius and the Goddess* (1955) and, most explicitly, in *Island* (1962). The mysterious presence is something, says Gumbril (xɪɪ), 'inexpressibly lovely and wonderful' yet 'inexpressibly terrifying', for should it 'engulf you, you'd die'. The death he has in mind is death to the self, the catastrophe all of Huxley's egotists fear most.

The central irony in the novel is that in a moment of crisis, when the opportunity to control events occurs, Gumbril Jr. chooses contrivance and coincidence over a chance for genuine contact. Despite his masquerade as Toto, Gumbril remains the parasite of events, and thus the genuine heir of Gaveston in a less flattering sense. Instead of goat-feet, he has cold ones. Although a rational theology where God is $2+2 = 4$ dismays him (ɪ) and he hungers for something more physical and emotional, Gumbril cannot confront what Eliot calls 'The awful daring of a moment's surrender/Which an age of prudence can never retract' (404–405). His pose as Complete Man could always be dropped, but his commitment to Emily would have to be permanent. In an atmosphere of withered values, Gumbril lacks sufficient faith. The chance to be Keats rather than a parallel line comes, but he retreats. He sends Emily a telegram – just as Denis sent himself one – saying he will join her a day late because of a slight accident. The slight accident is Myra Viveash, the novel's siren, whose desire for company lures Gumbril from his intended visit to Emily. Gumbril also telegrams Rosie to arrange a rendezvous, but purposely gives her Mercaptan's address and Coleman's name. As she proceeds to have affairs with each of them, the futility of Gumbril's affair with her is underlined. Through connivance, Gumbril equates the genuine contact he has made with Emily with its farcical counterpart in Rosie and strips himself of both.

As Myra and Gumbril dance, the band, parodying *Hamlet*, blares 'What's he to Hecuba?/Nothing at all' (xv). Prufrock protested he was no Hamlet, nor is Gumbril. He feigns an accident; like Hamlet, he procrastinates; but it leads to missed opportunity rather than climactic confrontation. The relevant play he watches in the night-club with Myra after the band has finished (xvi) does not catch his conscience as Hamlet's did the king's. He is not shaken by the lines: 'Somewhere there must be love like music. Love harmonious and ordered: two spirits, two bodies moving contrapuntally together.' For Gumbril, as well as Huxley, love is never sufficiently aesthetic. Gumbril accepts the band's song as a summary of his relations with both Myra and Emily. When her letter arrives next morning to put off his trip forever, Emily describes Gumbril's accident as a warning sent *by Providence* to show her hope for happiness was 'hopelessly impractical' (xvi). Gumbril's failure to confront the situation and Myra's ability to disrupt it cast them both in the role of Providence. That Gumbril should be described as the controller of events he has always desired to be at the moment he is most disloyal to his dream is exquisite irony. Had he come, Emily writes, 'I'd have twisted myself into the threads of your life.' Instead, Gumbril realizes, he has for-saken the one person with whom 'he might have learned to await in quietness the final coming of that lovely terrible thing': from which 'ignobly he had fled' so many times. Like Denis, Gumbril remains an escapist, a separatist. In the last chapter, he plans to flee to the continent to sell the pneumatic trousers he has invented. These and not Emily, comprise the threads of his life. He invented them to put cushioned material between humanity's posteriors and hard wooden benches and they signify his willingness to place some barrier between himself and the hard surfaces of reality.[6]

III

In *Those Barren Leaves*, his third novel, Huxley moves Crome to Vezza, Italy. The characters in the book seem to succeed where those in Huxley's previous novels failed. The novelist Calamy, whose arrival at Vezza seems to be a return from a flight-journey similar to that undertaken by Gumbril at the end of *Antic Hay*, has more success with women than his two male predecessors combined. So too, Francis Chelifer, instead of living in a private world, at first seems completely identified with his environment. Even Mary

Thriplow, though a flourishing novelist and a woman of many pretences, does not always put art before life. She does regard most experiences as material for her novels, but she has the experiences first, and then arranges them into patterns. Though Huxley severely satirizes her, her novels do not keep her from life as thoroughly as Quarles' do. Like Calamy, however, Huxley is dissatisfied with these 'successes'. Whereas Denis and Gumbril Jr. were satirized for raising shields against reality, Calamy's final retreat into solitude and speculation is favourably counterpointed against their flights.

Huxley's first three novels thus contain in miniature one of the major movements of his career: from a desire for involvement and unity to a later preference for properly motivated escape. The burden of inadequacy shifts in the course of these three novels until it rests less on the Prufrockian heroes and more on the society in which they live. In *Those Barren Leaves*, Huxley seems at times to suspect, perhaps even to discredit, the very things *Crome Yellow* and *Antic Hay* pursued.

Unlike Gumbril Jr., Calamy regards passion and its fulfilment as the barrier between himself and higher things (Part 1, IV). As the novel and his routine affair with Mary proceed, Calamy's dissatisfaction increases. He 'couldn't at the same time lean out into the silence beyond the futile noise and bustle – into the mental silence that lies beyond the body ... and himself partake in the tumult' (Part 3, XIII). If one compares Calamy's statements with some of the more basic advice to the yogi contained in the *Bhagavad-Gita*, it becomes clear that Calamy is discussing a few fairly fundamental contemplation procedures. He concludes that in 'thinking really hard about one thing – this hand, for example – . . . one might be able to burrow one's way right through the mystery and really get at something ...' (Part 5, 1). (The yogi is supposed to sit in some isolated spot and, while holding the senses and imagination in check, to keep the mind focussed on its object. The yogi's heart will then become pure.) For as Calamy realizes, his hand exists simultaneously in a dozen parallel worlds. He resolves to search for relationships between 'different modes of being', for what exists in common between life and chemistry, a collection of cells and the consciousness of a caress. Like many Huxley heroes, Calamy is after a vision part Keatsian, part Blakean, in which staring at one object in all its aspects with sufficient intensity can lead to an explanation of all things. Quarles' notebook in *Point Counter Point* insists 'the meditative eye can look through any single object and see, as through a window, the entire cosmos' (XIX). Even something insignificant, such as 'the smell of roast duck' can furnish 'a glimpse of everything, from the spiral nebulae to Mozart's music and the stigmata of St. Francis of Assisi', Quarles writes, purposely exaggerating his point. Like the author of *Point Counter Point*, and unlike the parallel-line-characters in that novel, Calamy desires to see a dozen worlds simultaneously and to discover the relationships between them. Both elements in Huxley – that which inclines towards the ideal of completeness and that which prefers mysticism, or, in other words, the extrovert and the introvert – encourage him and Calamy to search for links between different modes of being. But where Denis and Gumbril failed to resuscitate the romantic imagination and its capacity for sympathetic projection, Calamy initiates a new approach to the problem of how to transcend one's personal limitations: he opens gulfs between people and between things. To discover relationships, he dissociates his mind from his body and resolves to rely solely on the former.

In his flight to the mountains and in his hermit's existence there, however, Calamy seems to leave half of himself, the physical half, behind. Huxley is reluctant to sanction such a move and Calamy himself dreams of a 'graceful Latin compromise' featuring 'cultivation of mind and body' (Part 3, XIII). Then D. H. Lawrence appears (he and Huxley became friends in 1926, a year after *Those Barren Leaves* was published), and possibly seems to be that compromise personified. The shift from Gumbril and Denis' attempts at involvement to Calamy's exaltation of the contemplative life is arrested. The ideal of the whole man, fleetingly personified by Gumbril as Toto, enjoys a triumphant resurgence. But the Huxley novels from the mid-1930s onwards have their origins in the intentionally celibate Calamy. After his Lawrencian interlude, Huxley returns to Calamy's mountain top and the rudimentary outline of the perennial philosophy Calamy has already formulated. Calamy insists the axes 'chosen by the best observers have always been startlingly like one another. Gotama, Jesus and Lao-tze, for example; they lived sufficiently far from one another in space, time and social position. But their pictures of reality resemble one another very closely' (Part 5, IV). This is clearly a foreshadowing of the perennial philosophy's contention that 'Thou art That' is at the base of all religious experience and that mystics in all eras have enjoyed the same basic vision.

The chapter entitled 'Escape' in *Texts and Pretexts*, Huxley's attempts to combine the explication of poetry with the personal essay, seems written from Calamy's point of view: 'The world in which our bodies are condemned to live is really too squalid, too vulgar, too malignant to be borne. There is no remedy save in flight. But whither?'[7] Chelifer flees to the world's navel or Gog's Court, Gumbril Jr. departs for France, and Calamy climbs to a mountain top. Denis Stone returns to London and Shearwater pedals his bicycle in a perspiration experiment that is really a futile attempt to escape his desire for Myra Viveash. The novels present three major encounters with the phenomenon of other people, but none of the three main heroes, each patterned on Huxley himself, comes to terms with his world. Each hero seems to start where his predecessor left off: Denis never makes contact; Gumbril has a more than golden opportunity, but fails; Calamy, finding the encounters modern society provides unsatisfactory, tries to make contact with higher things.

Crome Yellow, Antic Hay, and *Those Barren Leaves* thus form a natural trilogy containing Huxley's initial explorations of egotism and alienation within the self. Each of the three main heroes reacts differently to the chasms that separate people. In their different responses and their variant forms of flight, the heroes encourage a reading of Huxley's first three novels as an exercise in counterpoint in which, as Quarles' notebook in *Point Counter Point* was later to prescribe (XXII), similar themes are pushed into different shapes from one novel to the next. In 1928, these three novels might have been written as one.

IV

Huxley's first three novels thus show him becoming increasingly ambitious in his use of counterpoint. He begins to exploit his themes in terms of a multiplicity of similar situations and to view these situations as simultaneously as possible. In *Crome Yellow,* Mary Bracegirdle's often disastrous search for a meaningful relationship is a simple variation on Denis' attempts to make contact with Anne and Jenny. The novel, with its many caricatures and exuberant inset tales from the history of Crome that Henry Wimbush is writing, stands as Huxley's freshest and possibly most amusing work. *Antic Hay,* a more serious comic novel than many critics suppose, is more complex in its use of variation. As Rosie proceeds from her self-absorbed husband to Gumbril, Mercaptan, and Coleman, she brings out their variant forms of egotism and one-sidedness. Like Grace Peddley of

'Two or Three Graces',[8] Rosie has no substantial character of her own and is transformed into the ideas of each successive male she sleeps with. The collapse of traditional values is made apparent by the various roles the characters assume but cannot fill. The unreal happiness Gumbril continually desires is what Shearwater, at the start of the novel, is never aware of and what every act of Coleman, the inverted idealist, tries to violate and refute.

Though still technically distant from *Point Counter Point*, *Those Barren Leaves* constitutes a decisive move in the direction of that novel. Calamy and the intentionally non-sapient Chelifer are obvious counterparts, while Irene's indecision over whether to make her own underclothing ('illicit love and rebellious reason') or write poetry ('spirit, duty, and religion') (Part I, VI) parodies Calamy's dilemma when he must choose between Mary Thriplow and spiritual progress. Part 3 of the novel, entitled 'The Loves of the Parallels', tries for similarity in situation and simultaneity in action (Part 3, II). The use of what Quarles later calls 'parallel, contrapuntal plots' or situations (XXII) re-enforces Huxley's opinion that the characters themselves are parallel lines. On different terraces, one above the other, Huxley presents Calamy and Mary Thriplow, Mrs. Aldwinkle and Chelifer, Mr. Cardan and Mr. Falx. The chiefly physical love of the first pair is compared with Mrs. Aldwinkle's possessiveness. Cardan and Falx are in love with ideas and learned discussions, but their inability to converse without arguing reveals them both as parallel lines. The terrace effect is meant as a rather rudimentary schematic statement of theme. The final variation is provided by Irene and Lord Hovenden who are in the country, but seated 'at the edge of a little terrace' (Part 3, IV) scooped out of the slope. Their love affair, a mixture of the comic and the idyllic, is handled with sympathy as a positive though only faintly reassuring counterpoint to the loves already mentioned. If one imagines all these events occurring at once, something resembling the effect produced by related but different melodies in a musical composition begins to emerge.

All three novels move towards or stem from moments of insight. The themes of missed opportunity and bungled epiphany seem closely related. Denis has his experience with Jenny's notebook, while Chelifer sees his whole life as a series of negative epiphanies in which he discovers the banal nature of reality. His recognition of Barbara's true character, of the extent to which, despite her physical allurements, she personifies the stupidity of modern life (Part 2, V), is a prime example. Gumbril Jr. never has sufficient courage to wait for the mysterious presence whose coming he often senses. He and Denis never take the chances they are offered, whereas Shearwater unearths the value of proportion but applies what he has learned about the need for physical and emotional contacts to a fruitless pursuit of Mrs. Viveash. When he finally realizes the epiphany may have relevance for himself and his wife, Rosie has too many liaisons on hand to notice him. By pedalling his stationary bicycle as part of a perspiration experiment, he tries to reduce himself to sheer water, to his former unknowing one-sidedness.

Crome Yellow is largely a high-spirited Peacockian novel, whereas the waste land atmosphere of futility and ennui in *Antic Hay* makes it a less exuberant work. *Those Barren Leaves*, in the barrenness of its characters and in Calamy's renunciation of them, seems darker yet. It remains a comic novel, but much of its comedy comes from parodies of Dickensian situations, parodies as effective as Evelyn Waugh's in *A Handful of Dust* (VI).[9]

In a lengthy critique of Dickens, Chelifer accuses him of being one of 'the jolly optimistic fellows' (Part 2, 1) who become 'chronically tearful' when they find virtue in the midst of squalor. But these virtues, Chelifer argues, are only of the animal variety and men inherit them from their animal forefathers. They are not the 'peculiarly human virtues', such as open-mindedness, complete tolerance, reasonable pursuit of social goods, and they are therefore not worth celebrating, according to Chelifer. The animal virtues Dickens lavishly praises reveal not merely his vulgar sentimentalism, Chelifer implies, but, more important, his basic escapism. The squalor, Chelifer argues, is the result of a lack of *human* virtues. Thus when Dickens condescends to look at reality, Chelifer says, he seizes on the purely animal virtues in order to avoid the real picture. The anti-escapist Chelifer must discredit Dickens lest it appear he himself has chosen to live in Gog's Court for sentimental reasons. In *Those Barren Leaves*, Dickensian scenes are re-done in an anti-sentimental manner, the way Chelifer would agree they ought to have been written. Barbara, for example, whom he pursues but never permanently attains, is Chelifer's Estelle, but for him there is no revised ending (Part 2, V).

The scenes at Miss Carruthers's boarding house are patterned after those at Mrs. Todgers's in *Martin Chuzzlewit*. Dickens' novels often present, within the larger world of the novel itself, a little world in which a ludicrous figure struts as cock of the walk. Mr. Lillyvick, the collector of water-rates in *Nicholas Nickleby*, is one such figure, as is Mr. Jinkins, that 'man of superior talents', at Mrs. Todgers's in *Martin Chuzzlewit*. Similarly, the witty sallies of the 'Inimitable Brimstone' make him the oracle of Miss Carruthers's table. The pretentiousness and egotism of a little world such as this is immediately apparent in both Dickens and Huxley, good-humouredly in the first and more satirically in the second. Huxley takes Brimstone and his domain as a microcosm for society's break-up into countless private worlds. In addition, the squalor in Gog's Court produces vulgarity, not virtue. Mrs. Cloudsley Shove is permitted to darken the doorway with her widowhood, but Mr. Dutt's black skin deprives him of the right to an opinion.

Miss Elver, a comic blend of Oliver Twist, Smike, and Little Nell, is not the waif who merits a fortune; in fact, she already has one. Instead of Mr. Brownlow, Cardan turns up to rescue her from her brother's plots. Miss Elver, despite her clumsiness, is named 'Grace', and to Cardan, she and her £25,000 seem sent from heaven to stave off his poverty. The wooing of this unattractive idiot child, who is actually thirty years old, by the cynical realist Cardan becomes the most memorable episode in the book. Their courtship is appropriately included as another variation in the section entitled 'The Loves of the Parallels'. Grace's death from food poisoning is intentionally 'disgusting', though no less amusing than some of the grotesque deaths in Waugh. In killing Grace off, Huxley makes a premeditated attack on the 'consoling serenities' (Part 4, IX) that palliate the deaths of Paul Dombey and Little Nell.[10] Though disgusting, Grace's death is not without pathos, and Cardan seems, at one point, genuinely moved. 'Blessed are the fools . . . for they shall see nothing', he reflects, possibly having two sets of fools in mind: those whose concern with consoling serenities blinds them to the real nature of an event, and those who see the real nature (disgust plus pathos) but miss the irony. Miss Elver's brother wished to kill her for her money. After rescuing her, Cardan unwittingly accomplishes her brother's design and Philip Elver becomes Grace's heir.

Huxley may share Chelifer's unfair views of Dickens, but not Chelifer's view of himself. As Calamy perceives, Chelifer is also a fool who sees nothing, the type who vanishes into the mess rather than have to cope with it. Ultimately, though he does not escape from reality, Chelifer flees from responsibility. He becomes, as Calamy charges, Dickens inside out and that is his form of escapism. Calamy's withdrawal, unlike the other retreats, is not a renunciation of responsibility. One can neither put a jolly face on reality nor merge into it, Huxley decides. In Denis, Gumbril Jr., Chelifer, and Dickens, Huxley considers alternative responses to reality and different escapes from it. Although at the end of *Those Barren Leaves* it seems by no means certain that Calamy will remain an isolated hermit until and beyond Cardan's next visit some six months hence, Huxley finds Calamy's act the only justifiable one. In the previous chapter, Huxley's development towards mysticism was assigned to the period following *Eyeless in Gaza*, and this is still correct. Yet Anthony Beavis, the hero of that novel, is clearly a modified version of Calamy and Huxley's development from 1936 on is partially a return to elements already present in his novels of the 1920s. In between, there is Huxley's Lawrencian interlude, in which the theme of completeness has its apotheosis.

CHAPTER IV

Huxley's Lawrencian Interlude:
The 'Latin Compromise' that Failed

'What I complain of . . .' are Mark Rampion's first words in *Point Counter Point* (VIII). And they are as much his tag as 'I'll never desert Mr. Micawber' is Mrs. Micawber's. For the next twenty-nine chapters, Rampion, an easily recognizable sketch of D. H. Lawrence, complains incessantly. Sexual relationships, mechanization, and, in fact, the whole trend of modern civilization come under his vituperative scrutiny. He seems to assume the role of professional curse-hurler, or, as Huxley euphemistically phrases it in *The Olive Tree*, to speak 'ex-cathedra'.[1] How the other characters in the novel stand him is difficult to determine, for Rampion dissects everyone he meets. To Spandrell he says: 'You like stewing in your disgusting suppurating juice. You don't want to be made healthy. You enjoy your unwholesomeness' (VIII). Yet the characters in *Point Counter Point* seek Rampion's companionship and expand in his presence. 'Without realizing it,' Spandrell 'had quite suddenly begun to feel happy.'

What, then, is to be made of Rampion? Is he, as was argued earlier, the centre of *Point Counter Point*, the standard from which the rest of the novel's characters have departed; or is he the boring gas-bag[2] Lawrence found him? No matter which alternative one chooses, the fact remains that Huxley often has tongue in cheek when Lawrence-Rampion appears.

In fact, beginning with Kingham in 'Two or Three Graces' (1926), and extending through Rampion of *Point Counter Point* (1928), Miles Fanning of 'After the Fireworks' (1929), and the Savage of *Brave New World* (1932), Huxley presents – and presents at times satirically – four protagonists who partially resemble D. H. Lawrence. This is surely odd behaviour on the part of the Huxley William York Tindall summarizes as 'Lawrence's disciple'.[3] On the other hand, Diana Trilling's assertion in 1958, that Huxley's Introduction to *The Letters of D. H. Lawrence* (1932) is 'the best single piece of Lawrence criticism that has been written'[4] cannot be maintained. But between these two opinions – Tindall's subservient Huxley and Mrs. Trilling's view of him as Lawrence's best interpreter – one can locate a Huxley who was both deeply influenced by and often astutely critical of his friend and fellow novelist. One can locate a Huxley who at times understood Lawrence all too well and at others not at all. In Mark Rampion, Huxley's ambivalent attitude towards Lawrence is most apparent, for Mark is both an idealized version of the Lawrence Huxley admired (but not necessarily the *real* Lawrence) and a satiric caricature embodying certain Lawrencian traits Huxley disliked.

Whether early or recent, critical estimates of the Huxley-Lawrence interchange contain no suggestion of friction between the two novelists. The common assumption is that Huxley served as Lawrence's bulldog in the same fashion that his grandfather, T. H. Huxley, was Darwin's. John Hawley Roberts insists Lawrence's friendship for Huxley in 1926 was a god-send since, in that year, Aldous 'desperately . . . needed a leader'.[5] Yet Aldous had been following Lawrence since the early 1920s and began satirizing him in 1926. John Atkins dismisses the increasingly critical comments on Lawrence that Huxley voiced in the early 1930s with the explanation that Lawrence's influence on Huxley naturally weakened after his death.[6] Yet the critical comments began much earlier. Whenever a critic appears aware of conflicts between the two novelists, the Huxley-Lawrence relationship is generally examined from a viewpoint friendlier to Lawrence. Thus in his biography of Lawrence, Edward Nehls furnishes Rolf Gardiner's statement that Lawrence enjoyed trying to frighten 'Aldoose' from his rationalist perch. Nehls also records Brewster Ghiselin's recollection of Lawrence sadly shaking his head over 'Huxley's preponderance of intellect'.[7] That Huxley considered Lawrence the opposite (i.e. the emotional) extreme is never mentioned.

It is unfortunate that most critics who have written on Lawrence know what he said about Huxley, but that few of Huxley's readers have examined his comments on Lawrence. For Huxley is often reduced to a Lawrencian satellite and the Huxley-Lawrence interchange dwindles to what Lawrence said about Huxley in letters or conversation. Thus if Lawrence writes or says he is offended by *Point Counter Point*, too many critics are prepared to find the novel offensive. In actuality, however, although there is no question that Lawrence surpasses Huxley as a novelist, their relationship comprises the most amusing friendship-antagonism of the present century's literary history. Huxley was more deeply influenced by Lawrence than has yet been realized. And his evaluation of Lawrence was often as perceptive and frequently more effectively satirical than Lawrence's estimate of him.

In effect, Huxley knew two D. H. Lawrences and liked the first of them better than the second. The first meeting between the two novelists, the essay in *The Olive Tree* states, took place in 1915. Lawrence asked Huxley if he would come to Florida where Lawrence planned a utopian settlement and Huxley quickly agreed. Huxley later expressed relief when the scheme fell through. In 1915, Huxley had as yet done little. His first volume of poems, *The Burning Wheel*, appeared the following year. Lawrence, by contrast, had just completed *The Rainbow* and was already in motion towards *Women in Love*, his greatest novel. The consequences for Lawrence's reputation of the uproar over *The Rainbow* were not yet fully apparent and it was a self-assured and as yet undaunted Lawrence that Huxley met.

The pair apparently did not meet regularly, if at all, nor did they formally correspond until 1926, a full eleven years later. Huxley's essay on Lawrence mentions only one meeting of the two novelists between 1915 and 1926 and their friendship may thus be said to begin when Lawrence wrote to Huxley in 1925 and when the two writers spent time together in Italy the following year. By then, Huxley had published three novels and was soon to attempt *Point Counter Point*, his most ambitious work. The year of this second meeting, Lawrence, recently returned from Mexico, published *The Plumed Serpent* and did his first draft of *Lady Chatterley's Lover*. In 1928, *Point Counter Point* was to make money as the Book of the Month in America, while the impoverished Lawrence would receive only opprobrium for *Lady Chatterley's Lover*. Richard Aldington finds Lawrence's letter to Huxley about *Point Counter Point* (*Letters*, pp. 765–67) full of envy and claims that Lawrence, after reading the novel, assured him Huxley would be in a lunatic asylum within a year.[8]

The influence of Lawrence's finest work – *The Rainbow* and especially *Women in Love* – on Huxley's writing is quite extensive. *Crome Yellow*, *Antic Hay*, and *Those Barren Leaves* have a strong Lawrencian strain– in theme, though not in style or structure, and it is clear that the Lawrence of 1915 and the early Lawrence novels were very much on Huxley's mind. It is possible to assume that under the impact of renewed acquaintanceship with Lawrence, Huxley, in 1926, makes an about face from the semi-mystical conclusions

Calamy comes to at the end of *Those Barren Leaves* (Part 5, IV) and resumes his previous concern with Lawrencian themes.

Both Rupert Birkin in *Women in Love* and Calamy in *Those Barren Leaves* express their disgust with the existing order of things and strive for something new. Both escape from society. Yet in Calamy's case, the escape is towards a philosophical outlook greatly resembling Huxley's future mysticism; whereas Birkin is after something beyond physical passion and even beyond love but still, in fact, rooted in the coming together of a man and woman. For Birkin and Lawrence, integration of the individual's mind, body, and spirit is still as potentially possible as it was for George Meredith. But Calamy wishes to escape his physical nature in favour of his mental or contemplative self. And Huxley, though reluctant, seems to agree with Calamy's decision. The mind-body dichotomy – a theme throughout Huxley's first three novels – is about to be resolved in favour of mind and spirit. When Lawrence reappears in Huxley's life, however, the theme of wholeness reasserts itself and one of the meanings of the title *Point Counter Point* is that passion and reason must be kept in the true counterpoint of balance or equilibrium.

Paradoxically, the year 1926 is also the date of Huxley's first satiric sketch of Lawrence as the over-emotional Kingham in the novella entitled 'Two or Three Graces'. In *Point Counter Point*, Huxley returns to *Women in Love* for his major themes and, to a lesser degree, for his structure (despite recent attempts to derive the novel from André Gide's *Les Faux-Monnayeurs*). But the Lawrence whom Huxley idolizes in *Point Counter Point* (1928) is closer to the Birkin-Lawrence of *Women in Love* (written in 1916, published in 1920), than to the Lawrence of 1926. Though the writer who celebrates Quetzacoatl in *The Plumed Serpent* (1926) and the novelist who created Ursula and Gudrun Brangwen in *Women in Love* are clearly similar, significant alterations have taken place. And although Huxley was anxious to go forward with Birkin and Ursula towards 'new life' (XII), he refused to go back with Cipriano and Ramón Carrasco of *The Plumed Serpent* in search of 'that timeless, primeval passion of the prehistoric races' (VII). Some of the satire directed against Lawrence in 1926 can thus be traced to Huxley's feeling that Lawrence is no longer pursuing the themes Huxley previously regarded as their common concern, even if, in retrospect, their positions on what constitutes wholeness seldom seem identical.

Brave New World is, among other things, a repudiation of *The*

Plumed Serpent since the Savage, who resembles Cipriano, fails to survive in anything other than a primitive milieu. With his lengthy commentary on Lawrence in *Beyond the Mexique Bay* (1934), Huxley rejects the influence of his fellow novelist entirely. Only in *Ape and Essence* (1949) and in his last work of fiction, the utopian *Island* (1962), does Huxley make his peace with Lawrence. Although Lawrence always professed a strong attachment to Huxley, he felt that Aldous' loyalty to him did not go very deep.[9] On his part, Huxley felt towards Lawrence the way characters in *Point Counter Point* feel towards Rampion or the way the Prufrockian Dick Wilkes admires the emotional Kingham in 'Two or Three Graces': 'He was in some way important for me, deeply significant and necessary.' Yet in view of the frequent opposition between them, Lawrence and Huxley, despite Huxley's feeling that Lawrence supplied him with a missing part of himself, could not have been the closest of friends.

I

Hermione Roddice (a fictional version of Lady Ottoline Morrell, whom both Huxley and Lawrence knew) appears in two of Huxley's first three novels. One-sided, a person composed almost entirely of intellect and will, she makes up for her lack of success with Rupert Birkin in *Women in Love* by returning to haunt both Calamy and Chelifer as the egoistic, possessive Mrs. Aldwinkle of *Those Barren Leaves* (1925). Her first appearance as Mrs. Wimbush in *Crome Yellow* (1921) is only a bit part compared to her function in Huxley's third novel. There, her outrageous conduct convinces each of the novel's two male protagonists that his view of society is correct. Along with Mary Thriplow, Mrs. Aldwinkle is one of the factors behind Calamy's renunciation of society and the physical life in favour of hilltop contemplation in the Wordsworthian manner. To Chelifer she is another demonstration of the banality and egotism that constitute the core of the modern world. Calamy (Huxley) and Birkin (Lawrence) flee, Gerald Crich (who is John Middleton Murry in *Women in Love*) and Chelifer (who, at times, is Murry in *Those Barren Leaves*) embrace the worst.

A major theme of Huxley's first three novels is the question of whether or not the complete life is still possible in a century of disintegration such as the twentieth. It is a theme roughly analogous to the search by three different generations of the Brangwens in *The Rainbow* for what Lawrence calls 'consummation' or fulfilment.

Egotism and the breakdown of societal standards – a breakdown that critics cite as a major concern in *The Rainbow* – are the chief obstacles in the way of any individual in Huxley's world who strives to become an integrated personality. By the end of *Crome Yellow*, Denis Stone has been momentarily shaken out of his egotism, but he has also discovered he is a split-man. In Anne's presence he is 'wild inside; raging, writhing – yes "writhing" was the word, writhing with desire. But outwardly he was hopelessly tame; outwardly – baa, baa, baa' (X). As a man whose intellect restricts his emotional response, Denis is as split as Gerald Crich. He does not immediately remind us of Crich because he lacks the latter's dynamic appeal. Gerald, Lawrence writes in *Women in Love*, was 'limited to one form of existence, one know-ledge, one activity, a sort of fatal halfness' (XVI). After succeeding as an industrial manager, Gerald feels his 'mind' needs 'acute stimula-tion' before he can be 'physically roused' (XVII). Though less manly and often harder to sympathize with than Gerald because he is so Prufrockian, Denis nevertheless has a similar problem: 'I have to invent an excuse, a justification for everything that's delightful. Otherwise I can't enjoy it with an easy conscience' (IV). Denis is the first of many Huxley characters who, like Hermione Roddice and Gerald Crich, allow one element of their being to dominate all the others. But Huxley, unlike Lawrence, is unable or unwilling to make these split individuals at all appealing, except, of course, as comic figures.

In *Antic Hay* – a novel in which Philip Heseltine, the Halliday of *Women in Love*, reappears as the diabolical Coleman – Huxley's characters again struggle towards wholeness, this time on the assump-tion that proportion is the answer. Shearwater puts it succinctly when he advises: 'Render therefore unto Caesar the things which are Caesar's . . . There must be a working arrangement' between a body and mind kept 'in proportion' (XI). In *Women in Love*, inci-dentally, Birkin laughingly suggested something similar when dis-cussing Minette with Gerald: 'Render unto Caesarina the things that are Caesarina's' (VIII). But neither Shearwater nor Gumbril Jr. attain proportion and Huxley tries for it again in his third novel just as Ursula, in *The Rainbow*, makes a third attempt to achieve fulfilment as the representative of the Brangwens, two generations of whom have previously failed in the search for 'consummation'.

Many of the discussion groups Huxley satirized in *Crome Yellow* seem actually to have met at Garsington, Lady Ottoline's residence.

From one of Lawrence's notes to Lady Ottoline (*Letters*, p. 224) one gathers that these discussions were often as oddball and unsatisfactory as Huxley's novels claim. In *Those Barren Leaves*, the discussion group moves to Mrs. Aldwinkle's villa in Italy, but many of the people present and the opinions expressed first appeared in Lawrence's novels at Shortlands and Breadalby. 'I begin to think that you can't live unless you keep entirely out of the line,' Birkin remarks (XVI). This bears comparison with Mr. Cardan's insistence in *Those Barren Leaves* that one now has to live 'in reaction against the general trend of existence' (Part 3, V). Calamy's conviction that Cardan is right influences his eventual flight.

Both Calamy (Part 1, IV) and Birkin (V, *passim*) want more than physical passion, more than personal love. They are both after something more fulfilling, something beyond the individual ego. But with these two characters Huxley and Lawrence appear about to go separate ways. In *Women in Love*, Birkin expounds his notions about 'ultimate marriage' to Ursula and, in the brilliant give-and-take between them, a new method of life begins to work itself out. A misogynist by comparison with Lawrence and his respect for the questing female (Ursula Brangwen, Kate Leslie in *The Plumed Serpent*, Connie Chatterley), Huxley parodies 'Excurse' and other chapters from *Women in Love* as he chronicles Calamy's failure with Mary Thriplow.

Like Birkin with Ursula, Calamy, although in pursuit of higher things, cannot resist 'the old blood' aroused by the physical attractiveness of his fellow guest at Mrs. Aldwinkle's. But whereas Birkin decides his love-making with Ursula has saved him from becoming a 'word-bag' (XIV), Calamy regards Mary Thriplow as another obstacle in the way of the contemplative life. Their bedroom scenes are a series of ironies. Though physically present, he is mentally elsewhere as he explains to Mary, between love bouts, his theory that the physical is an impediment to his search for knowledge, a search that can only be carried out by his contemplative faculties (Part 1, IV; Part 5, 1). The love scenes in Huxley – and many in Lawrence – often seem the work of a metaphysician. Mary, unlike Calamy, is having this affair only to gather material for a forthcoming novel. Already in Italy, the place Birkin and Ursula ultimately escape to at the close of *Women in Love*, Calamy becomes a solitary and begins to work out the basic tenets of what eventually constitutes Huxley's perennial philosophy. Left behind, Mary attempts to practise Calamy's method of contemplation, but soon finds herself thinking of her dentist (Part 5, III).

Although Gerald Crich and Francis Chelifer are very dissimilar, both have much in common with John Middleton Murry. Crich is a highly idealized sketch of Murry. It is a sketch more tolerant and less realistic than the caricature of him as Burlap in *Point Counter Point* or than the nasty opinion of Murry that emerges in Lawrence's letters to him. The equation of the *Adelphi*, one of two important magazines Murry edited, with Chelifer's *Rabbit Fanciers' Gazette* is one that Lawrence must have heartily enjoyed. Both Crich and Chelifer have sold themselves to what their creators consider the worst aspects of modern life: Crich to mechanical materialism and the triumph of man's will over Nature, and Chelifer to the prevailing chaos, eccentricity, and egotism of modern life.

After Chelifer's instalment at the villa, Mrs. Aldwinkle transfers her attentions from Calamy to him. Mrs. Aldwinkle 'tried to take possession of Chelifer; she ... tried to make him as much her property as the view, or Italian art' (Part 3, I). Mrs. Aldwinkle and Chelifer are members of the same species, as were Hermione Roddice and Gerald Crich, although Chelifer, unlike Crich, is all too conscious of his deliberately chosen failings. Hermione 'suffered when she felt her day was diminished, she felt she had missed her life. She seemed to grip the hours by the throat, to force her life from them' (VIII). Mrs. Aldwinkle constantly fears she is missing something. If one could only stay up an extra five minutes, the all-important event, she muses, might occur. She 'didn't want her guests to lead independent existences out of her sight' (Part 1, II).

It is Gerald's failure to escape from a 'one-sidedness' (XXIII) similar to Hermione's – he apparently has the potential – that seals his doom. Even with Gudrun Brangwen he seldom relaxes his will or surrenders to his unconscious. In his final love scenes with her, he closes over Gudrun 'like steel' (XXIX). Finally, he skis to his death in a world of whiteness that Lawrence calls the world's navel (XXIX) and that is, in being all white and all snow, the true mate for Gerald's lopsidedness. And it is Chelifer's inability to disentangle himself from Mrs. Aldwinkle that signifies yet again his acceptance of a world full of possessive egoists. Such is the microcosm he lives in when in London: Gog's Court, a place he himself describes as 'the navel of reality' (Part 2, II).

Birkin and Calamy are saved, Gerald Crich and Francis Chelifer choose their own damnation. But Birkin and Calamy rescue themselves in different ways. If Rupert is on his way to becoming, as some critics insist, 'the wholly integrated man', Calamy appears to be a second Buddha. Had Huxley followed *Those Barren Leaves* with *Eyeless in Gaza* (1936) and Anthony Beavis, its mystic hero, the development would have been a logical one. Instead of Beavis, however, Huxley presents *Point Counter Point* and Mark Rampion. Rampion's ideal is the sane and harmonious Greek who penalized neither mind nor body. The best explanation for this has to be Huxley's budding friendship with Lawrence. Before renouncing the physical, Calamy expressed his preference for some 'graceful Latin compromise' (Part 3, XIII) in which mind and body would be reconciled. Surely Lawrence must have appeared to Huxley as that compromise personified, as Birkin in the flesh.

From 1926 to the mid-1930s Lawrence is seldom out of Huxley's mind or work. What Lawrence is as a person, what he personifies for Huxley, often becomes of more concern to Huxley than Lawrence the literary artist. Huxley's Lawrencian interlude begins as Huxley's version of Lawrencian themes enjoys a resurgence in *Point Counter Point* and Huxley continually looks to Lawrence for encouragement and approval. *Do What You Will* (1929), for example, was written under Lawrence's influence and even, it appears from the *Letters* (p. 724), at Lawrence's instigation. The interlude consists of two parallel developments: Huxley's re-adoption of Lawrencian themes and his growing awareness that Lawrence and Birkin are no longer identical. The interlude runs from *Point Counter Point* (1928) through *Brave New World* (1932) to *Eyeless in Gaza* (1936). Although it includes much of Huxley's finest writing, it is, in retrospect, only an interval between the mystical tendencies of Calamy and their fullfledged realization first in Anthony Beavis of *Eyeless in Gaza*, then in Mr. Propter of *After Many a Summer Dies the Swan*, and in Sebastian Barnack of *Time Must Have a Stop*.

A thorough re-reading of *Point Counter Point* fails to disclose many themes that it does not hold in common with *Women in Love*. Observations critics have made about Lawrence's novel apply surprisingly well to Huxley's, despite the fact that as a satirist and a novelist of ideas Huxley is unable and unwilling to develop his characters to the fullness most of Lawrence's attain. The following comparison of the two novels ignores factors that perhaps make Lawrence's novel superior. Nor does it praise Huxley's abilities as a satirist – an ability Lawrence generally lacked, except for some brilliant self-satire in *Women in Love*.

At the root of Lawrence's novel is a contrast between two couples: Birkin and Ursula, Gerald and Gudrun. In *Point Counter Point*, Huxley replaces Gerald and Gudrun with Philip and Elinor Quarles. He substitutes himself and his wife for J. M. Murry and Katherine Mansfield, relegating the latter couple to a less central position. Murry remains in the novel as Burlap but Susan Paley, who is Katherine, is already dead, and much of the satire against Burlap accuses him of exploiting the memory of his wife. What Lawrence did to the Murrys, Huxley proceeds to do to himself. When Lawrence inserted his friends into a novel he often interpreted their psychology in a very unflattering way by adding insulting emotions and motives to the original life-like sketch. Huxley apparently includes himself in the novel as an exercise in self-analysis, an exposure of his own shortcomings. He tries to portray himself as he feels he would appear to Lawrence, whose judgments he respects. But *Point Counter Point* also attempts to show that Huxley-Quarles is closest to Rampion-Lawrence, that it is Quarles who understands Rampion most clearly and who is, after Rampion, the sanest consciousness in the novel. Huxley usurps for himself the primary place in Lawrence's affections that Murry at one time apparently held.

Both *Point Counter Point* and *Women in Love* attempt to dispense with the traditional device of a plot. Both depend heavily on the success of discussion scenes in which the way each character participates in an argument reveals his strengths and weaknesses. Gerald Crich is repeatedly attacked by Lawrence for the alacrity with which he starts, or rushes to enter, a serious discussion. Huxley's unique achievement as a discussion novelist is to make the discussion process into a major technical device through which each character or isolated little world is shown egoistically distorting every topic in the discussion to make it fit his private scheme. The egotism for which Huxley satirizes his characters is thus shown in operation. When at his best as a discussion novelist – in *Women in Love* and parts of *Lady Chatterley's Lover* [10] – Lawrence's achievement is the skilful incorporation of good discussion scenes into the essentially poetic and symbolic rhythm of his novels.

The integration of the total self is what Birkin aims at and what Rampion apparently has achieved. One may see, as some critics have done, the theme of *Women in Love* as a struggle between Will (either sensual or spiritual) and Being (the total self). Similarly, Huxley presents innumerable instances of the self-division that results from failure to reconcile passion and reason. To Birkin, Ursula offers 'emotional intimacy' and Hermione 'spiritual intimacy' (XXIII). For Rampion and Huxley, Quarles is all intellect, Burlap a case of sickening spirituality, and Old Bidlake a creature of almost mindless flesh. As Mark Spilka realizes, Lawrence's characters, like Huxley's, distort their lives by relying on one or two elements of their total being.[11] The eagerness with which Loerke and Gudrun prefer art to life in *Women in Love* (XXX) returns in *Point Counter Point* as a basic problem for Quarles and Walter Bidlake, both of whom find life more disappointing and harder to cope with than art.

What is surprising if one reads *Point Counter Point* and *Women in Love* back to back is the amount of what Huxley calls counterpoint or musicalization that Lawrence's novel contains. The theme of dissolution or disintegration, for example, is explored in terms of workmen (Crich's), their masters (Gerald Crich himself), the leisured classes (Hermione and her circle), and Bohemians and artists (Halliday's group, Gudrun, Loerke). Different people confront similar situations (Birkin and Gerald on love) and similar people face different situations (Hermione and Gerald with, respectively, Birkin and Gudrun). Birkin's escape from Hermione in the early chapters is balanced by Gudrun's movement towards Loerke at the end. These are only a few of the ways in which *Women in Love* anticipates some of the more basic theories about reduplicating situations and characters put forth by Quarles in *Point Counter Point* (XXII). One fails to notice this aspect of *Women in Love* because the skeleton of Lawrence's novel rarely shows through the flesh, whereas Huxley's ability to manipulate the skeleton of his novel is his strong point.

Other borrowings and similarities abound: for example, Clifford Chatterley realizes in *Lady Chatterley's Lover* that some of his friends are gods of industry but 'of a mental age of about thirteen, feeble boys' when it came to 'the emotional and human life' (IX). This realization, along with Gerald's inability to make love except 'like a child . . . as an infant' (XXIV), underlies many of the grotesques Huxley sketches, such as the child-like Burlap or the scientist Edward Tantamount, who is professionally an adult but sexually and emotionally little more than a foetus.

Huxley feels he and Lawrence are engaged in the same fight not only because both are on occasion thesis or discussion novelists, but also because the bedrock element in both men's philosophy is an unstinted hatred for egotism. To Lady Cynthia Asquith, Lawrence wrote (*Letters*, p. 251), what could serve as a blueprint for the world of the Huxley novels: Most people and political parties 'want the same thing: a continuing in this state of disintegration wherein each separate little ego is an independent little principality by itself'. One of the objections both Birkin (xxv) and Rawdon Lilly (*Aaron's Rod*, IX) raise against conventional marriage is that it amounts to '*Egoisme à deux*'.

Nevertheless, where Huxley equates ego and personality, Lawrence, more firmly than Huxley, links both with the mind.[12] In an essay entitled 'Love' (1936), Lawrence contends it is necessary for man 'to separate and distinguish' himself into 'gem-like singleness' while paradoxically and simultaneously fusing into oneness with a woman. Any drive towards the Not-Me, any urge to 'eliminate the Self', horrifies Lawrence.[13] But eventually, in *The Perennial Philosophy* (1945), the mystical Huxley feels it is the not-self in a person, the particle of divine otherness, that guarantees union with the Divine Ground. His assertions that one paradoxically retains individuality in this process often seem perfunctory.

One could go on to compare Huxley and Lawrence's preference for the novel as the form best suited to life's multiplicity and their mutual quarrel with the one-sidedness of tragedy,[14] but these general comparisons between the two novelists become a bit tedious. They succeed at times in reducing one's estimate of Huxley as an original novelist, but they ignore his satiric talents. They answer one or two basic questions, but add nothing to one's grasp of Lawrence. Two things, however, are unmistakably clear. First, Huxley, up through 1926, regarded himself as Lawrence's co-worker. In his own fiction, he repeatedly raises the problems Lawrence deals with and tests the validity of what he takes to be Lawrence's answers. Also, by 1926, Huxley needed a living example of wholeness because he felt he himself was not one, nor could any of the characters in his first three novels become one. This, then, is the role he thrusts on Lawrence. For Rampion in *Point Counter Point*, Blake is the last complete man; but for Huxley, the last one is Lawrence.

It is doubtful Lawrence ever realized how important he was to Huxley. He never saw that Huxley's allegiance to him was the latter's last enthusiastic romance with the idea that the complete life was still possible in the twentieth century. Lawrence admired Huxley as a satirist but considered satire one of the lesser arts. He praised *Point Counter Point* as a novel that burns out dead forms of life through satire. It gives, he felt, an honest picture of sordid society, but that is also its limitations. Finding positive replacements for dead forms is a higher role, and Lawrence justly saw himself in it. That Huxley too sought positive alternatives does not seem to have been part of Lawrence's understanding of Huxley.

Thus the questions that have been raised so far but have yet to be sufficiently examined are the following: Why is the resurgence of Lawrencian themes in Huxley's novels accompanied by an exchange of personal satires between the two novelists? Heretofore they had put some of the same people into their respective novels; now they insert each other. Did Lawrence, when seen up close and on frequent occasions, fail to personify the Latin compromise Huxley had insisted on making him? Why did Huxley have trouble seeing the Lawrence of 1926 and Lawrence's previous novels in the same light? Why was Huxley's allegiance often distasteful to the virtually ally-less Lawrence of 1926–30? Did Huxley misunderstand Lawrence, was there more to his fellow novelist than he perceived?

II

On the basis of an exchange of personal satires, it is tempting to view Huxley's Lawrencian interlude as a period in which Huxley and Lawrence came to personify the body-mind conflict both wrote about. Despite Huxley's re-adoption of Lawrencian themes in 1926, despite his return to *Women in Love* as a model, he seems to see Lawrence himself as a person lacking all the judgment and restraint a cultivated intellect should bring to bear on the emotions. Huxley, on the other hand, strikes Lawrence as an intellectual pervert who lives only with his mind.

Huxley's impudence in doing a fictional portrait of D. H. Lawrence as Kingham in 'Two or Three Graces' bothers no one who recognizes Huxley as the 'tall thin fellow' named Hammond in *Lady Chatterley's Lover* (IV). A cutting but still humorous version of Huxley, Hammond defines sex as 'a matter of misplaced curiosity'. If the novelist took no more notice of sex than of the fact that men use the W.C., the whole problem, Hammond maintains, would vanish. Charles May voices Lawrence's main criticism of Huxley when he tells Hammond: you talk about sex but 'too little of you goes that way . . . Your pure mind is going as dry as fiddlesticks.' In a letter to Aldous about *Proper*

Studies (*Letters*, p. 701), Lawrence made the charge directly, finding fault with Huxley's 'funny dry-mindedness and underneath social morality'. The accuracy of Lawrence's indictment Huxley never doubted. He continually satirized himself on similar grounds. Philip Quarles, Huxley's best fictional self-portrait, is accused of using his mind as a 'shield' and of speaking an 'intellectual language of ideas' that cuts him off from much he would like to experience (VI).

Through Kingham, however, Huxley asserted that Lawrence, by contrast with his own dry-minded self, was all emotion. 'Two or Three Graces' (1926), a long short story or novella, pictures Kingham wallowing in his feelings, exercising his emotions as one might flex one's muscles. Huxley often regretted his own 'asceticism of the mind'. In *On the Margin*, he expressed the desire to 'enjoy all the dear obviously luscious, idiotic emotions without an afterthought'. But Kingham is satirized for being at the other extreme, for taking emotional baths in which his 'intellect was put into blinkers, the most manifest facts were ignored.'[15] If Huxley originally considered himself the mathematical half of Richard Greenow, in 1926 he would have associated Lawrence-Kingham with Dick's emotional half, the fragment of his personality that gains independent existence as Pearl Bellairs.[16] Kingham forms intuitive judgments about people and becomes 'incapable of recognizing the facts that would have upset his prejudices'. He classifies the harmless Grace Peddley as a devil-woman and fails to remark her love for him. When he has an affair with her, it is his notion of her as a 'modern' (i.e. abandoned) woman that lures him on.

Huxley apparently accepted Lawrence's criticism, but how accurate is Huxley's attack on Lawrence? Although partially based on misunderstanding, it seems more justified than Lawrence's supporters have been willing to allow.

In his remarkable defence of Lawrence as a literary critic, David Gordon begins by explaining that for Lawrence true knowledge was rooted in the blood, not the mind, and was impersonal rather than personal.[17] This ties in with Gordon's subsequent assertion that in his theory of criticism Lawrence 'wants to avoid any word or phrase which too clearly suggests mental consciousness', since the primary consciousness and the one best suited to judgment is the 'emotional'. So far, whether one accepts Lawrence's theory or not, he does seem, as described by Gordon, to be doing with literature what Huxley attacks Kingham for doing with people. The difference, of course, is that Lawrence (and Gordon) find Lawrence's method sound while Huxley does not.

Later, however, Gordon argues that although Lawrence satirized one-sidedness, he had no intention of refurbishing the classical ideal of body-mind balance. Instead, Lawrence was in pursuit of a new centre of consciousness that would transcend the dualism of body and mind, that would enable body and mind to become one.[18] If this is true – and Gordon's evidence is considerable – then Huxley chose his candidate for the 'Latin compromise' most unwisely, for Huxley is clearly interested in balancing body and mind, passion and reason, feeling and rational thought. What should be remembered, however, is that Lawrence gave Huxley ample grounds for considering him a fellow advocate of body-mind balance. What is also clear is that in criticizing certain Lawrence novels for upsetting the body-mind balance he felt the early novels recommended, Huxley was still striking at a vulnerable point in Lawrence's thought. For even if the later novels (those after *Women in Love*) are not concerned with balancing the rival claims of body and mind but with fusing the two halves of the dichotomy into a new whole, very little of what Huxley would consider mind finds its way into the product of this fusion.

Lawrence was against one form of imbalance: the mentalization of one's instincts and feelings. Huxley comes to feel that Lawrence's alternatives increasingly tend towards another form of imbalance: the emotionalization of the mind. Gordon's statement that Lawrence's blood-mind anti-thesis is really a 'distinction between spontaneous and mechanical mind' does not explain many of Somers' comments in *Kangaroo* (1923), nor could it be safely inserted in the mouth of Don Ramón in *The Plumed Serpent* (1926), or stand as a summary of Kate Leslie's relationship with Cipriano in that same novel.

Gordon observes that by searching for a new centre of consciousness where body and mind are one, Lawrence became 'the last romantic'. By comparison, Huxley can be called a neoclassicist, at least in his insistence on balance, if not also in the value he places on wit and satire. If one does not forget that Lawrence, like many romantics, has a tough intellect and that Huxley has definite romantic tendencies, Huxley's effort to adjust to Lawrence is a rare instance of two opposed temperaments – romantic and neoclassic, the pioneer and the would-be traditionalist – attempting to co-exist. By reacting against Lawrence's later novels and pointing out the extent to which what Lawrence aimed at, be it fusion or balance, fails to come off, Huxley impairs his own quest as well as Lawrence's. His final refusal to see Lawrence's suggestions as anything but another form of imbalance also leads to his rejection of body-mind equilibrium as an ideal. He feels forced to choose between what he considers two types of imbalance, between the lack of proportion he comes to see in Lawrence and the imbalance deliberately adopted by Calamy. Whatever Lawrence began by recommending, fusion or balance, his later novels are an illustration of neither. Because Lawrence, in Huxley's opinion, failed as the 'Latin compromise', the compromise itself was largely abandoned.

It was only 'in his later years', according to Gordon, that Lawrence talked about the physical and the mental in terms of balance. 'But I regard such statements,' Gordon continues, 'as hasty journalism.'[19] One could produce quite a few examples of such haste, not all of them from later years. Nor did Lawrence's mind become enfeebled towards the end of his life, as the phrase 'in his later years' may imply. Huxley was not the only one Lawrence's haste misled. In his conclusion to *The Life and Work of D. H. Lawrence* (1951), Harry T. Moore insists Lawrence was 'trying to revive emotional values, to restore a balance'. Gordon summarizes Lawrence's position with more definiteness than Lawrence himself ever employed or than even Huxley hazarded in his many attempts to come to grips with Lawrence's volatile genius. In *Apocalypse* (1931), Lawrence muses: 'Maybe all basic thought takes place in the blood around the heart, and is only transferred to the brain.' In 'Apropos of *Lady Chatterley's Lover*,' he suggests his readers, 'make a balance between the consciousness of the body's sensations and experiences, and these sensations and experiences themselves'. In 'Introduction to His Paintings' (1929), he claims the mind 'can assert anything, and pretend it has proved it. My beliefs I test on my body, on my intuitional consciousness, and when I get a response there, then I accept.' What is striking about these randomly chosen passages is not only their different shades of meaning, but the different tone of voice, the different degree of assurance in each.

As early as 1915, in 'The Crown,' Lawrence, according to one critic, defined life as a warring of opposites, of flesh and spirit, emotion and reason, organic instinct and spiritual insight, with the crown symbolizing wholeness of being. To Dorothy Brett Lawrence wrote (*Letters*, p. 634): 'We are creatures of two halves, spiritual and sensual – and each half is as important as the other.' Lawrence was also capable of describing *Lady Chatterley's Lover* as 'a novel of the phallic consciousness versus the mental-spiritual consciousness: and of course you know which side I take. The *versus* is not my fault. There should be no versus. The two things must be reconciled in us.'[20] In short, Lawrence often presents himself as the redresser of a balance, the advocate of a reconcilement – not a fusion – of opposites. May's criticism of Huxley-Hammond in *Lady Chatterley's Lover* as a man too much of whom goes one way implicitly endorses the idea of balance.

Yet, in retrospect, despite the preceding passages, one must concede that Huxley and Lawrence were after different things. Lawrence was more interested in the recovery of vitality, Huxley in the regaining of balance. Lawrence, at least at times, was more concerned with fusing body and mind, Huxley with keeping them in equilibrium. Lawrence always took the term integration more literally than Huxley. The Huxley-Lawrence interchange developed into a struggle in which each novelist saw the other as more and more of an impediment to his own conception of the ideal relationship of body and mind. Lawrence became more and more convinced that Huxley was irretrievably rooted in the mental and Huxley claimed Lawrence went too far in the opposite direction.

The Lawrence of *The Plumed Serpent* (1926) is a more formidable impediment to Huxley than Birkin-Lawrence of *Women in Love* (1920). Having returned to Lawrencian themes in 1926, Huxley began to discover that Lawrence was moving in new and, for Huxley, disturbing directions. Under the impact of friendship with Lawrence, Huxley had re-adopted themes he considered to be Lawrence's but which he now saw Lawrence abandoning. Mark Rampion is Huxley's audacious attempt to make the Lawrence of 1926–28 into the Birkin of 1920, and to make both into a spokesman for the Huxley philosophy. To those who agree that Lawrence, by 1926, had changed in directions Huxley did not anticipate and was right in disliking, the effrontery of creating Lawrence as Rampion is not without its medicinal intent.

Each of Lawrence's novels is an open doorway to its successor. No matter how many difficulties resolve themselves at the end of any one book, one problem is left standing until the next. The symbol of the rainbow in the novel of that name is associated with all three generations of the Brangwens. Yet only Ursula experiences an actual vision of it. Only she seems capable of a male-female relationship arched in the blood and alive in the spirit. With Birkin in *Women in Love*, the Ursula of *The Rainbow* achieves this ideal relationship, but Birkin's desire for ultimate friendship with Gerald is frustrated. In *Aaron's Rod* and *Kangaroo*, the possibility of ultimate friendship becomes the central concern and the ideal coming together of a man and a woman either disappears or receives scant attention. The offer of discipleship Lilly is about to make to Aaron Sisson at the conclusion of *Aaron's Rod*, is rejected by Richard Somers when it is made by the improbably named Kangaroo.

The *Plumed Serpent* (1926) reveals Lawrence's admiration for the primitive peoples he often considered still vitally in touch with the living cosmos. It treats the friendship ideal in terms of Cipriano and Ramón and revives the man-woman theme in Cipriano and Kate Leslie. But in its preoccupation with the men who worship Quetzacoatl (half eagle, half serpent) and the old impulses Ramón tries to revive, the novel brings to a head the interest Lawrence expressed as early as *Twilight in Italy* (1916) in more primitive people and the ways of knowing he felt they still retained.

Lawrence's novels thus pass through three phases. The first ends with *Women in Love*, his last novel before *Lady Chatterley's Lover* in which insight outweighs nonsense. The second begins with the leadership or friendship theme of *Aaron's Rod* and touches bottom in *The Plumed Serpent*. With Mellors and Connie of *Lady Chatterley's Lover*, however, Lawrence creates a couple Birkin and Ursula would have admired and recaptures some of his earlier greatness. In reacting favourably to *The Rainbow* and *Women in Love*, in condemning the trend of the next two novels that climaxes in *The Plumed Serpent*, but responding with qualified sympathy to Lawrence's last novel, Huxley matches the pattern modern criticism has established in its assessment of Lawrence. At a time when Lawrence was having difficulty finding publishers, Huxley was already formulating posterity's opinion of Lawrence's novels.

As early as 1912, writes Huxley in *The Olive Tree*, Lawrence was already expressing his belief in the blood:

> My great religion is a belief in the blood, the flesh, as being wiser than our intellect. We can go wrong in our minds. But what our blood feels and believes and says is always true. The intellect is only a bit and a

bridle. What do I care about knowledge. All I want is to answer to my blood direct, without fribbling intervention of mind.[21]

But there is little in Ursula's quest in *The Rainbow* (or in Birkin's philosophy in *Women in Love*) that can readily be construed as an illustration of this belief, unless one reads 'blood' very metaphorically for spontaneous, non-egoistic response. Ursula Brangwen turns down the attentions of anyone who literally answers to his blood direct, such as Maggie's brother Anthony. His 'neighing laugh' and 'prance of triumph' (XIV) affiliate him with the imaginary stallions who later pursue Ursula (XVI) and, subsequently, with the horse called St. Mawr in the story of the same name. Although Lawrence's statement that Anthony is 'cleaner' than Ursula because he has no soul is ominous of future developments, Ursula is clearly after some combination of the mindless unity with organic creation (blood intimacy) possessed by the early Brangwen men and the life of moral effort, intelligent awareness, and spiritual power the early Brangwen women longed for. In the course of three generations, the Brangwen family's failure to achieve the second half of this combination increasingly vitiates the first.

The successive Brangwen generations (Tom Brangwen and Lydia, Will Brangwen and Anna, Ursula Brangwen and Skrebensky) are thus, among other things, symbols of the breakdown of the old male-female connection and of the world's unsuccessful search for a spontaneous relationship in which each person achieves maximum individuation. Ursula becomes a female picaro who tests several possibilities (teaching, college, lesbianism and Winifred Inger, and Skrebensky), but 'Always the shining doorway was a gate into another ugly yard' (XV). Surprisingly, especially when one tries to read *The Rainbow* in light of the 'belief in the blood' passage cited above, the 'sordid people' who cover the earth in Ursula's final vision already have the rainbow arched in their blood; it is in their spirit that it has yet to 'quiver to life' (XVI).

The crucial points in *Women in Love* are those in which Birkin formulates and revises his theory of 'ultimate marriage' in preparation for the climactic scene in 'Excurse' (XXIII) where he and Ursula Brangwen accept one another. The real challenge comes when Birkin recalls an art object, an 'elegant figure from West Africa' (XIX). The relationship between senses and mind has long since broken down and the carved woman figure, says Birkin, possesses in herself the 'mindless progressive knowledge through the senses' that Africa has attained over centuries. Is this, asks Birkin, the direction modern industrial society, having gone as far as it can the mental way, will select? Birkin insists there is another way, 'the way of freedom'. This is a new concept of love in which, paradoxically, as Ursula realizes, there is 'mutual unison in separateness'. The 'mingling self-abnegation' of modern life yields to the pure duality of polarization. Birkin criticizes Hermione and Gerald for allowing their minds, wills, or consciousnesses to control their feelings and emotions. In this sense only, their intellects are a bit and a bridle.

However, *Women in Love* also contains an anti-physical bias. Birkin tells Ursula he does not want physical things (XIX). When they make love in the 'Excurse' chapter, it is a 'perfect passing away for both of them, and at the same time the most intolerable accession into being', as each finds the other 'a palpable revelation of living otherness'. Birkin and Ursula seem to have gone beyond body and mind, to have become one while remaining separate. They seem to have escaped both egoism and self-abnegation. But they have transcended these four things (body, mind, ego, self-abnegation) by somehow satisfying the demands of all four. Their relationship, rooted in the blood, fulfills the self while simultaneously taking each out of the self and into an awareness of the other – all of which Huxley could eagerly approve of, whether or not he could reach similar heights in his own work.

In *The Plumed Serpent*, however, Lawrence reconsiders Birkin's question (XIX) and answers it the other way. The inadequacies of *Aaron's Rod* and *Kangaroo* – as well as their minor strengths – have been sufficiently explored by other critics and need not be re-examined. Yet one must note that after *Women in Love* the roles of social prophet and possessor of sexual wisdom, both of which Birkin played, are not concentrated in the same man again until Mellors appears. In *Aaron's Rod*, Birkin splits into Aaron Sisson and Rawdon Lilly; in *The Plumed Serpent*, into Cipriano (sexual wisdom) and Don Ramón (prophet). Neither *Women in Love* nor the two novels that follow it manage to incorporate the ideal of ultimate friendship with that of ultimate marriage. Lawrence presents the second but not the first in *Women in Love* and the first but not the second in *Aaron's Rod*.

Just as he preferred rewriting a novel to revising it, Lawrence, with characteristic courageousness, rewrites his philosophy in *The Plumed Serpent* to see what potential the other of Birkin's two choices contains. Father Tiverton and other critics to the contrary, Lawrence goes back.[22] His fiction, always an exercise in exploration, now attempts to discover if it might not have been better for Birkin to have recommended, with a few alterations, 'mindless progressive knowledge through the senses'. Perhaps that can lead to a relationship between two men as well as to one between a man and a woman.

In *The Plumed Serpent*, for what is probably the first time in Lawrence, one finds characters who deliberately try to live by the blood philosophy (now sometimes called the phallic consciousness). Although they have intellects, the characters are trying to become similar to the early Brangwens of *The Rainbow* and to the Anthony Ursula rejected. Ramón and Cipriano are the inevitable outcome of Rawdon Lilly's growing fondness for Aztecs and Red Indians in *Aaron's Rod* (IX), as well as of Somers' longings in *Kangaroo* for 'the great dark God . . . of the first dark religions'. Ramón and Cipriano's primitivism, although deliberately and consciously chosen by Ramón, seems a direct reversal of Birkin's choice of 'the way of freedom' over the African retreat into 'mindless progressive knowledge through the senses'.

The increased concern with darkness and loins in *The Plumed Serpent* and the recurrent, approbatory use of 'primitive' and 'mindless' are amply foreshadowed as early as *Women in Love* (IX): Gudrun encounters 'the voluptuous resonance of darkness' in the 'mindless' miners who arouse in her 'a strange, nostalgic ache of desire'. The nostalgia is also Lawrence's and in *The Plumed Serpent* it prompts him to join Ramón in an excursion into the past. Huxley's nostalgia, by contrast, is seldom for a period before the Renaissance. One often feels that for him disintegration is a fairly recent, post-Victorian development, even if the list of the grand orthodox perverts in *Do What You Will* goes back over a hundred and fifty years. Lawrence also dated the disintegration process from the Renaissance, but sometimes pushed it back as early as the era of Plato and Socrates. To the Australian politician named Kangaroo, Somers, who is a persona for Lawrence himself, speaks of 'a re-entry into us of the Great God, who enters us . . . not through the spirit [but] from the lower self, the dark self, the phallic self' (VII). He accuses Kangaroo of using 'the lower self as an instrument of the spirit', and refuses to follow him since it is now 'time for the spirit to leave us again'.

In the Mexico of *The Plumed Serpent*, Ramón brings all of Somers' prophecies to pass. Accompanied by a proliferation of banal poetry and bathetic ritual – modelled on the Indian dances Lawrence actually saw in Mexico – Ramón replaces Christ with the new god Quetzacoatl (half serpent, half eagle). All of Lawrence's goals are accomplished: the men of Quetzacoatl have a strong sense of community; Ramón, as a sort of president and chief priest of Mexico, and Cipriano, as the general of his army, attain ultimate friendship; and with Cipriano Kate achieves a satisfying relationship (although at one point (xxv) she appears to covet Ramón). Yet it is hard to imagine anyone deriving a sense of unity with the cosmos from Ramón's new lifestyle and rubrics. Cipriano, though devoted to Ramón, is, as Lawrence suspects, a very dangerous individual with marked Fascist tendencies. Kate's relationship with Cipriano involves 'no personal or spiritual intimacy whatever'. In their 'mindless communion of the blood', Lawrence obtains less than he bargained for and something Birkin would only partially have understood.

Huxley objects to the conclusion of the novel:

> ... in the end, we are asked to renounce daylight and fresh air and immerse ourselves in 'the grand sea of the living blood' – that blood whose natural and spontaneous flowering is hatred of spirit ... We cannot accept the invitation. Lawrence's own incomparable descriptions of the horror of unadulterated blood has [sic] made it impossible.[23]

Yet Kate Leslie does accept the invitation and one can hear Kate and Lawrence, as Huxley charged, shouting down their own doubts. Kate's admiration for the fact that Mexicans resemble men who existed 'before the mental-spiritual world came into being' (xxvi) supports Huxley's contention that Lawrence is unfairly slighting the rational. Ramón seems to stand for a sort of physicalization of the mind and Kate herself at times realizes this. She insists we 'must go back to pick up old threads' (viii), and tells herself Ramón does not advocate an out and out return to the primitive: he is after 'a new conception of human life, that will arise from the fusion of the old blood-and-vertebrate consciousness with the white man's mental-spiritual consciousness' (xxvi). Here surely is Gordon's *locus classicus*, but the fusion in the novel is one that pays little attention to 'mental spiritual consciousness'. Kate's statement is one that the action in the novel only imperfectly conveys.

When Kate insists that Ramón's movement is not a helpless panic reversal, but conscious and carefully chosen, she accepts the blood philosophy with her consciousness. She seems to *will* her immersion in the grand sea of the living blood. Here paradox, for once, works against Lawrence. For in so doing, Kate, not unlike Hermione Roddice in *Women in Love*, makes the sort of act of the will that Lawrence regarded as the unpardonable sin. One does not believe in the blood through an act of the mind.

By the time of *The Plumed Serpent*, Lawrence seems to be taking 'blood' more literally than Birkin did when he discussed knowledge in the blood (III). Although Birkin sounded a bit like Ramón, he took blood knowledge to mean awareness of oneself as a sensual being, an awareness one gets after escaping the tyranny of the conscious self. Where Birkin claimed Westerners spend all their lives with 'the electricity switched on', Ramón seems intent on permanently switching it off. Body and mind seem to have become a dichotomy that Lawrence is resolving not through fusion but by ignoring the mind. In the passage quoted above, Huxley finds 'blood' and 'hatred of the spirit' synonymous and one suspects Ramón does too. The two halves of Quetzacoatl, eagle and serpent, roughly parallel the two supports of the rainbow's arch. In *The Rainbow*, it was the spirit portion that had yet to quiver into life. The old form of spirituality, as signified by the cathedral Will Brangwen communes with (VII), had worn itself out. In *The Plumed Serpent*, the eagle half of the new god is largely neglected, both in Ramón's philosophy and in Kate's marriage.

The striking scene in *Eyeless in Gaza* where the fornicators, Helen Amberley and Anthony Beavis, are splattered with the blood of a dog dropped onto their roof from a passing plane as a cruel prank, is an immersion, for them, in the sea of the living blood (XII). Helen realizes how strictly physical their affair has been. Even Anthony, who categorically resists entangling alliances, is suddenly prepared to 'love the suffering person within that all at once irrelevantly desirable body'. But Helen's horror prompts her flight to Toulon. And it is only at the end of the novel that Anthony seems likely to re-establish a relationship with her on a more complete basis. By the end of the novel, Huxley, along with Beavis, is ready to prefer the oneness of the spirit to its opposite.

In *Lady Chatterley's Lover*, by reversing direction once again, Lawrence turns from conscious primitives to a man and a woman critics are willing to compare to Birkin and Ursula. Unfortunately, too much of Cipriano survives in Mellors, whose mind exists chiefly to evaluate his sexual acts. His attempts at sententious wisdom are often asinine ('the root of sanity is in the balls' (xv)), but he nevertheless emerges as the novel's most interesting, most vital character. Connie's flight with Mellors, like Birkin's with Ursula, is an escape to a new and more complete life.

In 'Apropos of *Lady Chatterley's Lover*' (1928), Lawrence wrote:

> ... I stick to my book and my position: Life is only bearable when the mind and body are in harmony, and there is a natural balance between them, and each has a natural respect for the other.

This comment, however, does not apply to Lawrence's three preceding novels and it applies only tenuously to *Lady Chatterley's Lover*. It seems quite the opposite of Connie's assertion, under Mellors' influence, that 'the life of the body is a greater reality than the life of the mind' (xvi). But the passage from 'Apropos', as compared with Connie's statement in the novel, aptly illustrates what Huxley responds to in Lawrence and what he reacts against. It is clear that Huxley, in 1928, would second the comment from 'Apropos' more heartily than he would endorse Connie's viewpoint. Yet as Lawrence argues, it is the tale that should come before the teller. What Lawrence says about *Lady Chatterley's Lover* in the above quote from 'Apropos' is, in fact, closer to Rampion's opinion than it is to Mellors' or even Birkin's. In *Point Counter Point*, Rampion insists that the 'sane man' tries to 'strike a balance' between his conscious soul and the physical, instinctive part of his being (x). Where Lawrence, in *Etruscan Places* (1932) and *Apocalypse* (1931), continued to speak with admiration of the peoples who were the predecessors of the men of Quetzacoatl, Huxley's Rampion endorses the Greeks and the idea of balance.

Despite Lawrence's return to something of his earlier self in *Lady Chatterley's Lover*, Huxley, in *Brave New World, Beyond the Mexique Bay*, and *Eyeless in Gaza*, continued to criticize the Lawrence who wrote *The Plumed Serpent*. In 'After the Fireworks', he often pokes fun at *Lady Chatterley's Lover*. Huxley returns to Calamy and refuses to resume Lawrencian concerns a second time. Thus if Huxley was often wrong in assuming Lawrence was an advocate of balance, he had some grounds for doing so, both in Lawrence's own statements and in his fellow novelist's early novels. And he was right in taking exception to Lawrence's development after *Women in Love*, for it was towards something that was neither balance nor fusion.

Not until *Ape and Essence* (1949) and *Island* (1962) do Lawrence and his concerns with the physical life receive some reconsideration. The escape Alfred Poole and Loola effect from the sex-less society of post-World-War-III-America bears comparison with the flight of Mellors and Connie. But there is one important reservation: Poole has only recently stumbled onto the phallic consciousness, yet he sees the spontaneous relatedness he and the terribly simple Loola have achieved as a mere first step to something higher and more spiritual. When something resembling the phallic consciousness re-enters Huxley's novels, it is coloured by his mysticism. The union of male and female (of Poole and Loola) at the end of *Ape and Essence* is destined, Poole feels, to be replaced by a higher, mystical union of the individual with the Divine Ground. The revelation of otherness Loola brings him cannot match the otherness revealed in any contact with the deity.

The inhabitants of Pala, in *Island*, are really the first people in Huxley since Mark and Mary Rampion to grant the importance of physical relationships. One fears, however, that Lawrence would have found the Palanese promiscuous. Nor would he have appreciated the Palanese blend of sex and mysticism. It is quite likely that Pala's concepts of love and marriage stem less from Birkin and Mellors than from the Oneida Community and John Humphrey Noyes' theory of male continence.

III

Throughout *Point Counter Point*, Mark Rampion is presented as the embodiment of what Huxley considers to be the Lawrencian position on the body-mind relationship. Perhaps Rampion was intended to remind readers of Birkin at a time when Lawrence himself had just presented Ramón and Cipriano. However, Rampion is, at times, more of a mouthpiece for the idea of balance than even Birkin ever really was. In presenting Mark, then, Huxley may have seen himself functioning as a corrective to the Lawrence who appeared less and less of an ally and by whom Huxley may have felt betrayed. Huxley is creating the Lawrence he admires, but it is a Lawrence who differs somewhat from the Birkin-Lawrence of 1916 and drastically from the Lawrence who celebrated Quetzacoatl.

To the question this essay began with – whether or not Rampion is the centre of *Point Counter Point* – the answer is affirmative. Mark is the standard that Burlap and Old Bidlake depart from in one direction (physical) and Quarles in the other (mental). But when he is the centre, Mark is a modified version of Lawrence. Rampion never substitutes the blood philosophy of *The Plumed Serpent* or the ideal of a new centre of consciousness for Huxley's theory of balanced contradictions. The definition of man as 'a column of blood' and of woman as 'a valley of blood' in *The Plumed Serpent* must be compared with Huxley's opinion in *Do What You Will* that the 'perfected man' is 'the complete man, the man in whom all the elements of human nature have been developed to the highest pitch compatible with the making and holding of a psychological harmony within the individual and an external social harmony between the individual and his fellows'.[24] By comparison with Lawrence, Huxley may sound here like a dry sociologist. Yet by Huxley's definition, few Lawrence characters after Birkin approach the well-roundedness and balance Huxley equates with wholeness.

Despite some alterations, Huxley captures much of the real Lawrence in Rampion. There is nothing tame about Mark's steep profile, his 'hooked fierce nose like a cutting instrument' and his 'pointed chin'. His eyes are 'piercing' and his hair flutters in the wind 'like whisps of blown flame' (VIII). To Mary, Mark's eyes seem 'bright with power' (IX). The sketch may intentionally make Rampion a bit too demonic, but Huxley's envious admiration for Rampion-Lawrence's vitality is unmistakable.

In a satiric novel that otherwise spares no one, the description of Mark and Mary's first meeting, courtship, and marriage (IX) is almost idyllic in tone. Despite the depressing industrial town of Stanton-in-Teesdale, the courtship has a pastoral atmosphere that contrasts with the rest of the novel. Unlike the other lovers in *Point Counter Point*, Mark and Mary are truly complementary. Their marriage is a series of bridges spanning the gulfs between two social classes (Mary is something of a lady), between male and female, mind and body, soul and senses. The Rampions thus overcome most of the counterpoints (mind and body, life and art) that split the other couples in the novel.

Philip and Elinor Quarles, for example, are the body-mind struggle personified. He is a foreigner in the realm of emotions and depends on her to have the experiences from which he builds his theories. But Mary's role as a sort of Earth Mother or pagan principle and Mark's function as a man of intelligence and philosophy are not mutually exclusive. Mary is delighted by the way Mark 'understood', by his ability to bring out and make clear the obscure relevance of her own remarks (IX). Her 'spontaneous, natural, untroubled way of living' is a revelation to him as well, since she does instinctively what he can articulate in theory but must teach himself to practice. Mark learns her 'noble savagery'. At first his rebellion against his mother's puritanism is only mental and 'he was at war with himself'. But Mark becomes the one male in the novel for whom passion and reason are not self-division's cause. He becomes the ideal, but on Huxley's terms. Mark brings his thoughts and actions, his theories and his life, into satisfactory accord. Quarles and Elinor, Walter Bidlake and Lucy Tantamount, Burlap and Beatrice – all are perverted versions of the Rampions. Mark and Mary may be the only tolerably happy married couple, outside of the families in the utopia of Pala, in all of Huxley's fiction.

Why, then, does Rampion often appear the butt of Huxley's satire? Rampion seems difficult to pin down, one concludes, because Huxley has several conflicting reasons for presenting him. He desires to use him as a standard against which to expose the novel's other characters. He wishes to express his admiration for Lawrence as a thinker and a person – even if he seems at times to modify Lawrence's views. Thirdly, however, he wants to point out some of Lawrence's less appealing characteristics, to subject Rampion to the same satirical treatment John Middleton Murry receives as Burlap and Huxley himself undergoes as both Walter Bidlake and Philip Quarles. The paradox Rampion embodies is that of being apart from and above others on one hand while still having their failings on the other. Huxley's attitude towards Rampion is complex, not ambiguous.

Rampion is often comical because he seems to express sound sentiments under circumstances that modify their validity. Mark defines civilization as completeness and equates lop-sidedness with barbarism. Yet this takes place as one of Rampion's courtship speeches to Mary (IX). Huxley seems to see Rampion, and Ursula to see Birkin, as the world's most philosophical lover, as a man who cannot court a woman except, to use Ursula's terms, as part of his larger vision of himself in the role of 'Salvator Mundi' (XI). Rampion remarks: 'She's a barbarian of the soul . . . All soul and future. No present, no past, no body, no intellect' (IX). This is almost a paraphrase of Birkin's condemnation of Hermione (III), but Rampion is summing up the relatively harmless individual who is his mother.

Even when Spandrell's life virtually depends on whether Rampion feels Beethoven's *helige Dankgesang* can be taken as a possible proof of God's existence, Rampion continues to elucidate his own theories until Spandrell is summoned to the door to stop the bullets of the murdered Webley's avengers. The incident is partially based on a real event in which Huxley, not Spandrell, confronted Lawrence with Beethoven and received an answer similar to Rampion's assertion that Beethoven had 'the art of a man who's lost his body' and thus writes 'a hymn in praise of eunuchism' (XXXVII). Rampion is justly satirized for his inability to make the slightest alteration in his own philosophy even in view of the disparate needs of his friends. Spandrell, Quarles, and Burlap in Huxley's novels, Gerald Crich, Aaron Sisson, and Kate in Lawrence's books, and Murry, Huxley, and others in real life – all seem to turn towards the Lawrencian philosophy with at least some sincerity. And all are invited to swallow it whole or not at all.

Rampion thus has qualities which all the other characters in the novel desperately need. The others seem to admire him for possessing these qualities and to take abuse from him in the hope of acquiring some of his completeness. 'If I could capture something of his secret!' exclaims Quarles (XIV). Yet Rampion is satirized as a man who will take any opportunity, no matter how absurd, to express his own theories about living naturally and spontaneously. Spandrell observes that twentieth-century sculpture could convince future archaeologists that people in London embraced one another naked in the park. Rampion replies: 'I only wish they did' (X).

What Huxley does capture and satirize in *Point Counter Point* is the lecture-like tone of voice Lawrence often adopted when at his worst. Rampion is always defining something – mystical experience, asceticism, God, civilization. He interrupts Spandrell's remarks about mysticism to ask if he has read Anatole France's *Thaïs*. He orders: 'Read it and then come and talk to me again about asceticism and mystical experiences' (X). After listing the perversions of Burlap, Spandrell, and Quarles in the climactic scene of *Point Counter Point*, Rampion all too truthfully labels himself a 'pedagogue-pervert. A Jeremiah pervert. A worry-about-the-bloody-old-world pervert. Above all, a gibber pervert' (XXXIV).

Worse things were said about Birkin in *Women in Love*. Some of Ursula's appraisals of Birkin, and especially the scene (XXVIII) where Halliday reads one of Birkin's philosophical-prophetic-religious letters aloud to the clientele of the Pompadour Cafe, reveal Lawrence as a sound self-critic and, for once, a skilled satirist. Birkin's dislike of mankind, Lawrence writes, 'amounted almost to an illness' (v). Halliday's coterie call him a megalomaniac and find him almost as bad as Jesus (XXVIII). Though Lawrence subsequently fails at satire in the Bloomsbury chapters of *Aaron's Rod* (V–VII), many of the scenes involving Birkin are frankly more amusing than those in which Rampion is criticized. The difference, of course, is that Birkin is satirized most heavily, although not most amusingly, in the novel's earlier chapters. His fellow characters always find him a bit amusing, but they become increasingly aware of his greatness. By the time of the Pompadour scene, one can afford to laugh with Halliday because Birkin's soundness is unshakable. Even Gudrun, in many ways the opposite of Birkin's ideal, has been influenced, since it is she who snatches the letter from Halliday's grasp. In *Point Counter Point*, the reverse is true. Rampion first appears in an idyllic chapter. He is then intermittently satirized until at the novel's climax, although his perversion is much less damning than Spandrell's or Burlap's, there is an assertion of Rampion's resemblance to those he himself has taken apart.

The ruthless assessments Rampion makes of his fellow characters in *Point Counter Point* seem based on Lawrence's actual practice. A glance at Lawrence's letters shows Huxley had merely to record, perhaps slightly exaggerate, Lorenzo's frequently Rhadamanthine remarks. Rampion dismisses Shelley as a man filled with 'a bloodless kind of slime'. He went to bed with women, Rampion charges, and pretended it was like two angels holding hands. In the essay entitled 'Introduction to His Paintings', Lawrence said Shelley stood for 'pure escape' in which 'the body is sublimated into sublime gas'. Compare the attack on Shelley (or any of Rampion's dissections of Burlap and Spandrell) with the following extracts from Lawrence's letters:

> Your articles in the *Adelphi* always annoy me. Why care so much about your own fishiness and fleshiness? . . . Can't you focus yourself outside yourself? Not for ever focused on yourself *ad nauseam*? . . .
>
> You know I don't care a single straw what you think of me. Realize that, once and for all . . . Leave off being emotional . . . Leave off having any emotions at all. You haven't any genuine ones . . .
>
> (To John Middleton Murry, *Letters*, pp. 601–603)

> I hate and detest his ridiculous imitation yokels and all the silly hash of his bucolics; I loathe his rather nasty efforts at cruelty . . .
>
> (On Abercrombie's poetry, *Letters*, p. 168)

To the rubbish heap with all unfortunates. A great *Merde*! to all latter-day Joan-of-Arcism. God, God, God, if there *be* any Youth in Europe, let them rally and kick the bottom of all this elderly bunk.

(*Letters*, p. 614)

One day, perhaps, you and I may meet as men. Up to now, it has been all slush. Best drop that Christ stuff: it's putrescence.

(To John Middleton Murry, *Letters*, pp. 636–637)

The majority of Lawrence's letters do not read this way, but those that do are fairly numerous. In both Rampion, as Huxley presents him, and in some of Lawrence's letters, one finds the same propensity for judging and advising, the same willingness to discuss and evaluate, the most intimate aspects of other people's lives. In Rampion's speech and Lawrence's letters, expressions such as 'slime', 'slush', and 'putrescence' often combine with a consistently imperative tone to make Rampion and Lawrence verbally offensive. Many of Lawrence's critical comments on other writers are in the same tone of voice as Rampion's evaluations of his friends. Thus Lawrence called Chekhov 'a willy wet-leg', and Dostoevsky 'a lilly-mouthed missionary'.

Some of the letters are extraordinarily funny because Lawrence exploits his own vehemence: 'That beastly —, why doesn't a shark eat him – not fit for anything else' (*Letters*, p. 753). Once a man called whom Lawrence did not wish to see again, 'so I told him he'd be raping little girls before ten years are out – don't think he wants to see me twice' (*Letters*, p. 798). Rampion's comments are equally insulting, though frequently less humorous. The Rampion who told Spandrell he enjoyed being unhealthy and the Lawrence who accused Huxley of wanting to be raped (*Letters*, p. 766) are strikingly similar. Rampion's tirades often seem about to topple over under the weight of their own vehemence. Satire once meant curse-hurling and Lawrence was indeed a modern Juvenal or a twentieth-century Carlyle with a sharp ear for vituperative slang and an apocalyptic tone. But Huxley's attitude towards Rampion's onslaughts, even when they fall on the eminently deserving, is not totally approving. Lawrence, Huxley wrote, was 'so blood-thirstily censorious'.[25] By the end of *Point Counter Point*, Rampion is in opposition to all the forces and movements of his time and has insulted virtually everyone else in the novel.

To record his reactions to *Point Counter Point*, Lawrence included in *Pansies* the short poem 'I AM IN A NOVEL':

> I read a novel by a friend of mine
> in which one of the characters was me,
> the novel it sure was mighty fine
> but the funniest thing that could be
>
> was me, or what was supposed for me,
> for I had to recognize
> a few of the touches, like a low-born jake,
> but the rest was a real surprise.
>
> Well damn my eyes! I said to myself.
> Well damn my little eyes!
> If this is what Archibald thinks I am
> he sure thinks a lot of lies.

The poem continues for two additional stanzas, but its main point is already clear. It registers Lawrence's surprise and mild indignation over the fact that Huxley's version of Lawrence differs from Lawrence's estimate of himself. These lines, along with Lawrence's assertion that Rampion is a boring gas-bag, recall Denis' reaction to the caricature of himself he discovered in Jenny's notebook (*Crome Yellow*, XXIV). It is tempting to suggest that one of the reasons for Lawrence's dislike of *Point Counter Point* was his recognition that Rampion's personality contained, in exaggerated form, some of his own less admirable characteristics.

Yet this is hardly a complete answer, since Birkin's weaknesses were also quite severely explored. Lawrence may, of course, have resented Huxley's satire because he felt only Lawrence should satirize Lawrence, but sufficient material has been presented to account for Lawrence's resentment on four grounds. First, Lawrence felt Huxley was making him a mouthpiece for Huxley's own version of Lawrencian themes. Rampion sums up the human situation thus: 'A man's a creature on a tightrope, walking delicately, equilibrated, with mind and consciousness and spirit at one end of his balancing pole and body and instinct and all that's unconscious and earthy and mysterious at the other. Balanced. Which is damnably difficult. And the only absolute he can ever really know is the absolute of perfect balance' (XXXIV). This is the sort of passage, had it been spoken by Lawrence, that Gordon would label 'hasty journalism'. Second,

Rampion was closer to the Lawrence of *Women in Love* (1920), closer to Birkin, than to the Lawrence of *The Plumed Serpent* (1926). Lawrence may have felt the chagrin of a prophet who catches his disciple preaching and preferring an earlier version of the present doctrine. Third, the sketch of Rampion ended with satire, whereas Birkin rose steadily in the reader's estimation. Birkin was triumphant, Rampion is at least partially unmasked. Finally, Lawrence may have recognized that if Rampion was indeed a bore, the portrait of himself was not therefore inaccurate. From one aspect, Huxley may have misunderstood or misinterpreted Lawrence, but from another he grasped him all too well. The first of the foregoing four reasons seems by far the most significant.

Rampion's drawings in *Point Counter Point* are generally allegorical and provide an additional perspective on the different estimates of the physical made by Lawrence and Huxley. They show Huxley re-interpreting Lawrence. The drawings usually stress the importance of a body-mind balance, of being no more or less than fully human. Lawrence's actual paintings, although often equally allegorical, stressed the physical or natural. Compare the Rampion drawings in x and xvi, two of the most anti-spirit drawings mentioned in *Point Counter Point*, with Lawrence's description of 'a nice canvas of sun-fauns and sun-nymphs laughing at the Crucifixion' (*Letters*, p. 756) and with Lawrence's intentionally comic description of his 'Unholy Family' as a *bambino* with *nimbus* watching a young man give a semi-nude woman *un gros baiser* (*Letters*, p. 680). Huxley tones down Lawrence's paintings. Indeed, the Rampion painting of '*physical* love' (xvi) is the most non-physical picture imaginable, given the pastoral, idyllic way Huxley describes it. Huxley mentions the man and woman and their naked bodies but spends the rest of the paragraph discussing the lighting like an art critic.

A glance at the *Letters* shows that many of Lawrence's comments about his paintings occur in letters addressed to Aldous or Maria Huxley. The canvas Lawrence writes that he has done especially for Maria is called 'Dandelions' (p. 729). It pictures a man 'pissing'. Lawrence later refers to 'Mango Tree' (p. 796) as 'that water-colour of which Maria said she couldn't hang it up in her bedroom when the boy was about . . .' Lawrence seems to have enjoyed offering the Huxleys paintings he knew they would feel qualms about hanging. Lawrence's paintings were often offensive by intent, eye-openers. But Rampion's sketches, despite their satiric nature and their ability to frighten Burlap, are, along with Rampion himself, advocates of a working arrangement between spirit and flesh.

To explicate the character of Miles Fanning and the twofold meaning in the title of 'After the Fireworks' one should recall Huxley's contention, in *The Olive Tree*, that Lawrence's philosophy is not suited to old age. For Miles Fanning is the Lawrencian hero on the brink of old age, about to become 'a superannuated faun'.

The story appears in *Brief Candles* (1930) and begins by contrasting Miles and his friend, Colin Judd, whom Fanning calls an unspeakable chastity-pervert. For some ten pages Fanning has everything his own way, until Huxley records Miles' 'horror when, a year before, he had realized that his own paunch was showing the first preliminary signs of sagging!' The real crisis develops when a young, rather attractive girl, Pamela Tarn, begins pursuing Fanning more overtly than her namesake in Samuel Richardson pursued Mr. B.

To appreciate the comedy, one must realize who Pamela really is. The answer is in Dodo's account of what Clare Tarn, Pamela's mother, once told her. 'How profoundly *satisfying*', Clare had said, 'to feel oneself at the mercy of the dumb, dark forces of physical passion! How *intoxicating* to humiliate one's culture and one's class feeling before some *magnificent* primitive, some *earthly* beautiful satyr, some *divine* animal! And so on *crescendo*. And it ended', Dodo says, 'with her telling me the story of her *extraordinary* affair with – was it a gamekeeper? or a young farmer? I forget.' In effect, Miles is possibly being pursued by Lady Chatterley's daughter.

Some of the satire may be directed against Pamela, whose notion of the Lawrencian hero is not much more accurate than her mother's. Yet Miles is also being satirized, and one feels Huxley is not unprepared to accept Clare's description of the '*magnificent* primitive' as an adequate depiction of the later Lawrencian figures, such as Cipriano in *The Plumed Serpent*, Mellors in *Lady Chatterley's Lover*, and the Mexican peasant in the short story entitled 'Sun'. The '*schwarze Bestie*', Cuesta, whom the cerebral Ethel Cane encounters in 'None of That' in *The Woman Who Rode Away and Other Stories* (1928) when she tries to prove her imagination is stronger than her body and its desires, is an additional example. Clare's description is not all that inaccurate when applied to some of the figures mentioned above. Through Pamela and Clare, Huxley implies that women, Connie Chatterley and Kate Leslie among them, do not want to be rescued from civilization. They merely want to take an occasional holiday from it.

It is Miles' reluctance, indeed his virtual inability, to react to Pamela as she expects, that provides the comedy. Fanning is quite different from the heroes in his own novels, and, by extension, almost the opposite of Cipriano and Mellors. One is tempted to suggest that Huxley is pointing out a difference between Lawrence himself and some of his heroes. For a time Miles staves off Pamela with sparkling conversation. He defines culture as knowing and thinking about what has nothing to do with us. He complains of the great split that broke life into spirit and matter. Pamela's mind, however, is on Fanning, not on his ideas. So is Fanning's mind, but with a sense of alarm: 'He got up and, as he unbent them, his knees cracked stiffly.'

The pair attend a fireworks display and after it, in the cab, Pamela cries 'Take me, Miles.' But Miles is already 'half out of the cab'. Thrusting money into the driver's hand, Miles 'almost ran'. He returns home, barricades himself in, and writes Pamela a long letter: 'Dear object, let's be reasonable – oh, entirely against all my principles.' When Pamela invades his stronghold, Miles finally realizes 'he would be her lover'. Their affair together, however, becomes broad farce as the ageing Miles must take a rest cure for his liver: 'He was on his way to becoming one of those pump-room monsters.' From this point on, Huxley provides excerpts from Pamela's diary in which she records her growing disenchantment with Miles and her preparations for leaving him to join a younger man. Her description of the rest home with its 'fountains of purgatives' and 'six hundred W.C.'s' and her realization that 'their roles were being reversed, that the desperate one was no longer herself, but Miles' are the best parts from the diary.

'After the Fireworks' thus refers both to an actual event in the story and to Miles' incipient physical decay. The title may also be a slap at the phallic titles Lawrence often used for his novels. Although it is largely a clever farce, the story contains a serious point. It records Huxley's growing dissatisfaction with what might be called the unperennial quality of the Lawrencian philosophy. Lawrence never doubted that his views applied to men and women at all stages of their lives. The fire of sex, he wrote in 'Sex versus Loveliness' (1928), burns inside us if we live to be ninety. In 'Apropos of *Lady Chatterley's*

Lover', he found there was a balance and harmony in existence between a man and wife whether they be thirty, forty, or seventy. But for Huxley this is not enough. 'Man dies, and woman dies', said Lawrence in 'Apropos', and 'perhaps separate the souls go back to the Creator. Who knows?' But Huxley will not entertain this uncertainty. He must know. And if there is an after-life in which the souls go back to God, Huxley reasons, then one should experience as substantial a foretaste of the next world as one's present life will allow. Taking Lawrence's blood-philosophy in a fairly literal sense, Huxley contends it does not provide either for old age or anything beyond. It is not sufficiently perennial, it is not complete. What the mystics know has been known by all the greatest religious figures in all eras, Huxley decides. It is in a definite sense traditional and it applies beyond the grave.

Part of Huxley's purpose in *Brave New World* is to explore the possibilities (and absurdities) of making the Lawrencian view – or Huxley's interpretation of it – world-wide. Birkin felt humanity was an aggregate lie and that the individual was more important than the community because he alone was capable of truth (xi). Yet in *The Plumed Serpent* Lawrence tried to prescribe for the community and it is that prescription *Brave New World* satirizes.

By 1932, Lawrence is not so much an influence on Huxley as he is a force Huxley was once influenced by but is now defining himself against. *Brave New World*, an extended critique of *The Plumed Serpent* and of Lawrence's post-1920 thought, juxtaposes the direction the industrial West appears to be taking with the path Lawrence, who may be loosely identified with the Savage, would prefer it to follow. Though Lawrence recovered from *The Plumed Serpent*, Huxley sometimes seems never to have done so. *Brave New World* is doubly a dystopia. London is anti-septic ('civilization is sterilization'), while the Indian reservation is 'pulsing with the indefatigable movement of blood' (vii). But neither place will do. The novel brings the scientific future forecasted by H. G. Wells into collision with the primitive past Huxley takes as Lawrence's alternative and repudiates them both.

There is a good deal of initial sympathy for the Savage in *Brave New World*. John's criticism of the new society as 'civilized

infantility' (xi), a world where 'Nothing costs enough' (xvii), represents Huxley's view and recalls Kingham's desire, in 'Two or Three
Graces', for a utopia built on ecstasy and fear rather than security.
The new society is indeed a world without feelings, as Lawrence
charged all Europe was. 'When the individual feels,' Lenina recites,
'the community reels' (vi). The Savage's fight to restore the maggoty
Deltas to some semblance of manhood (xv) has Huxley's support,
though it is from the start a futile manoeuvre. Huxley's objections to
the life-style of a scientific *Brave New World* have already been
treated in chapter one and will be examined at length in chapter
seven, but his criticism of Lawrence and the Savage is twofold: the
primitivism he makes them represent comes too late, is too atavistic;
and neither Lawrence nor the Savage, Huxley contends, are completely convinced by their own philosophies.

Huxley confessed that 'try how I may, I cannot very much like
primitive people'.[26] He did, however, try. *Beyond the Mexique Bay*
describes Huxley's journey to many of the places Lawrence himself
had visited. It is as if Huxley were trying to determine whether
Mexico and its people might not be the utopia some people claimed.
But Huxley concludes that there is no going back, no chance of revert-
ing to the life style of some prior era. To prove it, he takes the Savage,
who would have been at home in *The Plumed Serpent*, and confronts
him, in the London of *Brave New World*, with the world Don
Ramón's men wished to turn their backs on. The Savage is modelled
on the Cipriano of *The Plumed Serpent*. John is a mixture of the
modern and the primitive. His parents are English, but his upbringing
is Indian. He is a partially uncivilized person who speaks perfect
Shakespearian English. Cipriano is the undying Pan. Beneath his
restrained exterior, he has 'the crudity of the semi-savage' (iii). His
education – he speaks English the way he learned it at Oxford – 'lay
like a film of white oil on the black lake of his barbarian consciousness' (v).

Yet Cipriano is more fortunate than John. He seems capable of
maintaining his equilibrium even with one foot in the cultured world
of the whites and the other in the barbaric world of his Indian ancestors. John, more realistically, is only partially at home whether
among Indians at the reservation or in London society. In *The
Plumed Serpent*, Ramón and Cipriano seem to spread their philosophy over Mexico with fantastic ease. The extent to which this is
wish-fulfilment on Lawrence's part, or the result of underdeveloped

Mexico's susceptibility to extensive change, is pointed out by Huxley in scenes where John has little effect on modern society while it has a corrupting effect on him. Disgusted with modern civilization and defeated by his desires for Lenina, John retreats to a lighthouse. Instead of shedding renovating light on an insane civilization, John becomes as much of an escapist as Denis Stone was at the end of *Crome Yellow* or Gumbril Jr. at the conclusion of *Antic Hay*.

The confrontation of the Savage and Mustapha Mond, the new world personified, results in victory for neither (XVII). The society Mond describes has little appeal; but the Savage's rejection of comfort, his willingness to take, among other things, syphilis and cancer, is equally deplorable. In a rather Swiftian way, Huxley is pushing Lawrence's admiration for primitive peoples farther than Lawrence ever went and connecting that admiration with the unsanitary conditions Lawrence of course knew about but did not consider central to his concerns. To deflate modern society, Huxley has only to contrast their ease and immorality with John's more perceptive, poetic, and basically moral outlook. To deflate John and Lawrence, Huxley points to advantages that only a modern, scientific society can enjoy. The scene between the Savage and Mond is an example of the typical Huxley situation wherein two people, each of whom is partly right and partly wrong, refuse to see each other's viewpoint and become parallel lines. Mond's world needs an infusion of danger, sin, and poetry; but the Savage's could use some penicillin.

At best, Huxley writes in *Beyond the Mexique Bay*, one can 'introduce a salutary element of primitivism into our civilized and industrialized way of life', but no choice of one to the exclusion of the other is possible. Birkin, Mellors, Ramón – any Lawrence character who is willing to sweep away the industrialized way of life – are, Huxley would argue, impractical critics with escapist tendencies. Although Huxley hates modern society as much as John does, he accepts it as a given which can be changed for the better but cannot be totally removed or avoided. The Savage's attempt to return to his reservation way of life by isolating himself in a lighthouse is treated as an absurdity. In a society where Alphas use their own helicopters, John begins to make a bow and arrow.

Although Lawrence wrote 'eloquently', even 'overemphatically', about Oaxaca, Lake Chapala and 'the natural man', Huxley notes that Lawrence 'spent only a few months in Mexico'. In fact, 'whenever he lived among primitives', Lawrence 'found it necessary, in spite of the principles he had made his own, to refresh himself by occasional contacts, through books, through civilized men and women, with the lillies of the mind and spirit'.[27] Huxley still admires Lawrence's vitality, but he has come to see Lawrence as a man whose statements and actions fail to coincide and to see himself as a representative of the things Lawrence supposedly hates but cannot do without. For Huxley, Lawrence has become Cipriano, but a Cipriano whose connection with Oxonian pursuits is furtive yet consistent.

The concluding statement that *Beyond the Mexique Bay* makes about Lawrence must be quoted at length:

> The advance from primitivism to civilization, from mere blood to mind and spirit, is a progress whose price is fixed; there are no discounts even for the most highly talented purchasers. I thought once that the payment could be evaded, or at least very greatly reduced; that it was possible to make very nearly the best of both worlds. But this, I believe, was a delusion. The price that has to be paid for intellect and spirit is never reduced to any significant extent. To Lawrence it seemed too high, and he proposed that we should return the goods and ask for our money back. When man became an intellectual and spiritual being, he paid for his new privileges with a treasure of intuitions, of emotional spontaneity, of sensuality ... In practice, [Lawrence] found that it was psychologically impossible to return the new privileges or be content with the primitivism that had been paid away for them. It was even impossible for him to make fictious [sic] personage do so, at any rate convincingly.[28]

Huxley clearly implies that the mystic heroes who displace Rampion in the later Huxley novels occupy a higher rung on the evolutionary ladder than either the natural or complete man. The natural, primitive man whom Huxley feels Lawrence ultimately sides with, is dismissed as an anachronism. The complete man, who makes the best of both worlds, who was the ideal for a time, who was, in fact Rampion-Lawrence himself, is now a 'delusion'. Huxley returns to Calamy. Having charged Lawrence with abandoning the theme of body-mind balance in favour of the blood and the body, Huxley abandons this theme in the opposite direction. The novels after *Brave New World* generally regard the body as an impediment to spiritual advancement. Lawrence's advice, Huxley decides, 'though admirable as far as it went,' was 'inadequate'.[29] Lawrence was 'so wrong for all his gifts, as well as so right'.

Yet the lengthy passage above remains a disturbing one. It will do as a perceptive criticism of certain aspects of Lawrence, but can hardly stand as a total summation. It foists on Lawrence a very narrow and literal primitivism and defines evolution as a process in which serious gains have equally serious unfavourable consequences. It is naggingly, insistently commercial in its diction, if not its thought. One is tempted to say it was Huxley, in his contacts with Lawrence, who found it psychologically impossible to return the new privileges. Thus although the passage hits several of Lawrence's weak points and inconsistencies, and although Huxley is evidently trying to assess the situation objectively, there is a sense in which this part of *Beyond the Mexique Bay* was written by Philip Quarles. And it is a Quarles who seems rather relieved to discover that Lawrence's quest was a futile one and that mind and spirit are the guidelines for future progress.

Throughout his early novels, then, and during his Lawrencian interlude, Huxley strove to become as much like Lawrence as he could. Admittedly, Lawrence changed in directions Huxley disliked. But even had Lawrence gone on producing novels similar to *Women in Love* Huxley could not have ignored Calamy forever. What is ironical is that in the above passage Huxley seems to see himself as Birkin and to make Lawrence the advocate of what Birkin refused to accept: 'mindless progressive knowledge through the senses'.

Gradually, Huxley discards even the aspects of Lawrence he once approved of. Lawrence is no longer considered an ally in the war against egotism. In *Eyeless in Gaza*, after re-reading Lawrence's *The Man Who Died*, Beavis concludes that Lawrence was in favour of a sub-mental passion best described as 'impersonal egotism' (XXVI). Beavis sees Lawrence advocating a mode of being no better than James Joyce's: one can be a 'Personalité de nuit, création de Lawrence' or a 'Personalité de bain, par Joyce' (XI). Both are, Huxley contends, reductions of man's completeness. The realm of mind and spirit, paid for with a treasure of emotions, is a reduction in one sense, but, supposedly, a step up in another. In addition, the purchase has been made and cannot be withdrawn. Huxley's overabundant price and money metaphors seem intended to disarm any assertion, such as the Savage's objection to the insufficiently costly life led by the inhabitants of *Brave New World*, that the realm of intellect and spirit does not cost enough. It costs plenty, Huxley insists, but he resolutely pays.

IV

As one looks back over Huxley's writings, it becomes clear that Lawrence, as he appears in Huxley's works, has all along been evolving into the typical character Huxley – and Lawrence himself – often satirized. Once the evolution is complete, Huxley's Lawrencian interlude is over.

Kingham, Huxley writes in 'Two or Three Graces', virtually wore intellectual blinkers. This ties in with the essay in *The Olive Tree* where Huxley relates how Lawrence would stick to his own theories in the face of scientific proof to the contrary. The theory of evolution was Lawrence's particular bugbear, for it stood in the way of his insistence that men were drying up. To Huxley's request that he consider the evidence, Lawrence reportedly would point to his solar plexus and reply: 'But I don't care about evidence. Evidence doesn't mean anything to me. I don't feel it here.' Like the characters satirized in Huxley's fiction, Lawrence, in *The Olive Tree*, is said to be the victim of 'limitations which he seemed to have imposed upon himself',[29] to have created a private world in which all is twisted into accord with one's private scheme of things.

Huxley often seems to be apologizing for Lawrence: if Lawrence was as one-pointed as the lop-sided people Huxley and Lawrence both hated, it was because, as the essay in *The Olive Tree* argues, 'Loyalty to his genius left him no choice.' The methods of science and critical philosophy 'were incompatible with the exercise of his gift' and Lawrence, like Shearwater in *Antic Hay*, could not give to Caesar what was Caesar's. Shearwater permitted his absorption in kidney research to rule out interest in his own body and in other people. Huxley contends that Lawrence's concern with the natural, spontaneous life he wanted people to lead made science and philosophy his blind spots. Lawrence was not water, as Huxley feels many people are (Shearwater for example); instead, Lawrence was wine. Unfortunately, Huxley adds, half of the glass was spilt.[30]

Huxley satirized Philip Quarles for turning everything into a mental exercise. Even to love Philip can respond only in terms of ideas gleaned from books. In *Those Barren Leaves*, Chelifer reduces reality to matters concerned with *The Rabbit Fanciers' Gazette*, the magazine he edits. Throughout *Point Counter Point* Rampion often seems equally one-pointed in regarding spontaneity and completeness as the *summum bonum* (admittedly rather a large one-pointedness) and in relentlessy defining everything in terms of it. To Spandrell, Rampion defines God as 'the total result, spiritual and physical, of any thought or action that makes for life, of any vital relation with the world' (XXXVI).

Huxley felt that 'Lawrence deliberately cultivated his faith in the blood; he wanted to believe.' When doubts came crowding in upon him, says Huxley, the questioning voices had to be shouted down. Like the typical Huxley eccentric, Lawrence is seen imposing his views on reality at all costs. Most damning, however, is Beavis' charge, already cited, that Lawrence, ostensible foe of egotism, is really recommending a sub-mental passion that can be branded 'impersonal egotism'.

In *Brave New World*, the Savage and the modern world of Mustapha Mond are two parallel lines, as were Denis and Mary in *Crome Yellow* (XXIV). Lawrence, Huxley feels, is no longer communicating, but has become, in fact, an escapist. The Savage's retreat to a lighthouse and his suicide recall Huxley's assertion that Lawrence 'died remote and unconnected as he had lived'.[31] To Aldous and Maria Huxley, the disillusioned and embittered Lawrence of 1929 wrote (*Letters*, p. 805): 'The world is lovely if one avoids man – so why not avoid him! Why not! Why not! I am tired of humanity.'

There were, however, several aspects of Lawrence that Huxley always admired. As the essay in *The Olive Tree* makes clear, Huxley felt Lawrence had discovered that in sexual experience 'the immediate, non-mental knowledge of divine otherness' could be found. Huxley himself was always in pursuit of such knowledge, whether as a disciple-critic of Lawrence or as a student of mysticism. Furthermore, Huxley felt Lawrence never lacked vitality. To the intellectual Huxley, he always seemed, for that reason, a being of a higher order. Like Keats, Lawrence appeared to know what it was like to be a tree or a daisy. Huxley felt Lawrence could get inside the skin of an animal. According to some critics, this was not a talent Lawrence set great store by, but Huxley always desired such power. Denis Stone in *Crome Yellow*, Grumbril Jr. in *Antic Hay*, along with many other Huxley characters, are satarized for lacking negative capability, while Sebastian Barnack in *Time Must Have a Stop* is redeemed by acquiring something roughly resembling it. The admiration Dick Wilkes felt for Kingham and Quarles had for Rampion is echoed in Huxley's direct statement in *The Olive Tree*: 'Lawrence was one of the few people I feel real respect and admiration for.'

In *The Olive Tree*, Huxley states that it 'is impossible to write about Lawrence except as an artist' because Lawrence was an artist first and foremost. By comparison, Huxley felt he himself was no artist at all. Judged aesthetically, Lawrence's writings seemed infinitely superior to his own. But Huxley appears to have regarded himself as the better thinker, the man with a clearer conception of the world's problems and of man's final end. By comparison with Lawrence, however, Huxley seems to be a man of learning and assimulated thought, who knew his subjects exhaustively before writing on them, whereas Lawrence was the man of insight and originality who seldom allowed what he learned about a subject to nullify his initial feelings for or against it. Since Huxley was often prepared to judge literature on the basis of its thought content, it is possible he ultimately envisioned himself as Lawrence's superior.

What the Huxley-Lawrence relationship does reveal, however, is the extent to which the 1920s and part of the decade that followed can be viewed as an era of personal satire in which novelists inserted themselves and their friends into their novels with a gleeful vehemence unseen in England since the Augustan age and the *Dunciad* of Pope. From D. H. Lawrence's *Women in Love* (1920) and *Aaron's Rod* (1922) through *Those Barren Leaves* (1925), *Point Counter Point* (1928), and the writings of Wyndham Lewis, to Somerset Maugham's *Cakes and Ale* (1930), no writer's person or theories were safe from the malicious enthusiasm of his fellows. The discussion novel, as devised by Thomas Love Peacock, used by Huxley, and employed more sparingly, in certain scenes and sequences, by Lawrence, traditionally tolerated the satirizing of an individual's physical appearance, but chiefly as a prelude to a caricature of the victim's mind and ideas.

Thus John Middleton Murry, a recurrent target in the early Huxley novels, appears as Burlap in *Point Counter Point* and at times is Francis Chelifer in *Those Barren Leaves*. Burlap's manner of holding his head to one side and egotistically talking past other people as if to 'an emanation from himself, a little Doppelgänger' (v), as well as his natural tonsure, a sign of oncoming baldness, are all copied from Murry's actual behaviour and appearance. There is even a well-aimed blow at the cult of Katherine Mansfield: at what

Huxley considered Murry's perverse use of his deceased wife's reputation as a means of ingratiating himself with other women. Ethel Cobbett, who writes to Burlap about his wife, Susan Paley, after Susan's death from influenza (XIII), is based on a woman Murry almost married within two months after Katherine died of tuberculosis. Miss Cobbett had known Susan at school and so she and Burlap agree 'to found a kind of private cult for poor Susan' (XIII), but Ethel soon perceives Burlap is only interested in 'slimy spiritual promiscuities'. Ethel Cobbett's consequent suicide, however, is entirely Huxley's invention.

Murry's war-time job editing *The Daily Review of the Foreign Press*, an estimate of the enemy's economic status and morale based on a reading of enemy newspapers becomes for Chelifer, in *Those Barren Leaves*, a position in the contracts department of the Air Board. Where Murry relished his job, Chelifer is unhappily in charge of 'celluloid, rubber tubing, castor oil, linen, and balloon fabrics' (Part 2, v). Murry's work editing *The Athenaeum* (on which Huxley worked as an assistant editor just as Bidlake toils for Burlap on *The Literary World*) and *The Adelphi* helped make him by 1923 the most influential literary critic in England. Yet these successes are parodied by Huxley as he instals Chelifer as editor of *The Rabbit Fanciers' Gazette* and satirizes him for having consciously succumbed to all the worst aspects of modern life. Even Katherine Mansfield may be included in *Those Barren Leaves* since Mary Thriplow, the novelist, writes to her dead brother, Leslie, in a diary as did Katherine in her *Journal*.

The major impetus behind the assault on Murry-Burlap, whom Huxley calls a 'mixture . . . of a movie villain and St. Anthony of Padua . . . of a card-sharping Lothario and a rapturous devotee' (v), is Murry's lack of emotional balance. Not only did Murry bring out the mother in women, F. A. Lea writes in Murry's official biography, but his intellectual precocity was offset by an emotional immaturity.[32] And thus for Huxley, Murry is another example of imbalance, a man whose emotional immaturity causes him, when he appears as Burlap, to use his mind, his position as editor, the reputation of his dead wife, and even his spiritual leanings and cherubic appearance to penetrate the defences of the female. What may have been Murry's genuine sense of Katherine's loss and what was possibly a sincere but misguided desire to evolve a religious basis for his belief in physical love became in Burlap a search for a sort of mother-wife and a willingness to employ the spiritual as a prelude to the gratification of the body. Burlap turns up in *Point Counter Point* as a split-man whose emotional and sexual life has swallowed up or subjected his intellect. The rapturous devotee with the Christ-like physique who writes about *St. Francis and the Modern Psyche* is really a card-sharping Lothario who is not interested, as Murry claimed to be, in transfiguring sex through religion but who, like Shelley, disguises his sexual drives in religious terminology. Huxley dismisses Burlap's attempts at mysticism as 'incessant spiritual masturbation' (XIII). Although Murry later pretended indifference to the picture of himself as Burlap and to the accusation his love for his wife was 'child-like' and perverse, his initial reaction was to threaten to challenge Huxley to a duel.

The list of Huxley's contemporaries who turn up in fictional form in his novels is considerable and could probably serve as a *Who's Who* for the 1920s. The sensualist painter, John Bidlake, in *Point Counter Point* is probably modelled on the painter Augustus John and the affair between Bidlake and Lady Tantamount must be a literary echo of an actual event that the better-informed members of Huxley's original audience would instantly have recognised. More so than his other novels, *Point Counter Point* is a *roman á clef* whose breath of scandal can still be appreciated. Everard Webley, also in *Point Counter Point*, may be a fictionalized version of Sir Oswald Mosley, although Mosley's Fascist tendencies did not take the form of an actual political movement until the early 1930s. However, the National Fascists were founded in 1928 and were fond, as is Webley, of parading with drawn swords. The same year saw the start of Arnold Leese's Imperial Fascist League. Huxley thus had several available models for Webley's British Freemen and he may have, prophetically, put Mosley, an admirer of Mussolini, in charge. Illidge in fact calls Webley a 'Tinpot Mussolini' and Webley, like Mosley, spent time in Parliament before becoming disillusioned with that form of government. H. G. Wells appears as Mr. Scogan in *Crome Yellow* and returns, in terms of his ideas, as one of the major satiric targets throughout *Brave New World*.

There are, however, three things that must be kept in mind about Huxley's personal satire. First, the 1920s for Huxley, Murry, Lawrence, and others was an era marked by an absence of a communal philosophy and thus in many ways the start of the modern period. In a time when each man – in particular Huxley, Lawrence, and Murry – was trying to formulate his own frame of reference, an attack on the man was also a destructive assault on his philosophy. For it was a personal philosophy and not likely to recover its prestige as readily as Existentialism and Thomism can do despite the defeat of a representative proponent of either of those outlooks.

Second, the notion of personal satire, with Huxley and to a lesser degree with Lawrence, must always be expanded to include the satiric presentation of the self. In their early novels, Huxley and Lawrence treated their own failings at least as harshly as they condemned those of others. Finally, it should be obvious that Huxley's novels can be read and enjoyed without paying any attention to the identity of the persons in real life who provided the inspiration for some of the characters. But an awareness of at least some of the personal satire involved tempts one to generalize that while Huxley's sense of what was wrong with society and the modern world may have dictated which of his acquaintances he would choose as examples of modern failings, this sense more likely originated from an unerring analysis of what was wrong with himself and his famous friends. The chief targets of his personal satire – Wells, Murry, and Lawrence – were chosen because of the ideas they promulgated either directly or through their behaviour. The many similarities between Huxley and each of his three major targets (there is a sense, for example, in which all four were utopians) must not blind one, as it did not blind Huxley, to the basic differences in their outlooks.

But Lawrence was the biggest challenge Huxley ever faced. In the relationship with Lawrence, all the themes, desires, and longings in Huxley's early novels came to a head. Lawrence, without explicitly intending to do so, offered Huxley the opportunity to find out how deep his anti-intellect, anti-tradition, and anti-science feelings really went. Lawrence seemed to possess qualities and hold opinions that Huxley tried to use as a means of widening his own point of view and redressing his severely felt limitations. Through conflict with Lawrence, Huxley found out what he himself really believed. He discovered he was not by any means a congenital or potential worshipper of the phallic consciousness, that his intellect and erudition would always take precedence over his emotions and intuitions, that he would approach even a subject as enigmatic as mysticism with as much rationality as possible. His answer to Lawrence's opposition to science, for example, is ultimately a demand for more science 'of a higher quality'.[33]

Huxley was certainly right in rejecting Lawrence as the 'Latin compromise' personified. It was a role Lawrence was only sporadically, if at all, interested in playing. Although much of Huxley's criticism, and even his misunderstandings, of Lawrence can be justified, one cannot but conclude that Huxley retreated from the challenge Lawrence offered. Lawrence was perhaps the central event in Huxley's life and art, and much of his later development can be credited to, if not explained by, his failure permanently to come to terms with the revolutionary quality of Lawrence's thought and personality. After 1936, when the Lawrencian interlude ends, Huxley still has another twenty-seven years of writing, including five novels, ahead of him. His is the unusual situation of a novelist who did much of his best writing under the influence of a writer he eventually felt a strong antipathy towards and whom he virtually excluded from his later works.

From Huxley's viewpoint, Lawrence was clearly the 'Latin compromise' that failed, even if one suspects Huxley is relieved when it fails. Having convinced himself that Lawrence is another form of incompleteness, Huxley can return to Calamy's form of it without qualms. Yet if it were not for Huxley's Lawrencian interlude, *Point Counter Point* and *Brave New World* would not exist, at least not in their present form. The temptation to sum up the Huxley-Lawrence interchange as a process in which they became parallel lines is checked by the realization that in several respects they had been so from the start.

CHAPTER V

Satire and Structure:
The Appropriateness of Counterpoint

Edouard, the novelist-protagonist of Andre Gide's *Les Faux-Monna-yeurs* (1925), remarks at one point that he would like to see in literature 'something like the art of fugue writing in music'. However, Sophro-niska quickly reminds him that 'music is a mathematical art' (Part 2, III). Her position receives support from Knud Jeppesen, who, in his counterpoint textbook, warns readers to 'avoid comparisons between music and other arts; they are on the whole so different in character and material that a comparison is apt to prove quite pointless'.[1] The ultimate effect of *Point Counter Point*, with its 'musicalization' of fiction, is, as has already been observed, probably more mathematical than musical. Yet the point that needs to be made is that there are numerous ways in which, despite Jeppesen, Aldous Huxley's choice of counterpoint as a structural principle and dominating metaphor is intellectually satisfying. Often the choice proves ideally suited to the discussion-novel-of-ideas Huxley wishes to, write. One must re-member that Huxley means counterpoint in a visual rather than an auditory sense. There is to be, as Quarles' notebook makes clear, no 'subordinating of sense to sound'. Instead, the counterpoint is to be utilized 'on a large scale, in the construction' (XXII).

In *Point Counter Point* – and later in *Eyeless in Gaza* and *Time Must Have a Stop* – Huxley is writing neither the straightforward novel of ideas nor the more dramatic discussion novel, but rather a clever combination of the two. In the novel of ideas, such as H. G. Wells' *The World of William Clissold* (1926), the author, having assumed the name Clissold, displays in essay form his own opinions and evaluates the leading notions of his era. Parts of several Huxley novels proceed in this fashion: Quarles outlines his theory of novel writing in a notebook in *Point Counter Point* and Beavis, in *Eyeless in Gaza*, records his developing thoughts in a diary. Mr. Propter's verbal essays in *After Many a Summer Dies the Swan* (Part I, VIII-IX) must also be placed in this category. In the discussion novel as practised by Thomas Love Peacock and W. H. Mallock, the fate of an idea is generally of little concern provided it has been discussed

124

amusingly by the assembled characters. But in the combination of the two genres that Huxley employs, each idea presented and discussed is vitally important. By attempting to modify the presented idea until it suits their own theories, the characters in the discussion reveal their own inadequacies and often become illustrations of the very theme they are discussing. The extent of their inadequacies is made clearer by the presence of a Mr. Propter or a Mark Rampion who speaks for Huxley as Clissold does for Wells.

The climactic scene of *Point Counter Point* (XXXIV), briefly discussed in chapter two, can now be seen in fuller perspective. In it, Rampion functions as *cantus firmus* when he insists mind and consciousness must be checked by body and instinct, that perfect balance is man's only absolute. As if they were second, third, and fourth voices in a polyphonic exercise analyzed by Jeppesen, Quarles, Spandrell, and Burlap all twist Rampion's comment to suit themselves. Quarles' version of Rampion's theme tries to shift the emphasis from balance to truth and intellect. Having recently murdered Webley in an attempt to prove good and evil exist, Spandrell, the diabolist, insists murder must be an absolute wrong, so that balance is not the only absolute. Burlap, who prides himself on his cultivated Christ-like qualities, advises Rampion to forget balance and teach obedience to Christ.

Rampion answers each objection as it arises and then proceeds to label each character's perversion. He concludes they are 'All perverts. Perverted towards goodness or badness, towards spirit or flesh; but always away from the central norm, always away from humanity.' Each character's perversion is evident in his reply to Rampion's cutting evaluation. The 'morality-philosophy pervert', Spandrell, responds by grinning 'like all the tragic characters in fiction rolled into one,' as if he were indeed as complex as Baudelaire or Dostoevksy and not a 'simple-minded zany'. Quarles, the intellectual-aesthetic pervert, tries to be ironic as he says 'Thanks for the compliment.' And the 'pure little Jesus pervert', Burlap, responds by smiling forgivingly. All of these characters, both in this discussion and in the scenes dealing with their public and private actions, are variations of Rampion. Counterpoint thus permits Huxley to discuss an idea in its variant, even its perverse forms without losing sight of it in its original and recommended version. Theme and technique become one. The way the scene in which balance is discussed is put together, the way the discussion proceeds, reveals the balance of Rampion and the imbalance of his listeners. Although the novel has no plot in the traditional sense of the word, it does build, in XXXIV, to a crescendo or climax.

What then, in terms of large scale construction, is the appropriateness of counterpoint? If one considers what counterpoint does and what Huxley's satire is attempting to do, it becomes apparent that the aims of both are similar. The concept of counterpoint (literally: note against note) provides a ready metaphor for a discussion involving conflicting opinions. Thus when Rampion and Spandrell discuss sex, marriage, and wholeness (VIII and X) or Webley and Lord Edward exchange views on progress (V), two speakers take up the same topic but express irreconcilable views in much the same fashion that two voices or instruments handle two different melodies or slightly different versions of the same melody. The disputants emerge, indeed one seems to visualize them, as the parallel lines Huxley charges they are. Musical counterpoint is thus quite compatible with Huxley's satire against egotism. It is the 'interplay of agreement and disagreement between the various factors of the musical texture' that Walter Piston identifies with 'the contrapuntal element in music'[2] and that is also the basis of a good discussion scene.

To have truly contrapuntal music, observes Arthur Tillman Merritt, 'each part must have the assurance that in the course of the piece as a whole, it is as important as any other part'.[3] The egoistic characters in the discussion analyzed above lack this assurance. Each wants to gain control of the *cantus firmus* or main melody and convert the conversation into an extension of his own theory. In polyphonic music, Merritt notes, the independent lines are supposed to be good individually but capable also of 'accommodating themselves to an ensemble over which no one of them has control or is unduly dictatorial'.[4] In a very real sense, musical counterpoint appears to be anti-ego. It permits no predominance by any one voice or instrument that has not been designated the main melody and it is thus the ideal form for indicating the preferred version of an idea and the degree to which variations of that version are tolerable.

Defenders of counterpoint insist it is a very pleasing variety of music. Looked at in one way, Huxley's novel is like counterpoint in that it pits opinion against opinion the way two instruments may be said to compete in a musical composition. But in another sense, if one stresses the pleasing aspect of counterpoint, then it is the failure of Huxley's characters to participate in true counterpoint, to take no more than their fair share of the pattern, that Huxley wishes to stress. *Point Counter Point* may thus be seen to depend on the tension between its construction or format and the inability or unwillingness of the characters to subordinate themselves to the book's design. Though the discussion sequences and the abrupt transitions within a chapter from one scene to another offer ample opportunity for differences of opinion and outlook to combine, provided they are sufficiently complementary, only opposition and disharmony result.

In musical counterpoint, according to Jeppesen, balance between the elements is indispensable and no one element can be emphasized at the expense of another.[5] In effect, true counterpoint demands the same sort of balance in composition and performance that Rampion recommends to all the split-men who are his listeners but that none of them can manage in the discussion scenes or in their private lives. All of the novel's counterpoints – between passion and reason, art and life, and mind and body – can be resolved by any character (though only Rampion succeeds) who brings both halves of each dichotomy into the true counterpoint of equilibrium (where the halves receive equal attention) or that of proportion (where the claims of one half exceed but do not exclude those of the other).

Counterpoint also offers Huxley the 'possibility of shifting from objectivity to life's subjective meanings', a possibility he felt should be 'built into the structure of almost every good novel'.[6] The discussion scene, with its exchange of subjective viewpoints, enables Huxley to examine a topic from numerous aspects while showing the incompleteness of each separate view by comparison with an objective standard stated by a spokesman or implied by the partial truths the speakers express. *Point Counter Point* deals with the counterpoint of subjectivity versus objectivity and characters who fail to temper the first with the second are consistently satirized. When Quarles (or Burlap or Illidge or Lord Edward) tries to interpret the world in terms of his own preoccupations or shortcomings, he inverts proper procedure. He fails, Huxley charges, 'to find ways in which to detect the whole of reality in the one illusory part which our self-centred consciousness permits us to see.'[7] Responding here to the loss of traditions and values most twentieth-century novelists regard as a major characteristic of the modern era, Huxley is suggesting a method, practical if not profound, of working outwards from one's personal opinion through the viewpoints of others to something resembling objective truth. What the musicians playing different parts of a piece never doubt but that the disputants in a Huxley discussion scene seldom realize is that each of them is dealing with only one aspect of a larger whole. Huxley's characters rarely comprehend that an objective standard, even if it is not identical with a perception of all the aspects of a thing, is primarily available to those who can see all the aspects.

Counterpoint is appropriate not only for the structural and thematic concerns of *Point Counter Point* but as a preparation for Huxley's eventual allegiance to the perennial philosophy as taught by the Vedanta Society of Southern California. Within ten years after *Point Counter Point* appears, Vedanta, in the late 1930s, provides Huxley with a religious basis for what his major novel tries to establish through its artistry. Where Huxley satirizes the selfish and incomplete viewpoints of his characters, Swami Nikhilananda insists that any man who 'separates an event from its cosmic environment and views it from his own standpoint' is bound to suffer.[8] The Huxley who attempts to see all the diverse viewpoints of his characters in the hope of discovering some common ground between them surely felt sympathy for Vedanta's claim that after attaining mystical union with the Divine Ground one no longer believes diversity to be real, 'seeing [instead] only unity and oneness'.[9]

What Huxley satirizes in *Point Counter Point* and throughout his earlier novels, Vedanta also disapproves of. What his structure aims at – an extensive picture of life's multiplicity but with a concordant awareness that there is an underlying unifer – Vedanta guarantees. In *Point Counter Point*, the underlying element is the true, harmonic counterpoint the characters violate but that is still implied. In Vedanta, it is Brahman or God, in union with whom, Swami Nikhilananda asserts, one 'sees all things at once' (as Huxley tries to do through abrupt changes of scene) 'and contemplates everything from the standpoint of eternity'. Other adherents to Vedanta have listed 'unity in variety' as its fundamental principle and called it 'the philosophy of *total* experience', a principle and an appellation Huxley could not help but admire.

If a musical score employing counterpoint is examined, the ease with which that score can stand as a structural representation or diagram of Huxley's novel is unmistakable. Although the construction of *Point Counter Point* is indeed mathematical rather than musical, logical and subject to analysis rather than melodious and auditory, the novel is nevertheless mathematical in an analogously musical way. The novel's thirty-seven chapters could be scored on paper, though such an exercise would soon prove tedious. Nor would such a literal 'musicalization' of Huxley's fiction change any reader's original estimation of the book. Yet a critic with an advanced knowledge of music might even detect in the rapid transitions, the changes of mood, the contrapuntal stories, the variations that reduplicate characters and situations – all of which Quarles describes (XXII) – imitations of actual compositions by Palestrina or, more likely, Bach and Beethoven. Huxley surely has these compositions in mind when Quarles advises: 'Meditate on Beethoven . . . (Majesty alternating with a joke, for example, in the first movement of the B flat major Quartet. Comedy suddenly hitting at prodigious and tragic solemnities in the scherzo of the C sharp minor Quartet).'

Although Quarles may have Beethoven in mind, he himself sounds more like Wagner here. The novel Huxley writes, rarely, if ever, deals with 'prodigious and tragic solemnities'. But if one tones down Quarles' comments, they suit *Point Counter Point* well enough. The critic scoring the novel could begin by abstracting the theme of marriage. This theme turns up with Walter Bidlake and Marjorie Carling (I), Lady Tantamount and Lord Edward (III), Philip and Elinor Quarles (VI), Mark and Mary Rampion who are the ideal couple or *cantus firmus* (IX), Burlap and an account of his relationship with his late wife (XIII), Sidney and Rachel Quarles (XX), John Bidlake and his third wife (XXVII), and, in the final chapter, with Burlap and Beatrice indulging in a relationship as illegitimate as Walter and Marjorie's. Once all the main themes are labelled, the pattern in which one theme alternates with another could be charted, as well as the interplay between the variant forms of each theme, such as that of marriage just outlined. The astonishing structural complexity of the novel would then be more apparent.

Similarly, if the theme of wholeness or balance is isolated, each new male as he appears is seen to be a new voice or instrument enriching the novel's texture. In almost every one of the first dozen chapters another male protagonist is introduced. As do many novels, *Point Counter Point* contains a large cast, but some members do not present themselves until half or even two-thirds of the book is past. Their appearance is dictated by musical concerns (by structure and design) rather than plot. Thus when Sidney Quarles enters (XX), he becomes another form of incompleteness and, with his wife, an additional example of unsatisfactory marriage.

Sidney's rather shabby sexual escapades (XX, XXXI), make him quite a different creature from his son, Philip, who cannot even carry on the affairs his wife arranges for him (XXVIII). The father-son contrast takes its place as one of several contrapuntal contrasts in the novel between generations of the same family (John Bidlake, his daughter Elinor, his son Walter, and his grandson little Phil, for example). The gaps that exist between characters are no more extensive than those that exist between parents and their children. Always the stress is on variation, where difference and sameness are simultaneously emphasized. Counterpoint – whether of opinions, characters, situations, or moods – has a vital ambivalence. It can bring out mutual opposition or cross-purposes and it can also suggest potential unity even among the most perverse variations of the standards that Rampion personifies and the other characters deviate from but still resemble. What Huxley says of Gesualdo's madrigals is true of *Point Counter Point*: 'The whole is disorganized . . . [but] . . . totality is present even in the broken pieces. More clearly present, perhaps, than in a completely coherent work.'[10]

II

As a structural device, counterpoint still has its virtues even for those who regard the musical metaphor, the whole notion of 'musicalization', as a counterfeit one. One of the prime values of counterpoint is its ability to encourage eloquent juxtapositions of moods and themes, to facilitate fine situational ironies. These remain even if one ignores the musical metaphor. *Point Counter Point* as a whole may leave one with an appreciative sense of the contrast between the musically structured novel the characters appear in and the inharmonious nature of their relationships, but it is the wit and irony in individual situations that propel one from page to page. The extent to which life's ironies are conveyed by the structure of *Point Counter Point* helps distinguish Huxley's novel from Gide's *Les Faux Monnayeurs*.

Often the change of mood Quarles values so highly in his notebook is accomplished within a chapter. Burlap and Rampion seriously discuss Mark's satiric drawings before the scene switches to Burlap at home working on his ludicrous life of St. Francis (XVI). In the latter part of the chapter Burlap virtually becomes an extension of some of Mark's sketches.

Perhaps an even better example is the shift from Philip's attempt to have an affair with Molly d'Exergillod to his wife's efforts at evading Webley's overtures (XXVIII). Not only do these two scenes form an excellent contrast but each is ironic in itself, the first comically so, the second more tragically. Although Philip is largely a man of intellect and conversation, he is presently striving to get beyond vocal preliminaries. He is making an attempt to save himself from one-sidedness. However, Molly unintentionally makes herself part of his problem by admiring love's 'almost infinite capacity for being turned into phrases'. As Quarles knows all too well, Molly joyfully realizes you 'could talk about it forever'. Elinor all along has been a consistent contrast to her husband's intellectuality, but here she suddenly realizes how closely she resembles his non-physical make-up. She seriously considers taking Webley as a lover to compensate for her husband's failures, but 'What her intellect found harmless, her stiffened and shrinking body passionately disapproved. The spirit was a libertine, but the flesh and its affections were chaste.' As some of the difference between Elinor and her husband vanishes, the contrast of Elinor and Mary Rampion is sharpened.

After Illidge returns from concealing the murdered Webley's body (XXXIII), he finds Lord Edward anxious to discuss the disposal of corpses in relation to the world's dwindling phosphorus supply. Though the characters refuse to act harmoniously (Illidge assists in killing Webley because he cannot tolerate his politics), the novel's structure still manages to establish ironic connections. The move from Webley's body to Lord Edward's conversation about corpses is not purely arbitrary, even if Webley and Lord Edward, when the former was still alive, were parallel lines (V). Instead, the move seems to be life's revenge on the militant separatist. The scene in which one first encounters Philip Quarles and learns that he is an 'emotional foreigner' is appropriately set in India (VI), in contrast to the London setting of the surrounding chapters (V and VII). The idyllic account of Rampion's courtship of Mary (IX) profits immensely from the contrast with Spandrell's description of his technique for seducing young women (VIII and X).

One of the most ironic chapters in the novel begins in a pub with Spandrell meeting a talkative gentleman who resembles an aging choir boy (XVII). The pair discuss the sanctity of marriage, in between scene shifts to Walter and Lucy, who are dining at Spisa's. The talkative gentleman turns out to be Carling, whose wife, Marjorie, ran off with Walter but is now being neglected by him. Spandrell and Carling form a perfect contrast. The former has defined himself in opposition to goodness as a result of his traumatic disapproval of his mother's re-marriage, whereas the latter's disappointment in marriage has resulted in his developing a maudlin sense of religion. Spandrell subsequently arrives at Spisa's to tell Walter and Lucy about Carling, much to Walter's discomfort. The suggestion of musical chairs is heightened by the recollection that Lucy was once briefly Spandrell's mistress. Thus, although the characters prove incapable of order and harmony, they are frequently reminded of how disruptive they are.

As in the later Dickens novels, the same sets of characters continually reappear in new combinations. They display what Huxley no doubt regards as life's propensity for ironic tableaux. Each new grouping is potentially another chance for true counterpoint, but always cacophony results. Most of the egoistic characters in *Point Counter Point* inhabit their own eccentric worlds and seldom tolerate opinions and disciplines contrary to their own. Yet their relationships with other characters are brought out in ironic ways they are powerless to stifle. In one sequence, Webley, Illidge, and John Bidlake are the major male figures (IV). One instantly realizes how unsuited these three are for conversation, yet all are soon to be ironically linked by death. Illidge will participate in Webley's murder (XXXII), and Old Bidlake is marked for stomach cancer (XXIV). Just as Webley does not realize Illidge's significance, Old Bidlake never suspects Webley is a possible lover for his daughter, Elinor. The connections between these characters remain ironic and, by them, unperceived. Little Phil's death from meningitis has no real connection with John Bidlake's stomach illness, but Old Bidlake convinces himself he will survive if little Phil does. When Phil succumbs (XXXV), Bidlake's stomach pains return. One of the very few connections Huxley characters make with each other is thus purely superstitious. It is also psychosomatic as Bidlake connects his body and mind but with disastrous results.

Spandrell, Beatrice, and Old Bidlake form an interesting pattern or minor melody even though the three never meet to form a trio in the course of the novel. Each has never recovered from a critical experience early in life. Shortly after Spandrell read *A Girls' School in Paris*, in which the sexual exploits of the military were 'pindarically' exalted, his mother married a Major Knoyle (XIII). Spandrell's life of self-degradation began from that moment. His absorption in whores and alcohol, as well as his enthusiasm for seductions, seem to him a sort of revenge he can take on life. Beatrice, on the other hand, has been afraid of males ever since a relative molested her as a child. And Old Bidlake, who meets his mistresses of thirty years ago wherever he goes, was once married to Isabel for two golden years until she died 'pointlessly' (xi) in childbirth. All three of these characters, either through perverse conduct or the avoiding of normal actions, are thus in full flight from certain physical realities of life. By contrast to Lucy Tantamount, Walter Bidlake, and Burlap, who have never grown up, Beatrice, Spandrell, and Old Bidlake grow up permanently warped by an early experience.

Point Counter Point begins with a Bach concert at Lady Tantamount's and practically concludes with Spandrell and Rampion listening to Beethoven. But between these scenes that serve as bookends, all is inharmonious. In fact, the musical content of both the Bach and Beethoven scenes is scrupulously undermined. The concert sequence (i–xi) seems a suitable beginning for a novel concerned with music and harmony, the metaphors for unity that it employs. Yet the cinematic shifts from one group of concert-goers to another, from the concert hall to Lord Edward's upstairs lab, from the music scenes to Rampion and Spandrell at Spisa's, only show how incapable these instruments are of producing anything similar to music. Huxley starts with a concert and shifts from one set of characters to another as if they were the concert instruments, but the characters ignore the conductor. They all take up their parts, but the result is not the melodic composition one expects and that, because of Rampion's presence, seems to lie just below the surface. Instead, the characters illustrate the disconnection and vulgarity of modern life. When Illidge greets Lady Tantamount, they remain members of two different classes. When Webley and Lord Edward cross paths, the scientific point of view and the political prove mutually impregnable. The characters assemble at a concert, but they lack grace and harmony and look, in Molly's words, 'like elephants' (xi).

The novel begins with a concert but ends even more disruptively than it began with a crescendo of deaths. Elinor is summoned to little Phil's sickbed while Everard Webley is murdered by Illidge and Spandrell (xxxii). Elinor reaches Little Phil as Spandrell disposes of Webley's body (xxxiii). Little Phil's death (xxxv) is followed by Spandrell's (xxxvii). If one recalls Miss Cobbett's suicide and the fact that Old Bidlake is doomed, the novel, though essentially plotless, contains at least five different and dramatic forms of death, most of them reminders that the unconnected die as unconnected as they live.

Webley's men shoot Spandrell in revenge at almost the same moment his record of Beethoven comes to an end with the needle making a rasping sound. Here, and frequently throughout the novel, the effect is one of excessive contrivance. Everything is too schematic, too mathematical. Still, the scene effectively underlines Spandrell's doubt of the existence of any supernatural unifying principle, for the record is supposedly Spandrell's proof that God exists. It is to obtain Rampion's opinion of this proof that the record is being played. The abrupt switch from music to a rasping sound is virtually a pattern for the course of any encounter in the novel between two or more characters.

The extent to which the characters in *Point Counter Point* instinctively exploit each other's weaknesses and distortions should not be overlooked. When Spandrell decides to tempt God's vengeance and possibly provoke the Deity into self-revelation by murdering Webley, he persuades Illidge to be his accomplice by playing on the latter's class prejudices. And he selects, though on the spur of the moment, Quarles' deserted house for the murder, as if aware that no more unlikely place for an act of physical violence exists. Ironically, it is little Phil's fatal illness that prevents Elinor from meeting Webley and makes Webley's violent death possible.

III

Philip Quarles' observations on his own art (XIV, XIX, XXII, XXVI, XXIX) constitute a sort of theme or recurrent melody all by themselves. Some of his comments, however, apply to more than the organization of scenes, which is mainly what has been considered so far. Quarles' remarks can also be brought to bear on Huxley's use of similar characters from novel to novel. The statement that a 'theme is stated, then developed, pushed out of shape' by each variation of it has already been quoted in a different context. Nevertheless, it also applies to a character from one novel who appears in a slightly different form in the next, who is pushed into different shape from book to book. Coleman of *Antic Hay* is more readily fathomed in light of Spandrell, his successor in *Point Counter Point*. Denis Stone of *Crome Yellow* becomes Gumbril Jr. of *Antic Hay* who turns into Walter Bidlake whom Huxley metamorphoses into Anthony Beavis of *Eyeless in Gaza*. There are 'sets of variations' (XXII) within any one

Huxley novel and between any two. Huxley's elderly men, Cardan in *Those Barren Leaves* and Scogan in *Crome Yellow*, begin as devil's advocates for other characters' opinions but evolve into Propter and Rontini, sages or gurus. As he reappears in one shape after another, the typical Huxley young men seems to seek, and with Beavis begins to find, essential maturity. Viewed in retrospect from Huxley's later Vedantic beliefs, these young men seem to progress towards awareness through a series of reincarnations. The older men, as they recur, appear to possess something more and more akin to wisdom. The Huxley canon is thus itself a counterpoint process in which similar, recurrent characters search from novel to novel for balance, maturity, and wisdom.

As Quarles suggests, Huxley modulates through all the aspects of each theme 'by reduplicating situations and characters'; but the same modulation is carried on verbally in the statements these recurring characters make and in the style Huxley employs throughout *Point Counter Point*. In this verbal counterpoint, characters who are themselves unsatisfactory variants of Huxley's spokesman make assertions, even outside the discussion scenes, that resemble yet ironically distort the spokesman's comments. 'One ought to have had all the experiences', says Lucy Tantamount (XII). She sounds very much like Rampion until she adds 'they might be amusing'. One of the British Freeman observes: 'Webley wants to keep all the classes and strengthen them. He wants them to live in a condition of tension, so that the state is balanced by each pulling as hard as it can its own way' (IV). This sounds almost identical with the checks and balances Rampion recommends for keeping body and mind in equilibrium and with the balance through excesses Gumbril Jr. momentarily achieves in *Antic Hay* (IX) as Toto, the Complete Man. Yet Webley's is a selfish political programme chiefly designed to keep people like Illidge in their place.

'A great artist,' says a Huxley character, 'is a man who synthesizes all experience' (V). Again it appears to be Rampion speaking, but the speaker is actually Burlap. By means of verbal counterpoint, the true standard is more carefully defined and the person mimicking it satirized. Through Lucy and Webley, for instance, Rampion's advocacy of the full, balanced life is distinguished from all traces of promiscuity and from political proposals. Burlap on the synthesis of all experience is Braggadocchio on Guyon's horse. The pseudo-Rampions are thus satirized by their own statements. Verbally, they step for a moment into Mark's shoes, just as in the discussion each tries to become the main melody; but once their actions are compared with their words they become dwarfs by comparison with Rampion.

Quarles contends that the novelist has 'the god-like creative privilege' of considering 'the events of the story in their various aspects' (XXII). This recalls Calamy's speculation, in *Those Barren Leaves*, that his own hand exists simultaneously in a dozen parallel worlds (Part 5, 1). For Calamy and Huxley, the question is how to perceive the unity that may underlie and thereby contradict life's surface diversity, its apparent meaninglessness. If one could think 'really hard about one thing', Calamy decides, one could 'burrow one's way right through the mystery' and unearth the relationship between all the 'different modes of being', whether moral, electrical, or chemical. Stylistically, as well as structurally, *Point Counter Point* insists on relationships the egoistic, eccentric characters refuse to acknowledge. Huxley attempts to scrutinize each theme from as many aspects, situations, and viewpoints as possible, not only to get closer to life's multiplicity but also to suggest that the aspects are components not counterpoints. Appropriately, the style of the novel is also multiple. Though the characters cling to their separate or parallel worlds, Quarles' notebook contains the following:

> I write one sentence: 'Summer after summer, from the time when Shakespeare was a boy till now, ten generations of cooks have employed infra-red radiations to break up the protein molecules of spitted ducklings; ("Thou wast not born for death, immortal bird, etc.").' One sentence, and I am already involved in history, art, and all the sciences (XIX).

In one sentence, Quarles' style accomplishes what the novel's characters fail to do in thirty-four chapters: it links several parallel worlds and breaks down the compartments into which individuals too readily divide different varieties of knowledge and experience. Huxley does stylistically what Calamy considers doing through contemplation and one has an unmistakable example of the proximity of Huxley's moral and artistic concerns.

The style in the above sentence seems to take on different viewpoints from phrase to phrase, moving from time's passage and cooking to science and then to poetry and art. Fortunately, such a sentence can only exist in a Quarles novel. Huxley is seldom equally extravagant, unless for comic effect. But to a more moderate degree, the cornerstone of Huxley's stylistic practice in *Point Counter Point* is deliberate violation of the injunction against mixed metaphors and the keeping of a constant vigilance against uniformity of diction. Huxley chooses his words in a given sentence or paragraph from as many different fields as possible until the sentence becomes a sort of bridge between separate disciplines. The novel's counterpoint of different viewpoints is also reflected in what may be called its contrapuntal style.

Huxley's favourite example of this is his scientific description of Bach's music working its way into Lord Edward's mind through the *malleus, incus,* stirrup bones, and auditory nerves of his ear (III). The passage results in excellent satire inasmuch as it reminds one that Lord Edward mistakenly reduces everything to science. Huxley's multi-aspect style, drawing here on science and music, suggests that the 'vast number of obscure miracles' that are performed in Lord Edward's ear and the miracle of music are not unrelated. Tantamount's previous assertion that life 'comes down to chemistry in the end . . . all chemistry' – a statement most of the other characters would make but in terms of their own pursuits – is completely overthrown.

In an equally impressive and perhaps more serious passage, Huxley writes that the painter, John Bidlake, 'was thinking of death; death in the form of a new life growing and growing in his belly, like an embryo in a womb. The one thing fresh and active in his old body, the one thing exuberantly and increasingly alive was death' (XXIV). The sentences derive their force and irony from the interplay of life and death, age and exuberant freshness. Huxley links embryonics with an ironic eschatological tone that would terrify Old Bidlake. From one aspect, Old Bidlake is dying of stomach cancer. From another, he is giving birth, an unusual, almost grotesque notion, but significant when one recalls that Bidlake always reduced life to the claims of his flesh. Ironically, Bidlake is conceiving his own death, just as his former wife, Isabel, died in childbirth. The sentences depend on the total opposition of life and death at the same time that the words 'alive was death' momentarily break down that opposition.

IV

Andre Gide's *Les Faux Monnayeurs* (1925) is often cited as the source of much of Huxley's technical skill in *Point Counter Point*. However, an examination of Gide's novel does not reveal a structure as intricate as Huxley's. Although Huxley learned a great deal from Gide[11] and possibly did not equal the latter's achievement, it would be a serious mistake to dismiss *Point Counter Point* as a·derivative novel.

There are indeed numerous similarities between the two books. Vincent's scientific discourse on plants and animals (Part I, XVII) may be responsible for Quarles' decision to make the novelist in his novel a zoologist (XXVI). Bernard's practice of taking any opinion he hears and writing it down in a column across from its opposite is not unlike what Huxley does by means of different characters in any discussion scene.

The main resemblance, of course, is between Edouard and Philip Quarles. Each is writing a novel as well as appearing in one. Edouard, Gide writes, 'understands a great many things, but he is forever pursuing himself – through everyone and everything. Real devotion is almost impossible for him'.[12] Like Quarles, Edouard cannot handle his emotions, cannot make real and lasting connections. Both men take an aesthetic view of people and events rather than a personal one. Neither has the ability to balance life and art without turning the former into the latter. Again like Quarles, Edouard possesses a sort of negative capability: 'I live only through others – by procuration, so to speak, and by espousals; and I never feel myself living so intensely as when I escape from myself to become no matter who' (Part I, VIII). Quarles, too, can become anyone with his imagination, but both men live parasitically on the emotions of others, Philip on his wife's and Edouard on a succession of individuals he seems attached to more for his own sake than theirs. The novels both men are writing reveal their personal limitations. Quarles' novel, in the few glimpses one has of it, seems emotionally dry and analytical. Edouard, who will resign himself to reality if it comes as a proof of his thought 'but not as preceding it' (Part 3, XX), thus rejects some of the prime material life offers him. He resolves not to incorporate the counterfeiting ring into his novel even though it ties in with his title and theme and he will not include the account of Boris' suicide, one of the best chapters in Gide (Part 3, XIX).

Edouard is quite correct in describing his subject as 'the rivalry between the real world and the representation of it we make to ourselves' (Part 2, V). But when Edouard pinpoints 'the manner in which we try to impose on the outside world our own interpretation' as 'the drama of our lives', he is also inadvertently defining the content of every Huxley novel since *Crome Yellow*. Denis Stone had Edouard's problem and suffered acutely when the real world broke through the patterns he imposed upon it. All of Huxley's novels are full of egoists, most of them less easy to sympathize with than Denis, who have little if any idea that their private worlds and reality are two different things.

In both Huxley and Gide, there is the strong suggestion that any idea, inasmuch as it is an abstraction, is a counterfeit and that all art is a process of substituting the unreal for the real. But where Gide equates the problems of life and art, where he contends that in both the struggle is between the given and what one wishes to make of it, Huxley often seems to feel life – either the full life of Rampion or later the contemplative life of the mystic – is different from art and indeed above it. Like Huxley, Quarles is sincerely suspicious of the intellectual life (xxvi) in a way that Gide and Edouard are not. Quarles advises Walter Bidlake that 'One shouldn't take art too literally. It's apt to be too true. Unadulterated, like distilled water . . . unadulterated with all the irrelevancies of real life.' (i).

Both Huxley and Gide expose disordered, almost decadent societies and each explodes his share of traditions, taboos, and forms of restraint. But with Bernard's anarchical conclusion, ultimately seconded by Edouard, Huxley could only respond with qualified approval. Bernard insists 'nothing is true for everyone, but only relatively to the person who believes it is . . . there is no method and theory which can be applied indifferently to all alike' (Part 2, IV). Edouard subsequently agrees with Bernard that one must find 'the rule in oneself' (Part 3, xv). While *Point Counter Point* often seems to illustrate Bernard's belief and although Huxley in *Brave New World* and elsewhere is revolted by regulations indifferently applied, he constantly satirizes his characters for taking themselves as the measure of all things. Despite being opposed to regimentation and all decreases in individuality, Huxley is continually in search of something perennial and universal.

Therefore, despite more similarities than it is possible to mention, the differences between Huxley and Gide cannot be emphasized too strongly. Gide is writing a novel about a man writing a novel about a novelist, whereas one of the chief functions of Quarles' notebook is to explain the book Huxley is better than half way through by the time the explanation appears. Quarles is indeed doing a novel about a couple based on Walter Bidlake and Lucy Tantamount, but his comments are clearly intended to clarify Huxley's book. Where Edouard's problems and Gide's novel are generally identical, Quarles' notes, though not Quarles himself, are often separable from

Huxley's novel. They are often more of a gloss on the novel than an episode in it, though the charge that Quarles is 'merely an excuse for writing essays' is extreme.[13] Quarles does take Gide's recommendation when he advises the novelist to include a writer in every novel. However, Huxley was acting on this advice even before it was offered. *Those Barren Leaves*, which appeared in the same year as Gide's novel, contained long excerpts from Francis Chelifer's autobiography as well as frequent glimpses into Mary Thriplow's notebook and diary. If one surveys Huxley's novels, one finds that the notebook-journal-diary element gradually increases, until in *Eyeless in Gaza* it forms possibly the most important part of the novel and the novelist of ideas virtually consumes the discussion novelist.

The tempting conclusion is that Gide helped Huxley to formulate what Huxley had been looking for and perhaps working towards all along. Indeed, what Huxley derives from Gide can be found more readily in the 'Journal' Gide kept while writing the novel than in the finished novel itself. On November 21, 1920, Gide wrote:

> I should like events never to be related directly by the author, but instead exposed (and several times from different vantages) by those actors who will be influenced by those events. In their account of the action I should like the events to appear slightly warped; the reader will take a sort of interest from the mere fact of having to reconstruct. The story requires his collaboration in order to take shape properly.
>
> Thus the whole story of the counterfeiters is to be discovered only in a gradual way through the conversations, by which all the characters will portray themselves at the same time.[14]

This comment is a fairly good outline of Huxley's method in *Point Counter Point*. It suits what Huxley does better than it fits the novel Gide completed some five years after making the statement.

There are numerous conflicts between different points of view in Gide, especially between older men and their sons, nephews, and grandsons. But Gide's novel, at least in terms of the definitions offered earlier, is not ultimately *about* points of view, is not, in short, a discussion novel at all. What Gide describes in his 'Journal' and what Huxley does in his discussion scenes are almost identical. Huxley's book is literally closer to Gide's directions than Gide's own novel. *Les Faux Monnayeurs*, wherein each new character or new grouping of characters necessitates a fresh chapter, has little of the cinematic quality Huxley captures in *Point Counter Point*. One suspects Huxley's disrespect for movies, rather than his respect for Gide, made him consider a cinematic technique ideal for expressing the disorder and vulgarity of modern life.[15]

In Gide's 'Journal' and to some extent in *Les Faux Monnayeurs* itself, Huxley could have found suggestions for a novel in which warp and incompleteness would be the process or method of the novel as well as its theme. Huxley had been working towards such a structural technique in his first three novels, for example in the section of *Those Barren Leaves* entitled 'The Loves of the Parallels', as well as in the exercise in counterpoint that Huxley's first three novels, considered as a trilogy, seem to constitute. Quarles was almost an inevitability in Huxley's fiction from the moment Denis appeared in *Crome Yellow*. Thus Gide may be a strong impetus behind Huxley's technical maturity in *Point Counter Point*, but it is not implausible that Huxley's novel would have attained something resembling its present form even if Gide had never published. Huxley undoubtedly sought inspiration in Gide, yet one cannot deny that much of what he found there was actually confirmation.

It was thus neither arrogance nor forgetfulness that made Huxley, at two different times late in his career, describe Shakespeare's method in such a way as to make the Bard seem like the real originator of the structural technique in *Point Counter Point*:

> What he gives us is not a religious system; it is more like an anthology, a collection of different points of view, an assortment of commentaries on the human predicament offered by persons of dissimilar temperament and upbringing. Shakespeare's own religion can be inferred in many cases from hints dropped by his characters.[16]

The passage on *Troilus and Cressida* as 'a vast repertory of life's multiple meanings' in *Literature and Science*[17] is an equally good example, although it is always easier to make inferences about Huxley's beliefs than it is to do so about Shakespeare's.

V

The foregoing comparison of Huxley and Gide has been included as a prelude to the question: What, after all, is a congenital novelist? That Huxley did not regard himself as one is sometimes inferred from the self-critical fashion in which Quarles dissociates himself from the species:

> The chief defect of the novel of ideas is that you must write about people

who have ideas to express – which excludes all but .01 per cent of the human race. Hence the real, the congenital novelists don't write such books. But then, I never pretended to be a congenital novelist (XXII).

Yet Quarles' statement can be read as self-praise just as readily as self-depreciation. It is the congenital novelists, not Quarles, who must deal with the 99.9 per cent of thoughtless humanity and the intellectually prideful Quarles is quite aware of this.

After one mentions Dickens, the list of 'born' English novelists is severely depleted, if not exhausted. To say Huxley grew too interested in promulgating one point of view to remain forever within the dramatic requirements of the novel does not mean he was never a serious novelist and craftsman. In *Point Counter Point* (and in *Eyeless in Gaza*) – his most experimental and perhaps his best novel(s) – he demonstrates a serious concern for technique and structure as he dramatizes with skill the interchange of opinions and ideas. 'I have always been interested in the subtleties of literary form,' Huxley once wrote. 'I have dallied with many literary forms,' he continued, 'taking pleasure in their different intricacies, studying the means by which great authors of the past have resolved the technical problems presented by each.'[18]

In *Point Counter Point*, satire and structure become synonymous. The novel's musical format becomes part of the satire directed against the characters as it exposes their eccentricity, their inability to abide by norms, their lack of harmony. As a metaphor for a discussion scene and as an overall structural principle, counterpoint often proves ideally suited to Huxley's thematic concerns. Yet 'Music', as Huxley notes, 'can say four or five different things at the same time, and can say them in such a way that the different things will combine into one thing. ... But ... there is no equivalent in literature of sustained counterpoints or the spatial unity of diverse elements brought together so that they can be perceived at one glance as a significant whole.'[19] Thus Huxley's attempts to achieve through rapid shifts of scene a simultaneity of scenes and events (simultaneity being a form of wholeness) are ultimately futile. The entire chapter that relates Rampion's past history (IX) supposedly takes place between the sentence Spandrell begins in VIII and concludes in X; but while one can understand what Huxley does here, no one can experience IX as though it did take place fleetingly in the interstices of Spandrell's words. If one could see and hear at once all the speakers at the concert sequence (I–XI) with the true counterpoint of Bach as the background, the effect Huxley is striving for would be perfectly attained. But Huxley, like Gide with his fugues, can only approximate. In the opening chapters, and throughout the novel, he is engaged in an experiment, perhaps suggested to him by Gide, that is predestined to be, at best, only partially successful. One cannot read more than one thing at a time or hear a piece of fiction. The structure of *Point Counter Point* is at best something only intellectually analogous to certain types of musical composition, but the analogy holds up. Huxley's limited success improves by comparison with the fugue section of *Ulysses* (it begins: 'Bronze by gold heard the hoofirons, steelyringing') or with the musical patterns critics have sought in Eliot's *Four Quartets*.

CHAPTER VI

The Art of Seeing

Eyeless in Gaza (1936) is *Point Counter Point* (1928) in microcosm. Where *Point Counter Point* asked if the society it depicted might not be a whole despite its surface diversity, *Eyeless in Gaza* questions Anthony Beavis' initial assumption that his life is not a single entity. In the course of the novel, all the pieces of Beavis' life fall into a unified whole both for him and for the reader. David Daiches contends Aldous Huxley's novel 'would have been much more effective as straight autobiography or as the straightforward history of the development of his hero'.[1] Nothing could be more at variance with the purpose of Huxley's novel. It is Beavis' refusal to confront the possibility of straightforward personal development, indeed his desire to frustrate it, that the novel's structure begins by mimicking but ends by satirizing.

Though *Brave New World* (1932) stands between them, *Eyeless in Gaza* continues, on a less ambitious scale, the experimentation of *Point Counter Point*. Beavis himself becomes a successor to the contemplative Calamy with whom *Those Barren Leaves* ended eleven years before. *Eyeless in Gaza* is thus an intentionally disordered novel with an original structure; it has much in common with the traditional *bildungsroman*, yet is also a satire against that form. It encompasses some of Huxley's finest writing, attests to his burgeoning concern with mysticism, and, ironically, contains the seeds of his dissolution as a discussion-novelist-of-ideas.

I

Huxley had more than one brush with blindness and his novels, not surprisingly, are obsessed with the problems of perception and viewpoint. Denis Stone, Shearwater, and Lord Edward Tantamount (in *Crome Yellow*, *Antic Hay*, and *Point Counter Point* respectively) are just a few of the characters in his novels who have epiphanic experiences. But although Stone discovers the existence of viewpoints other than his own, while Shearwater perceives the value of proportion and Tantamount has a vision of the solidarity of all life, these epiphanies are either subsequently ignored (by Stone) or misapplied (by Shearwater and Tantamount). Quarles' theory of the novel insists on 'multiplicity of eyes and multiplicity of aspects seen' (XIV) as a corrective to a one-pointed outlook and *Point Counter Point* is written accordingly. The theorist Quarles also encourages the presentation of scenes and events through which one can look, as if through a window or a Blakean grain of sand, at the entire cosmos (XIX). The short work, *The Art of Seeing* (1942), which Huxley wrote to recommend the Bates method of sight recovery, could thus give its title to all of Huxley's novels. In his first four novels, Huxley satirizes his heroes for neglecting the art of seeing, for refusing to develop negative capability, for never adopting viewpoints other than their own.

Beavis' problem, however, his metaphorically sightless or eyeless state, involves neither Keats nor Blake but Wordsworth, the roman-tic poet most frequently quoted by the characters in the novel. Wordsworth saw life as one long *bildungsroman*, a continual process of growing up but with recurring pauses in which one surveyed one's development to make sure it was still a continuum. Not so Beavis the sociologist who states: 'I would wish my days to be separated each from each by unnatural piety' (1). Beavis must be taught to see the unity of his own life and, as a consequence, the unity of all life. He must succeed where Denis Stone and Lord Edward failed, where Quarles partially succeeded through his structural technique but proved deficient in his personal life. The perception of this unity of all life, it becomes clear, is the highpoint of religious experience. It is practically mystical awareness itself.

That Huxley considers Beavis' redemption of great importance is clear from the novel's title which links Anthony with Milton's Samson, the 'great Deliverer'.[2] Beavis is also marked out as a deliverer, not only of the London he lives in, but for the entire world of fiction as well. He can teach the world pacifism and he can also save fiction, Huxley's novels in particular, from the predominance of the anti-hero. There is a singular lack of non-attached people in literature for us to pattern ourselves on, Huxley once wrote.[3] His own younger men (Denis Stone in *Crome Yellow*, Walter Bidlake in *Point Counter Point*, Alfred Poole in *Ape and Essence*) seem cut from the same material as Evelyn Waugh's inept males or T. S. Eliot's Prufrock. Beavis, and his successors, are to remedy this lack of imitable heroes.

In 1933, the year in which the novel opens, Anthony Beavis is another Philip Quarles. His mistress, Helen Amberley, accuses him, as Elinor accused her husband, of taking her love while refusing to commit himself in return (I). Despite his training as a sociologist, Beavis is an egoist who makes the world over into his own image: 'He had written of the world in general as though the world in general were like himself – from the desire, of course, that it should be' (XI). He is also, like the typical Huxley character, a confirmed escapist who shirks all forms of involvement and responsibility, including his own past and future. He wishes to go 'beyond the past and the future, beyond right and wrong, into the discreet, the self-sufficient, the atomic present' (III). His life, he insists, is not a unity, nor is his personality. He is split, as Miller, the doctor-anthropologist-pacifist, informs him (though not in order to substantiate Beavis' theory), into an unholy trinity: a manipulator of ideas, but a man ignorant of self-knowledge, and with a body unaware of its proper uses (II).

Initially, the structure or chapter arrangement of *Eyeless in Gaza* supports Beavis' philosophy. In his book, *Elements of Sociology*, Beavis insists personality is merely 'a succession of more or less incongruous states' (XI). Thus the child is not father of the man; or, as Beavis puts it, what right has the man of 1914 to commit the man of 1926? Apparently none, if one judges from the novel's opening chapters which jump at will from one phase of Beavis' life to another, from 1933 to 1902 and then to 1926, for example. Helen Ledwidge, in the first chapter, appears to be merely Anthony's mistress of the moment. There is as yet no definite indication that she is both the daughter of Mary Amberley, Beavis' first mistress, and the present wife of Hugh Ledwidge, Anthony's former schoolfellow. Nor do the brief references to such un-introduced characters as Purchas, Miller, or Beppo Bowles mean very much. Although Miller is mentioned early (II), Anthony's first meeting with him is not recounted until much later (XLIX). It is only after forty-seven chapters that Miller's full significance becomes clear. The structure of *Eyeless in Gaza* seems to be Beavis' accomplice. One suspects, wrongly, that the book illustrates his theory of personality and condones the replacement of responsibility by disorder and meaninglessness.

Yet there are problems for the wilful separatist. Anthony is repeatedly betrayed by his associational or Wordsworthian faculties. He touches Helen's skin and the 'firm ground of its sensual immediacy . . . opened beneath his feet and precipitated him into another time and place' (III) to thoughts of his mother and of Mary Amberley. A certain odour and, Proust-like, he recalls some words of Brian Foxe, another as yet un-introduced character who, in 1933 at the start of the novel, has been dead almost twenty years. That the separatist Beavis should be betrayed by his ability to make associations becomes all the more ironical in light of the subsequent discovery that he once betrayed his association with Brian and directly prompted his friend's suicide. As Beavis realizes, the possibility exists that a 'picture gallery' of past places and events has been 'recorded and stored away in the cellars of his mind for the sole and express purpose of being brought up into consciousness at this present moment' (III). But Anthony dismisses this theory in favour of the hypothesis that some lunatic in the mind shuffles a pack of snapshots and deals them out at random 'in different order, again and again, indifferently. There was no chronology.'

Any brief survey of chapter arrangement tends to support Beavis' hypothesis. Each chapter has a date rather than a title and by following these dates one realizes that according to strict chronology the first chapter should be moved back to the twenty-seventh whereas the fourth should really be the first. The only sections whose place in the novel correspond to their place in time are the last chapter and the twenty-fifth or middle chapter. Yet the novel actually has a fine sense of chronology and the reader's sense of the book's unity dawns on him at roughly the same moment that Anthony realizes it also and ceases to deny the integral nature of his life.

For one thing, despite its apparent chaos, the book's overall motion is forward. The first chapter begins on August 30, 1933 and the climactic chapter (LI) containing Anthony's conversion is dated February 7, 1934, less than one year later. The novel opens with the separation of Anthony and Helen and ends less than two years later in 1935 with their implied reunion on a more promising basis. In terms of straightforwardness, the book moves within a two-year period, but while dealing mainly with 1933 and 1934 the chapters flash back to cover the period from 1902 onwards. One can isolate six separate chronological threads:

(1) 1902–1904: IV (1), VI (2), IX (3), XV (4)
    Anthony's childhood, his mother's death, his schooldays.
(2) 1912: X (5), XVI (6), XIX (7)
    Anthony and Brian at Oxford, Brian and Joan Thursley.

(3) 1914: XXVII (8), XXX (9), XXXIII (10), XXXVI (11), XLIII (12), XLVIII (13), LII (14)

Anthony and Mary Amberley, Anthony's betrayal of Brian, Brian's suicide.

(4) 1926–1928: V (15), XI (16), XIV (17), XVIII (18), XX (19), XXII (20), XXIV (21), XXXIV (22), XXXIX (23), XLV (24)

A party at the Amberleys (V, XI, XIV, XVIII, XX, XXII), Helen and Hugh Ledwidge, Anthony's schoolfellows reappear as grown-ups.

(5) 1931–1933: XXV (25), XXIX (26), I (27), III (28), VIII (29), XII (30), XXI (31), XXVI (32), XXXI (33), XXXVII (34), XLI (35), XLVI (36), XLIX (37), LI (38), LIII (39)

From Helen and Anthony's early acquaintance to their affair and break-up to Anthony's conversion by Miller.

(6) 1934–1935: II (40), VII (41), XIII (42), XVII (43), XXIII (44), XXVIII (45), XXXII (46), XXXV (47), XXXVIII (48), XL (49), XLII (50), XLIV (51), XLVI (52), L (53), LIV (54)

Anthony a dedicated pacifist and mystic, excerpts from his journal, his developing ideas.

The roman numerals are the chapter numbers according to Huxley. The arabic numbers indicate the real order of events. If one reads the novel in the above order (starting with IV), it will be as straightforward as Daiches would prefer, but scarcely as meaningful or impressive.

As Huxley wrote it, the six different time periods are different melodies that alternate in a sort of counterpoint. Each date or period stands for a different (i.e. a changing) Beavis. The confrontation *Point Counter Point* obtained by contrasting different points of view and variant forms of the same mood or event is attained here by juxtaposing the Beavis of 1926 with that of 1934. The question of whether the former has any claims on the latter is omnipresent as Beavis is scrutinized from multiple aspects.

The chapters, though apparently arranged in haphazard order, cannot be reshuffled and dealt out differently. The first chapter in Huxley's arrangement presents the escapist Beavis of 1933 while the second involves the converted Anthony, part pacifist and part mystic, of 1934. It is this converted Anthony who commences a journal as 'the first step' towards greater awareness of his new self. Were the Beavis of 1933 correct, there would be no connection between these two selves. They would be separate, unrelated psychological states. But the subsequent chapters fall into an unmistakable pattern. Each is a missing link that increasingly explains both the Beavis of 1933 and that of 1934 as well as the connection between the two. From chapter to chapter, the gap between these two pictures of Beavis in the novel's first two chapters is progressively narrowed. The book begins with Anthony thoroughly fouled up and the chapters describing this state alternate with those in which his journal reveals him to be a purposeful individual with mature opinions. The novel reaches back to uncover the cause of each condition and finds them in two sets of adjoining chapters: XLVIII and XLIX, LI and LII.

From Chapters XLVII to LII, the Beavis who causes Brian's suicide in 1914 and the Beavis who is saved from his separatist and egotistic existence by Joseph Miller early in 1934 appear by turns. In the chapter dated January 10 and 11, 1934, Mark Staithes has a serious accident while he and Anthony are travelling by mule across part of Mexico (XLVII). In the chapter headed January 23, 1914 (XLVIII), Brian, on a walking tour with Anthony, receives a note from Joan Thursley in which he learns of Anthony's duplicity. Anthony had previously been asked to look after Joan, Brian's fiancée, in London during Brian's absence. But, to please a whim of his mistress, Mary Amberley, Beavis, ironically after escorting Joan to the deception-filled *Othello*, encouraged her to transfer her love from Brian to him (XXXIII). Shortly after receiving Joan's letter (Anthony has been unable to force himself to confess his transgression), Brian commits suicide by hurling himself from a cliff. Brian's possessive mother and his own inability to come to terms with his physical desire for Joan are also instrumental, but Anthony is chiefly responsible for Brian's suicide. Nevertheless, Beavis burns Brian's suicide note and young Foxe's death is ruled an accident; it is thereby connected associationally with Mark's mishap in the previous chapter. This is the nadir of Beavis' fortunes. An understanding of Brian's suicide explains the extent to which Beavis' theory of personality is an attempt to elude the consciousness of his past actions. It explains why, though willing to recall many things about Brian, the supposedly random card-dealer in Anthony's mind has refused for most of the book to review Brian's death.

Immediately following XLVII, however, are the incidents of January 12–14, 1934 (XLIX). Anthony, in search of a doctor for Mark, encounters Joseph Miller. The latter appears as providentially as the Leech-Gatherer did for Wordsworth in *Resolution and Independence* and is even more articulate. On February 7, 1934, at the end of a discussion chapter featuring Miller's pacifist sentiments and Mark's rebuttal of them, (LI), Anthony grants Mark some wisdom but concludes: 'I think I shall go and make myself ridiculous with Miller.' This decision, which seals Beavis' fate and accomplishes his redemption, is followed by an account of his failure, nearly twenty years before, to tell Brian's mother he was responsible for her son's death (LII). There too Anthony sealed his fate and began to live the lie he was still living when *Eyeless in Gaza* opened in 1933.

In brief, one strand of the novel moves through the period from April to October of 1934 while also reaching back to January of the year 1934 for the conversion scene. Another strand moves back from 1933 in the opening chapter to all the childhood and school experiences that culminate in the betrayal scenes of 1914 and that shape Beavis into the escapist of 1933. The betrayal chapters containing Brian's suicide and those containing Anthony's redemption at the hands of Miller occur alternately, suggesting that even the two stages of Beavis' life that seem most opposite are really similar and interconnected. It is at the point where these chapters alternate – in fact, at the point where Beavis elects to follow Miller – that the reader understands completely and for the first time the Anthony of 1933 (I) and the different Beavis of 1934 (II). The reader now has all the pieces of Beavis' life and can mentally put them into illuminating order at the precise moment Anthony himself is prepared to see his life as a continuing, developing whole for which he cannot avoid responsibility.

The methods of *Point Counter Point* and *Eyeless in Gaza* satirize the pretensions of their characters. In *Point Counter Point*, each egoist takes himself and his viewpoint as the centre of the universe. But the pitting of opinion against opinion, egoist against egoist, in the discussion scenes soon illustrates how warped and limited each of the self-styled centres really is. In *Eyeless in Gaza*, the unregenerate Beavis claims he is merely a succession of psychological states but the novel's structure, though at first glance chaotic, gradually reveals itself to be an integral whole in the Wordsworthian vein. The novel fights Beavis on his own ground. It appears to be a collection of scenes or cards dealt out in insane fashion, but one's sense of the book's organic nature grows with each additional chapter and Beavis' life eventually becomes an exemplum of a theory contrary to his own.

Beavis began as the unwilling hero of a *bildungsroman*, as a character who was unwilling to acknowledge the fact of growth and continuity. He is the sort of person Huxley says he himself once was.[4] Both Huxley and Beavis at one time apparently preferred thinking life meaningless to searching for its meaning. Despite Mr. Scogan's satirical account of the typical *bildungsroman* in *Crome Yellow* (III), Mrs. Foxe's description of Anthony immediately identifies him as the typical *bildungsroman* hero and as one who has definite physical resemblances to Huxley himself. Anthony seems 'so vulnerable', so 'terribly at the mercy of the world' (IX). He has Huxley's 'broad and candid forehead . . . tremulously sensitive lips . . . slight unforceful chin'. *Eyeless in Gaza* is thus a *bildungsroman*, a novel of a young man's growth and development, in spite of Beavis, since his struggles to keep his past and his present separate do not succeed. Because the novel also presents, in varying degrees of depth, the early youth and later manhood of almost all of Beavis' schoolfellows (and Helen Amberley's maturation too), it is perhaps the most multiple *bildungsroman* in English. Anthony's affair with Helen, for example, has its variations in Hugh's excessively idealistic love for her and in Gerry Watchett's seduction of her. With regard to Joan Thursley, Brian wants to feel the way Hugh does towards Helen but must continually struggle against desires similar to Gerry's. *Eyeless in Gaza* is the *bildungsroman* of a certain class of twentieth-century England, all of whom were born in the 1890s and grew up under the dubious guidance of World War I and its consequences. Beavis grows up as he grows old, but few of his schoolfellows are equally fortunate. The novel presents a sightless egocentric society in which only Miller and Beavis (and possibly Helen) have regained some vision. In view of the consequences of World War I and the imminence in the mid-1930s of World War II, Beavis and Miller's pacifism seems, in the novel, a crucial antidote as well as a bit of preventive medicine.

Beavis' journal promulgates several of Huxley's perennial ideas but in slightly different forms than they had in the earlier novels. Anthony once stated: 'I value completeness. I think it's one's duty to develop all one's potentialities – *all* of them' (X). The comment reflects Huxley's concern with completeness, but no longer in terms of the body-mind balance Rampion-Lawrence recommended. For Anthony makes the statement while reading the mystics at Oxford. The mature Beavis, echoing Calamy from *Those Barren Leaves*, later decides we must do what we can from the mental side since the physical will let us down (II). From now on, Huxley, even when he underscores *all* in 'all one's potentialities', generally means spiritual potentialities. Beavis continues the initial formulation of the perennial philosophy that Calamy began (Part 5, IV) and that Sebastian Barnack will complete with his 'Minimum Working Hypothesis' in *Time Must Have a Stop* (XXX).

Beavis defines the good man as 'a less completely closed universe than the bad; but still closed' (LIV). He equates evil with the accentuation of division and good with whatever makes for unity within the self and between individuals. The pacifist Beavis, who is now, along with Huxley, the foe of egotism, eccentricity and escapism, receives a threatening note the afternoon before he is to address an evening meeting. But his belief in the unity of all being is now so firm that he resolves to take this opportunity to practise the pacifism he has been preaching, even if it means death. The whole novel has been a prelude to the course of action Beavis will now take and which the reader will comprehend because he knows how Beavis has developed. Anthony insists unity is 'demonstrated even in the destruction of one life by another', and that final peace is 'the consciousness of being no more separate'. Huxley has always opposed the egocentric isolation of many of his characters, but here Beavis recommends a union that is ultimately spiritual, even if it can be experienced in the temporal, material order and made into a basis for practical conduct, such as the preaching and practice of pacifism.

However, the question of Huxley's mysticism, in itself a book-length subject, remains a puzzling one. It is highly doubtful that Huxley ever had a genuinely mystical experience such as Beavis has at the very end of *Eyeless in Gaza*. The scene is one of the very few attempts in Huxley's later novels to dramatize a character's mystical awareness. To Huxley himself, the consciousness of being no more separate, of having attained union with the Divine Ground, probably never came. Huxley's mysticism, one feels, amounts to knowledge rather than experience. He was a student of mysticism rather than an experienced mystic and his grasp of the basic mystic texts, like his knowledge of science, music, and art, was the result of extensive intellectual effort.

This conclusion is supported by Huxley's own optimistic expectations prior to taking mescalin for the first time: '... by taking the appropriate drug, I might so change my ordinary mode of consciousness as to be able to know, *from the inside*, [italics added] what the visionary, the medium, even the mystic was talking about'.[5] As always, Huxley was after a new way of seeing. Nevertheless, few authorities on mysticism would accept mescalin, soma (the holiday-inducing drug in *Brave New World*), or Will Farnaby's moksha-medicine (a sounder form of soma used by the Palanese in *Island*) as genuine paths to the state of being traditionally reached only through mortification and non-attachment. In a way Huxley may never have realized, his ability both to debunk science throughout his novels and yet to jump here at the chance it might offer for spiritual advancement is slightly incongruous. The mescalin incident indicates how ready Huxley always was to support even the most unlikely and unexpected allies.

It is highly presumptuous to decide what the extent of another person's religious experience has been, especially since at present there is little of Huxley's first-person testimony available. Even in the case of individuals who have explicitly presented themselves as mystics (something Huxley has not done), doubts persist. David Knowles writes that scholars disagree as to whether Master Eckhardt, whom Huxley accepts as a mystic, was 'a distinguished mystic or merely a theologian'.[6] Uninformed critics are fond of discussing D. H. Lawrence as though he were a mystic, and John Middleton Murry firmly but, according to Huxley, wrongly believed he had had, on occasion, genuine mystical experiences. Huxley's case becomes clearer, however, in view of his observation that 'Mystical religion is the ideal religion for doubters – those ultimate schismatics who have separated themselves from all belief'.[7] Yet even this remark, made in the 1930s, must be applied to the Huxley of the later novels only with extreme caution. Christopher Isherwood does echo Huxley's remark when he distinguishes between belief and hypothesis. Perhaps mysticism holds the same attraction for both novelists. One's religion 'remains an hypothesis', Isherwood writes, 'as long as you are not quite sure'.[8] Even the fairly advanced Sebastian Barnack in *Time Must Have a Stop* presents his views as a 'Minimum Working Hypothesis' rather than as a creed or doctrine. That a novel with a mystical hero need not be written by a mystic is amply illustrated by Somerset Maugham's *The Razor's Edge* (1944), and, even earlier, by the picture of Godbole in E. M. Forster's *A Passage to India* (1924).

What appealed to Huxley in mysticism was its ability to insure a valid escape from the ego, its contention that it could lead to an awareness of life's oneness and of one's own unity with the Divine

Ground. From *The Perennial Philosophy* (1945) it is clear that Huxley responded to, among other things, the traditional, almost institutional, aspect of mysticism, to the fact that mystics in all eras and countries have described their discipline in similar fashion. They have pinpointed the truth attained in mystical experience as a sort of common denominator for all religions. It is supposedly the common aspect beneath all aspects, the basic truth that all religions deal with in different ways. Mysticism, Huxley feels, is the direct experience of the basic tenet of the perennial philosophy: that Atman (the divine element in man) and Brahman (the ultimate religious principle or God) are one and the same. The proponent of the perennial philosophy can feel he is part of an ancient tradition while he still remains a sort of ultimate schismatic unconnected with any of the major religious institutions. Most important is the sense of having discovered the common denominator. Thus if one assembled William Law, St. Teresa, a Taoist, a Buddhist, and the authors of such diverse works as the 'Tibetan Book of the Dead', the *Upanishads*, and *The Cloud of Unknowing*, the resulting conversation would be the true counterpoint of mutual dependence and independence, of disagreement within agreement, rather than the egoistic clash of diverse views every encounter in *Point Counter Point* produces.[9]

That Huxley longed to have the mystical experiences he wrote about is quite clear, but one must conclude that he longed for them with his intellect, much as he had desired to be a life-worshipper along with D. H. Lawrence. As this and previous chapters make clear, mysticism thus offers Huxley answers to some of his major concerns: his desire to transcend the ego, his search for unity amid life's diversity, his longing for some form of religious belief, his yearning for a viewpoint that promised, to the successful mystic, something akin to complete vision and understanding.

Mysticism, in a way that pleases both Huxley and Beavis, exalts mind over body and even, in some of its less contemplative forms, dictates a programme of ethical concern. The 'proper use of self' for Beavis is not the balance of body and mind Rampion wanted but the 'power to cure bad behaviour . . . to inhibit and control' (XXIII), a power the occasionally promiscuous Calamy badly needed in *Those Barren Leaves*. Under the influence of Gerald Heard, who appears in *Eyeless in Gaza* as Joseph Miller, and of Swami Prabhavananda's magazine, *Vedanta and the West* (the organ of the Vedanta Society of Southern California), Huxley becomes quite concerned with the practical ramifications of mysticism. His essays, many of them contributed to Vedanta Society publications, are often written from what may be termed the mystic's viewpoint,[10] even when the subjects are world politics, demographic conditions, the state of the World's IQ or of its food supplies, or overpopulation. The perennial philosophy, and Vedanta as its most ancient expression, become not only an alternative to meaninglessness and sexual and ethical confusion, but also, in *Island* (1962), a blueprint for the society of the future.

Nevertheless, Huxley always remains of two minds about mysticism. His continual drive for multiplicity of viewpoint at times stands between him and the complete acceptance of the mystic's viewpoint that he would prefer to have. In *Eyeless in Gaza*, Beavis' mysticism plus pacifism seems the answer to the problems of a pre-World-War-II world, and in *The Perennial Philosophy* Huxley concludes that 'the existence of at least a minority of mystics is necessary for the well-being of any society' (XXVII). In *After Many a Summer Dies the Swan*, Mr. Propter is full of theories for starting co-ops of producers and consumers and for reactivating a sort of Jeffersonian democracy (Part I, X; Part 2, VII). Yet Propter's indictment of literature and culture – 'the enormous defects of so-called good literature' (Part 2, V) – is an indication that, unlike Huxley's, the mystic's list of the best that has been thought and said would be very short. In the ideal world of the mystic, just as in its converse in *Brave New World*, literature and indeed all the arts would be either unnecessary or too trivial to be important. This disturbs Huxley. Judging from Sebastian Barnack and Bruno Rontini in *Time Must Have a Stop*, Huxley clearly seems at some points to prefer a mysticism of complete detachment from social concerns such as those in which Propter and Beavis are involved. *Island*, again by contrast, is a fairly pragmatic mystic's utopia; but one never forgets the tragedy of Father Joseph of *Grey Eminence* (1941) who failed to maintain the mystical bent of his temperament due to the pressure of political policies and problems in the seventeenth-century France of his day. Though Huxley always feels the mystic is essential to the world's salvation, he vacillates between the saint who influences simply by being and one who has practical proposals to make, and he never ceases to wonder what will happen to art and literature should suffering and malaise finally be eliminated.

Eyeless in Gaza is a satiric *bildungsroman* because it treats Beavis as the typical *bildungsroman* hero despite his initial antagonism to the theme of growth and development upon which the *bildungsroman* traditionally turns. Huxley's novel also satirizes the genre's willingness to settle for discovery of self as a fitting conclusion. Of all the *bildungsromans* in print, *Eyeless in Gaza* would probably be most tolerant of Walter Pater's *Marius the Epicurean*. Beavis is possibly the only *bildungsroman* hero who develops into something of a mystic. As such, he does not only grow up, he does not merely discover himself, but also learns how to transcend the self and escape from the ego. He moves from his attempts to avoid responsibility to a realization of self and then on to ways of escaping the self properly through self-transcendence. This last involves the quieting of selfish cravings, the acquisition of humility, the learning of unity, love, and compassion through both action and contemplation. It also involves the search for the Divine Ground or Beatific Vision, for the peace that is the 'ultimate light ... source and substance of all things' (LIV). Anthony moves from one sort of detachment to another. He begins with detachment that is disconnection or self-centred separation and ends with something more akin to the non-attachment of true disinterestedness.

Unfortunately, *Eyeless in Gaza* is often a very undramatic novel. It may end with Anthony resolving to practise what he preaches but Huxley has been more concerned with the preaching. The counterpoint among the various stages of Beavis' life is hardly as intellectually stimulating as the collisions of opinion in *Point Counter Point*. Even the juxtapositioning and the constant ironies obtained by the unusual arrangement of chapters are not as impressive and never, except for XLVIII–XLIX and LI–LII, as powerful as those that result from swift changes of scene in *Point Counter Point*. The sequence in which Anthony and Brian discuss their sexual problems (XXVII) follows the chapter in which the mature Beavis picks apart D. H. Lawrence's *The Man Who Died* (XXVI). Beavis flees an attacker in Mexico (XLI) in between the chapter wherein he describes Miller's pacifism (XL) and one in which he gives his own views on William Penn and the Quakers (XLII). However, the chapter describing Anthony's betrayal of Brian by making love to Joan (XXXIII) and the scene in which Huxley jumps fifteen years to Anthony's visit to Mary Amberley for the first time since she encouraged him to deceive Joan (XXXIV) must be considered exceptional. The contrast between the Mary of 1914 and the drug-ridden Mary of 1928 is Huxley's comment on the life of pleasure. The Mary of 1914 has clearly committed the Mary of 1928, and Anthony is thus only one of several characters in the novel to be viewed from multiple aspects.

Most of the contrasts, even when as effective as the one just described, arouse less interest than those in *Point Counter Point* because the characters, other than Beavis, are themselves vaguer, less clearly defined. Many of them appear mostly in Beavis' journal. He does not need to describe them to himself, but the reader often wishes he would. On occasion, one learns a character's future before discovering his present or past. In one scene (xiv), Huxley records Hugh Ledwidge's growing fascination with Helen Amberley, but the book opened with her as Anthony's mistress. The reader thus knows the result of Hugh's marriage even before it takes place. The as yet unexplained event is implicit in the one under scrutiny and the book's contention that the lives of individuals and of society are a continuously developing organic whole is thus supported. Even if the novel presents events in an apparently disjointed fashion, for the reader it brings order out of the confusion just as Anthony does in his own life. For most of the other characters, the book's apparent confusion is not unlike the genuine disorder of their lives. The homosexual Bowles, Staithes, who is another version of Coleman from *Antic Hay* and Spandrell of *Point Counter Point*, and the inept lover Hugh Ledwidge – all are warped or deficient and remain so. Still, if Hugh Ledwidge himself were more interesting, the care Huxley takes with the novel's design would be too. As in *Point Counter Point*, there is an air of the mathematical about the structure and one never quite loses the suspicion that in unravelling the chronology one is solving a picture puzzle.

The novel's central weakness rests in Joseph Miller's failure as *deus ex machina*. By comparison with Rampion (or even with Propter and Rontini), Miller is a shadowy, colourless individual whose solutions to the world's problems seem to verge on the simplistic. The secret of politics, he explains, is that if you treat others well, they will reciprocate (LI). Miller's inadequacy would be less disastrous if Huxley did not seem to be working towards his appearance for over forty chapters.

Miller solves all of Anthony's problems and seems a divinely sent apparition. A professional anthropologist with a sound grasp of medicine, Miller is also a pacifist well acquainted with Buddhism. It is perhaps intentionally ironic that Anthony discovers mysticism and pacifism in the Mexican desert where Lawrence experienced an increase of admiration for certain qualities he professed to find in the rather primitive Mexicans he met there. Miller also seems to have solved the dualism of mind and body that bothers so many Huxley young men but is somehow as non-existent physically as Mr. Propter. Ultimately, one feels that Miller, though significantly heartier and more intellectual, could pass for one of the Cheeryble Brothers, whom Huxley, in 'Vulgarity in Literature', so vehemently detests.

What *Eyeless in Gaza* does accomplish is an examination of public issues in terms of private life. Anthony's flight from responsibility – a flight which has at its base the crumpled body of Brian Foxe – seems to stand for an entire generation's post-war sense of negligence and guilt. In fact, the events leading up to World War I did take place at about the same time as those that terminate with Brian's suicide. Through Beavis, Huxley wrestles with the whole problem of pessimism and disillusionment so prevalent in the middle 1920s and early 1930s. This has the effect of broadening the novel's significance while also slightly dating it. When Anthony faces up to the demands of his past, the consequences have a wider reverberation than the merely personal one. In his diary, Anthony reaches the conclusion that separation, or the avoidance or betrayal of contacts, is wrong not only on the personal level but also where international diplomacy is concerned (XXVIII). The individual who is a separate or closed universe and the country given over to a narrow nationalism are, both for Beavis and for Huxley, strikingly similar.

If one reads Huxley's works in order – if one examines *The Olive Tree* and *Eyeless in Gaza* (1936), *An Encyclopedia of Pacifism* and *Ends and Means* (1937), along with the earlier *What Are You Going to Do About It?* (1936) – the extent to which Huxley's non-fiction has managed to infiltrate his novels is unmistakable. There is no reason why the Beavis whose journal appears in *Eyeless in Gaza* could not be the author of all of the above books. Both he and Miller seem to be taking turns at quoting them. At one point, Beavis' journal anticipates the central tenet of *Ends and Means* by observing that means determine ends and therefore means different from ends achieve ends like themselves (XXIII).

Throughout Huxley's career, his fiction and non-fiction concerns run parallel. In the early 1920s, he often uses a short story or essay as an initial exploration of a theme later to occupy an entire novel. Usually, he cannot resist the need to say straightforwardly in his own voice whatever he dramatizes in his novels. *Do What You Will*

(1929), for example, puts many of the themes of *Point Counter Point* in essay form. By the middle of the 1930s, however, the distinction between Huxley's novels and his essays is rapidly breaking down. There is an increased impatience with the demands of the novel and the introduction of more and more material by means of devices (journals and notebooks) that are meant to cloak the non-fictional content is impossible to ignore. In fact, the development of the diary or journal as a device in Huxley's fiction would make an interesting study in itself. Both Chelifer and Mary Thriplow keep notebooks in *Those Barren Leaves*, as do Pamela Tarn in 'After the Fireworks' and Quarles in *Point Counter Point*. But in *Eyeless in Gaza* and *Time Must Have A Stop*, the notes of Beavis and Sebastian Barnack seem on the point of taking over their respective novels. Sebastian's actually do, although they do not appear until the final chapter. One can imagine *Point Counter Point* without Quarles' notebook but not *Eyeless in Gaza* without Beavis' journal. Paradoxically, as Huxley progresses, he becomes more and more adroit in his use of the diary: he incorporates it into his novels with greater skill and makes it serve an ever-widening variety of purposes; but the net result is a decrease in his novels of dramatic or novelistic content.

What happens is that Huxley's original combination of the Peacockian discussion novel and the Wellsian novel of ideas breaks down. The discussion novel, though it presents few developed characters, is at any rate somewhat dramatic. But with Beavis' journal, Propter's lengthy orations in *After Many a Summer Dies the Swan*, and Sebastian's notebook, Huxley moves towards the strict novel of ideas such as H. G. Wells' *The World of William Clissold*. Huxley becomes less and less interested in the confrontation of different viewpoints out of which the reader can attempt to construct the ideal position (or possibly learn it by deciding which of the characters is Huxley's spokesman) and more earnest in the direct presentation of his opinions. Thus, despite some fine sections, especially the scenes describing the funeral of Anthony's mother (IV, VI), *Eyeless in Gaza* can be said to contain the seeds of Huxley's dissolution as a novelist. In it, the drift towards that ultimate novel of ideas, the non-satiric utopia that is really a disguised essay, has already begun. In *Island*, a non-satiric utopia, Huxley writes a lengthy work in which several people, fairly unimportant as characters, answer the visitor Will Farnaby's questions with short essays delivered verbally. Intellectualizing the novel can go too far.

Where Wells and at times even Thomas Hardy and D. H. Lawrence suffered as novelists the more concerned they became with theses, Huxley, in the late 1920s, developed an excellent form for the dramatic presentation of ideas, whether serious or satiric, in terms of conflicting viewpoints that were almost like characters. But the novelist of ideas, the man with a programme to present, the writer who wishes to state his views rather than develop them dramatically in discussions, gradually wins out over the discussion novelist. The blend of discussion novel and novel of ideas ceases to exist. In the earlier novels, even where Scogan, in *Crome Yellow*, or Cardan, in *Those Barren Leaves*, spoke at length, they either did so in answer to another character or their views were presented in such fashion that the gap between them and Huxley's own provided the amusement. Between the Beavis who writes his journal or the Sebastian who frames a 'Minimum Working Hypothesis' and Huxley himself there is no difference at all, just as William Clissold is a pseudonym for H. G. Wells. Ultimately, as Huxley may have decided, you cannot discuss mysticism convincingly except in the first person.

II

Of the non-utopias Huxley writes after *Eyeless in Gaza*, only *Time Must Have a Stop* (1944) deserves some extensive treatment. In it Huxley briefly revives the counterpoint method of both *Eyeless in Gaza* and *Point Counter Point*. The novel is, in fact, a curious fusion of Huxley's two finest novels. The first twenty-nine chapters, dealing with the pre-mystical Sebastian Barnack, proceed by means of Sebastian's exposure to the conflicting theories of the other characters. But the last chapter or 'Epilogue', in which the youth has adopted the outlook of the mystic, Bruno Rontini, switches to Sebastian's notebook and becomes an extended essay in the style of Anthony Beavis.

Neither *After Many a Summer Dies the Swan* (1939) nor *The Genius and the Goddess* (1955) improve with re-reading. The opening chapters of *After Many a Summer Dies the Swan*, Huxley's first novel after moving to America, record the Englishman Jeremy Pordage's impressions of California. The satire against the amorphous crassness of Western America is continually amusing. Signs announcing 'Classy Eats' and 'Jesus Saves' occur ba :k to back. An element of the grotesque is seldom lacking, especially in Jo Stoyte's Beverley Pantheon Cemetery with its full-scale reproduction of the Leaning Tower of Pisa – 'Only this one didn't lean'. America's lack of taste and perception, symptoms of a larger moral failure, is everywhere visible, particularly in Stoyte's castle with its Vermeer in the elevator and in Virginia Maunciple's room: a 'Louis XV boudoir' with 'a fully equipped soda fountain in a rococo embrasure'. In countless ways, *After Many a Summer Dies the Swan* is Evelyn Waugh's *The Loved One* (1948) but done nine full years before Waugh. The attempts of Mr. Propter to instil some sense into Jo Stoyte's exploited migrant pickers vaguely recalls Steinbeck's *The Grapes of Wrath*, which appeared the same year as Huxley's novel.

After Many a Summer Dies the Swan, one of the few pieces of writing by Huxley where plot is of central concern, builds to a rather melodramatic climax which the reader has figured out long before the characters do. The novel contains, *Brave New World* to the contrary, Huxley's strongest satire against science as an inadequate religion for the future and as no antidote at all to one's fear of death. In *Eyeless in Gaza*, Beavis' friend, Mark Staithes, observed: 'Death's grown, I should say, now that the consolations and hopes have been taken away. Grown to be almost as large as it was when people seriously believed in hell' (XXXI). Death is Jo Stoyte's biggest fear, as it was Mr. Cardan's in *Those Barren Leaves* and will be Eustace Barnack's in *Time Must Have a Stop*. Stoyte, the symbol of all that is wrong with modern society, looks to Dr. Obispo's longevity experiments to keep him forever alive. Cut off from all taste and value, having made a supreme standard of his own ego and personality, Stoyte regards self-preservation as the only goal. The mention of his own cemetery is enough to terrify him. He is the modern Tithonus, as the novel's title, taken from Tennyson's poem, aptly suggests.

Early in the novel (Part 1, v), Obispo speculates that the intestinal flora of carp may account for their longevity and hold the secret of permanent life. Later (Part 2, VI), the Fifth Earl of Hauberk, whose autobiography Jeremy reads as part of the Hauberk Papers he is editing for Stoyte, notes that the carp in his moat live two or three centuries. A subsequent entry in the Earl's diary relates how, in the 1790s, he began to ingest raw viscera of carp. Immediately the reader guesses the Earl is still alive and the novel's epiphanic last scene (Part 3, II) is a foregone conclusion. In it, Stoyte's hopes for permanent life, science's potential as a panacea, and the Earl's boasts are all exploded. After nearly one hundred and fifty years the Earl has merely become the evolutionary process in reverse and has degenerated into an ape.

The Fifth Earl is a remarkable devil. His account of how he recovered his youth and virility to become younger than his heirs is more entertaining than the chapters that deal with Mr. Propter, Huxley's spokesman. Science, Huxley argues, can increase the span of one's life but cannot increase one's level of existence or provide higher goals than those life already offers. Although he attains a sort of permanent mortality, the Fifth Earl uses his regained youth to perform the same sort of detestable actions all over again. The prospect of evolution as a doctrine of inescapable progress is rejected. Gradually, the Earl degenerates into the beast he really is. Presumably Stoyte will do likewise if he adopts the carp diet. Science thus caters to the Tithonus element in everyone: the clinging to the self via a prolongation of life, the retention of the ego and personality at all cost. By contrast, Propter, in numerous orations, offers a way out of the ego, a mystical method of self-transcendence, and, perhaps, eventual union with something larger than the confining self.

In both *After Many a Summer Dies the Swan* and *Time Must Have a Stop*, Huxley, often in a manner that suggests the medieval preacher, holds the inevitability of death over the heads of his older characters as a reminder of the need for a set of values that apply beyond the individual's lifetime. Propter is the spiritual norm from which most of the novel's other characters have departed. By comparison with Rampion, however, Propter is more consistently boring. Thus although one feels Pordage sincerely needs the benefit of Propter's wisdom, Jeremy is probably right in detecting in the garrulous older man 'a bit of an Ancient Mariner' (Part I, XIII). The alternation of chapters which contrasts Propter's outlook with the rejuvenation of the Fifth Earl is only a faint echo of earlier successes with counterpoint and often works more to the Earl's favour than to Mr. Propter's.

The Genius and the Goddess (1955) is a thin book, even by comparison with *After Many a Summer Dies the Swan*. The novel is an attempt to describe the series of awakenings its hero, Rivers, experienced while in the household of Henry and Katy Maartens. Like Mark Rampion, Brian Foxe, and Jeremy Pordage, Rivers is the victim of a narrow, Puritanical mother. In the turbulent, pagan Maartens household that he enters to assist Henry, a famous scientist, Rivers has one eye-opening experience after another; each time the scales fall from his eyes, a new illusion waits to be dispelled. In a fairly conventional manner, Huxley, by means of Rivers who is an old man recounting the past as the novel begins, is still developing his thesis that one can never see everything but must keep modifying and broadening one's viewpoint in search of inclusiveness. Yet the outcome of Rivers' awakening seems virtually predestined. He is shocked when Katy – whom he calls 'Mrs. Maartens' even as she climbs into bed with him – needs his consolation in order to bear the strain of her husband's dependence upon her. Rivers is subsequently astonished to find how thoroughly this act of adultery rejuvenates the 'goddess' Katy, whom he previously equated with Beatrice and Laura. He is also astonished at how, for the first time, he has been taken out of himself. The neophyte in love is also the neophyte in spiritual experience.

The novel is full of latent mysticism. What is unusual about the book is that it chronicles all of Rivers' awakenings except the final ones. In old age Rivers resembles Mr. Propter. He has apparently adopted an outlook similar to Anthony Beavis'. Yet the novel gives in detail only the initial stages of Rivers' progress towards awareness. It is a novel containing a man's account of certain experiences in youth from which his later development can be inferred. By sleeping with Katy, the young Rivers felt an 'uprush from within of something strong and wonderful, something that's manifestly greater than yourself'.[11] This was the first step towards more serious awakenings that are never really described in the novel, but whose spiritual nature can be deduced from the high frequency of religious terms in Rivers' vocabulary as he recalls his affair with Katy.

Rivers' relationship with his wife, Helen, who is mentioned only once or twice, was apparently of even greater importance than the affair with Katy. Helen, like Katy, has been dead for some time, but, unlike Katy, Helen 'knew how to die because she knew how to live – to live now and here and for the greater glory of God. And that necessarily entails dying to there and then and tomorrow and one's own miserable little self'.[12] Rivers' comments here remind one of Mr. Propter in *After Many a Summer Dies the Swan* or Bruno Rontini in *Time Must Have a Stop*. After Katy's tragic death, says Rivers, the scientist, Henry Maartens, went from one woman to another. At his death, Maartens, who is sketched as the typical

Huxley egoist-eccentric and reminds one of Lord Edward Tanta-mount, was 'unprepared, by any preliminary dying, totally un-prepared for the decisive moment'.[13] By comparison, one supposes that Rivers is quite prepared, even if he often wondered but never learned whether Katy's affair with him was, for her, just one of many.

In her role as a sort of pagan goddess, Katy stands for the kind of frank vitality that Rivers missed in the narrow religion of his youth. As one of his era's foremost scientists, Maartens, despite being the stereotype of the absent-minded professor, represents the new religion of modern times. Through contact with the Maartens household, Rivers' own outlook is indeed broadened, but he also perceives that neither Katy's vitality nor Henry's genius are broad enough to stand as absolutes. They are in fact totally inadequate in the face of any serious crisis. In a manner reminiscent of Sebastian Barnack, Rivers seems aware that Katy's way of life and Maartens' intellect are both in time and that time, as Hotspur was aware, must have a stop (*Henry IV, Part I*, IV, iv, 81–83) at the moment of one's death. Thus it is advisable to stop time while one is still alive by dying to temporal concerns and focusing on the final reality that is outside time and above it. Huxley's experiments with time – the effort to obtain simultaneity of events in *Point Counter Point* and to regard one's personal life, in *Eyeless in Gaza*, as a continuum – were both aimed at time's capacity to divide and separate. These experiments find a sort of fruition in a mysticism that encourages an escape from time and that professes to nullify the separation that exists between temporal and eternal.

The Genius and the Goddess is thus not as thin as it at first appears, and the manner in which Rivers' development must be inferred from incidents of his early life is often intriguing, but the novel is less substantial than one would like it to be. The story depends, more so than most Huxley novels, on the creation of convincing, fully-developed characters – never a Huxley strong point. With the possible exception of *Ape and Essence*, it is the slightest of Huxley's novels.

In *Time Must Have a Stop* (1944), most of the major characters, like many in *Point Counter Point*, are in the grip of a particular viewpoint or theory. As young Sebastian Barnack passes from one to another's tutelage, each is given the opportunity to force a viewpoint upon him.

In two key passages, Bruno Rontini, the novel's mystic, explicates Sebastian's role. When Eustace Barnack, Sebastian's uncle, introduces them, Bruno notes that Sebastian has 'the name of fate's predestined target'. 'Somehow,' Bruno continues, 'I can't help thinking of all those arrows' (XI). Afterwards, when Sebastian seeks Bruno's help about a drawing he is accused of stealing, Rontini refers to him as 'Sebastian, the predestined target, the delicate and radiant butt of God alone knew what ulterior flights of arrows –' (XXVI). Like the saint whose name he bears, Sebastian is to be a martyr to the successive theories of his relatives and friends until such time as he matures into an outlook of his own. In a novel where Eustace Barnack is the target of a heart attack, while Mrs. Thwale is a victim of her lusts, Bruno Rontino of the Fascists, Mrs. Weyl of a bombing raid, and Fred Poulshot of Japanese bayonets, Sebastian is to be target (and test) for the conflicting viewpoints of the other characters.

Sebastian is an extremely talented young poet, somewhat on the order of Keats. He is puzzled for an explanation of why a certain chapel looks hideous by day and mysterious by night and concludes it is one of those 'questions' that 'admitted of no answer, the only thing you could do was to re-formulate them in terms of poetry' (III), as did Keats. This is as close as Sebastian comes to an outlook of his own in the early chapters. Though capable of good verse and clear thought, he is disappointed with his own immature appearance. At seventeen, he looks 'like a child', even though, by comparison with the other characters, he feels himself 'to be a hundred times abler than the oldest of them' (II). Sebastian has an inkling of his own potential, including his ability to project himself into others, but is at present no older mentally than he is in years. He watches a beetle's movements and wonders, Keats-like, 'what would the beetle say it was doing?' (XIV). Even after Bruno lectures him on the superiority of acting on one's knowledge over merely expressing it, Sebastian escapes the responsibility of considering the lecture as a guide to conduct by turning Bruno's reflections into a poem (XXVI). As hard as he tries to 'think less of himself' and live more with events and 'not so exclusively with words', he initially cannot get beyond 'the bliss of detached poetical contemplation' (XXVII), any more than Denis Stone could in *Crome Yellow*.

Nevertheless, Sebastian is the only character in the novel, besides the already mature Rontini, who truly comes of age. For in this *bildungsroman*, even more so than in all the later Huxley novels, age is figured in terms of one's years, one's intellectual development, and one's 'spiritual maturation' (x), with the third as the ultimate standard. Sebastian eventually brings his physical age and his spiritual maturity into accord. Both in years and in wisdom he becomes an adult, just as Rampion previously brought mind and body into the true balance of equilibrium. Unlike his uncle, Eustace, and unlike Jeremy Pordage whose sexual life in *After Many a Summer Dies the Swan* is 'simultaneously infantile and corrupt' (Part 2, i), Sebastian resolves the counterpoint of age-in-years versus degree of wisdom attained.

John Barnack, Sebastian's father and earliest formative influence, is a male Mrs. Jellyby. He supports liberal political organizations and exiled professors but is an unbearable skinflint towards his son. Sebastian is glad to escape him for a visit to Florence and Uncle Eustace. The novel's resemblance to a morality play becomes evident as Sebastian now passes through the hands of one character after another in a search, as yet unconscious, for a dependable mentor and an unfailing philosophy. In fact, it becomes increasingly obvious that Huxley is alluding to *Henry IV, Part I* in terms of structure as well as in Hotspur's speech. The psychomachia structure of Shakespeare's play, wherein Hal has the models of his father, Hotspur, and Falstaff to choose from is recaptured in *Time Must Have a Stop* as Sebastian undergoes the successive tutelages of Uncle Eustace, Mrs. Thwale, and, finally, that of Bruno Rontini. Virtue and Vice compete for control of Sebastian as they did for Prince Hal.

Uncle Eustace, a sort of decayed Oscar Wilde, advocates a life of pleasure, of 'Live and let live' (XII), in which 'Just keeping out of mischief' is 'the greatest of all the virtues' (V). Sebastian easily falls under Eustace's spell, for Eustace is worldliness at its limited best. He holds many opinions similar to Huxley's and is not a bad conjectural portrait of the mental attitude that might have been Huxley's own had the cynical elements in *Antic Hay* and *Those Barren Leaves* not yielded substantially to those novels' equally strong religious overtones. But Eustace's philosophy of 'Live and let live' is suddenly rebutted by the heart attack that ends his epicurean existence. In a series of after-death chapters (XIII, XV, XVII), Eustace struggles to retain his selfhood, his ego. He refuses to be absorbed into the centre of all things and, unlike Anthony Beavis, insists on remaining a self-centred separatist.

Even before Eustace's sudden removal, however, a new influence has begun to operate on Sebastian. Mrs. Thwale's theory of life is the complete opposite of Eustace's. One of countless women in Huxley who seem capable of devouring a male (she is a widow), Veronica Thwale advocates the outrage theory. Instead of living and letting others do so, she recommends that Sebastian overcome his shyness and get out of himself by saying and doing outrageous things. If someone asks how he writes a poem, he is to reply: on toilet paper with an indelible pencil (XVI). She advises that he 'do violence' to himself as if he 'were committing suicide'. The way to escape from oneself and one's shyness is to act as if it was the end of the world, as if, in effect, time was about to stop. To Sebastian's objections that the world does not thereby really come to an end, that there still are consequences, Veronica replies that the world does not end but is 'transformed', since the outrage creates an entirely novel situation.

Rather than face poverty as a widow, Veronica has consented to marry Paul de Vries. But she remains true to her outlook by virtually raping Sebastian the very night she tentatively accepts Paul's proposal. It is unfortunate, Mrs. Thwale reflects, that fans, the 'big white masks' they wore in Casanova's time, and the custom of 'talking from behind screens' have all gone out of fashion (VI). They would have been an immense aid to her theory, since, as she notes, you could do the oddest things behind a screen even while talking to the vicar. Yet by seducing Sebastian she unwittingly frees him from her influence. He at first sees her as the incarnation of Mary Esdaile (XI), his imaginary mistress, but soon concludes, unlike Rivers, that love-making is equivalent to the 'madness' of 'twin cannibals, devouring their own identity and one another's' (XXIV).

In addition to Mrs. Thwale, Daisy Ockham, Paul De Vries, and even the Dickensian Queen Mother take turns trying to influence Sebastian. Daisy, Eustace's only daughter and heir, sees in Sebastian a reminder of her dead son and resolves to mother him. As a dedicated maternalist, she is the fitting representative of her own religious belief in a personal, parental deity whom people approach to seek assurance and comfort for their egos (XXII). The Queen Mother's religious preferences run more to mediums and sham spirituality. For her, heaven's bourne is attainable through seance. A repulsively amusing eccentric, she summons a medium immediately after her son, Eustace, dies. 'I always like to have my first séance as soon after the funeral as possible. . . . Nothing like striking the iron while it's hot,' she explains (XVII).

Paul de Vries is as interested in building bridges between ideas as the Queen Mother is in connecting this world with the next. Yet he is as ridiculous and eccentric as she. 'Every one', de Vries says, 'ought to know something about Einstein' (VIII). But Paul's concern with bridge-building is as ineffectual as Sebastian's concern with the co-ordinating power of poetry (XIV). The theories for bridging gaps that are held by Paul, Mrs. Ockham, and the Queen Mother are as useless as the more self-centred practices of Eustace and Mrs. Thwale. Paul hopes to be a 'humble bridge-builder', to set up 'an international clearing house of ideas' in the hope of formulating some 'scientific-religious-philosophic-synthesis for the entire planet'. As de Vries continues to talk, he sounds more and more like a satiric portrait of the Huxley who wrote *Point Counter Point* in the hope of finding a musical composition in prose into which all the variations of characters, opinions, and events could fit harmoniously. He also reminds the reader of the Calamy in *Those Barren Leaves* who scrutinized the parallel worlds in which his hand existed simultaneously (Part 5, 1). At present, de Vries observes, the best one can do is 'just to skip from one world to the other – hoping, meanwhile, that someday one might get a hunch, an illuminating intuition of the greater synthesis . . . a thought-bridge that would permit the mind to march . . . from telepathy to the four-dimensional continuum, from poltergeists . . . to the physiology of the nervous system'.[14] Unfortunately, de Vries is more of a split-man than a bridge-builder. He quixotically recommends celibacy even though he is 'caught between his ideals and his desires'. Any influence he might exert on Sebastian is prematurely terminated by Eustace's death and by his proposal to Mrs. Thwale.

Most of the theories Sebastian is exposed to have a religious foundation. Eustace advocates the doctrine of harmlessness (a doctrine Jeremy Pordage embraces in *After Many a Summer Dies the Swan* (Part 2, 1) and that Propter seems to agree is the highest ideal the non-mystic can aspire to), while Mrs. Thwale is for defiance of conventional social and moral procedure. Daisy is for loving a personal God and the Queen Mother for a perverted spiritualism. All of these different views offer illegitimate paths out of the self, either through a plunge into pleasure in Eustace's case, or through a violent reversal of one's normal behaviour patterns in Mrs. Thwale's. To Sebastian,

Eustace is a substitute father, Daisy a second mother, and Mrs. Thwale a mistress or substitute wife; but only Bruno Rontini is capable of being Sebastian's guide and of teaching him a mode of life that is less limited than the other theories in the novel and that Huxley believes is as suited to the next life as it is to the present.

In *Point Counter Point*, Mark Rampion's views emerged as the standard for the full life, but here it is Rontini's outlook that survives the counterpoint of conflicting theories and appears superior even to the synthesis of ideas de Vries recommends and that the early Huxley might have gravitated towards. Significantly, Bruno at one point appears as Sebastian's guide to Florence. 'I shall be very happy to help you find your way about' (XXIV), he says as he assumes the role of Virgil. But Bruno has no tolerance for the sort of egoist's paradise wherein Dante could still rail about contemporary politics (XXVI). Instead, he offers the way towards 'achieved knowledge of the Divine Ground' (XXX), a path familiar to those who have perused Beavis' diary or listened to Mr. Propter. Bruno Rontini is thus not only Sebastian's Vergil, but, as the resemblance of his name to that of Dante's Brunetto Latini indicates, his teacher as well. The vision Eustace Barnack refuses to be absorbed into is clearly drawn from the closing cantos of the *Paradiso* and it is this vision for which Bruno will prepare Sebastian.

Those who consider Beavis' solution a highly personal one can easily find the same fault with this novel's 'Epilogue' of approximately thirty pages. In this longest of the book's chapters, Sebastian, now thirty-two, puts his version of Rontini's thoughts on paper. Undeniably, Rontini's viewpoint, like that of Beavis and Propter before him, is personal, of limited application. Where the other theories in the novel are limited by applying only to this life (and indeed to only certain aspects of this life), Rontini's is restricted to only a few fortunate individuals. As Rontini observes, only one out of every ten thousand herrings manages to break out of his carapace completely and few of the ones who do become full-sized fish (x). The odds against a man's bringing 'the process of spiritual maturation' to a successful conclusion, Rontini continues, are even greater. Most remain spiritual children all their lives, such as Uncle Eustace, whose mistress threatens him with a hairbrush (IX). No way of life which only one out of ten thousand will fully realize can appeal as an objective standard. *Time Must Have a Stop* is thus a *bildungsroman* in which its hero comes of age by a path that seems closed to the majority of its readers.

One should realize, however, that much of what Rontini says (and the same was true of Mr. Propter's discourses) can be adopted by those who are unprepared to follow all of his directions. As in the case of books depicting lives of the saints, the reader is not obligated to match the excellence of the model being offered. By comparison with Rontini, Sebastian has not achieved a very high plateau of awareness himself. Most important, however, is the fact that *Time Must Have a Stop*, despite occasional bad writing,[15] succeeds as fiction whether or not one accepts its philosophy. A major reason for this success is the presentation of contrapuntal theories, of which only Rontini's preserves some power to please. Something of the method in *Point Counter Point* and *Eyeless in Gaza* is revived in this novel as Huxley discredits viewpoints he dislikes and makes Rontini's the acceptable alternative, at least within the confines of the novel.

As in *The Genius and the Goddess*, Huxley skips over any direct presentation of Sebastian's maturation process. One never sees the stages by which he becomes Rontini's disciple and then his successor. Nor is any attempt made to dramatize any of Rontini's supposed contacts with God. Between two chapters (XXIX and XXX), there is a jump of fifteen years. World War II has come and gone, Rontini is dead. Perhaps the jump is an unabashed attempt to get past events that are hard to bring alive dramatically. Sebastian does provide an account of his meeting with Rontini after the war and of the latter's death some five years prior to the time of the 'Epilogue'. But even this must be done in terms of a first-person account in a notebook similar to Beavis'. Mystical experience is only valid as first-person testimony. Otherwise it is, as the numerous books about it illustrate, scholarship rather than first-hand information. All mystics have agreed that their encounters with God are indescribable in words. The contention that the God they attain union with is beyond the conventional notion of a deity to whom attributes can be ascribed makes the personification approach of Milton or the symbolic method of Dante equally undesirable.[16]

Nevertheless, the sharp contrast between the boy Sebastian of seventeen and the man of thirty-two, who has lost an arm in the war and is a widower, works powerfully. Some sense of the way Huxley insists time will stop abruptly at the end of every life and make all but one's spiritual status inconsequential is adequately conveyed by the missing decade and a half. The Sebastian who reappears as a man has stopped time in the mystic's sense. He is in search of 'the reality of one's own Atman', which he defines as 'the spiritual principle in us' (xxx) and which can lead to a foretaste of eternity. The switch from the counterpoint method of *Point Counter Point* to the diary or notebook device Beavis used in *Eyeless in Gaza* indicates that although the mystic attains union with an impersonal deity Huxley feels even the most inadequate account of that union demands the first person. Similarly, the movement from the psychomachia structure of *Henry IV, Part I* to situations that recall Dante is another indication of Huxley's contention that self-discovery, the goal of every *bildungsroman*, must be followed by self-transcendence. Just as Anthony Beavis might have written *Ends and Means*, Sebastian could easily have authored *The Perennial Philosophy* (1945). In fact, that appears to be the book he is at work on in the 'Epilogue'.

What is most noticeable about the mature Sebastian's position is the extent to which it is an amalgamation of what he learned from all the viewpoints he was exposed to throughout the first twenty-nine chapters. Rontini's thought is of course the largest contributor, but Sebastian, retaining some resemblance to the Huxley of *Point Counter Point*, has considered all the points of view in the novel and tried to resolve them. For Sebastian, this is both a maturer form of his early ability to project himself into those around him as well as a violation of Keats' preference for entertaining doubts and remaining in uncertainties. As he reads over his notes, Sebastian is seen advocating the avoidance of sensuality and pure aestheticism, the life-modes respectively of Mrs. Thwale and Uncle Eustace. He has also developed a formula for universal peace – a factor in the limited but still definite rapport he finally achieves with his aging, disillusioned father, whose political activities have had little success.

One of the 'indispensable conditions' for peace, Sebastian decides, is 'a shared theology'. He has put together a 'Minimum Working Hypothesis' he believes all countries and religions can subscribe to. It is, of course, a condensation of Vedanta's version of the perennial philosophy. Surely Huxley means this as a more practical version, for this world and the next, of the grand synthesis or common denominator de Vries lengthily described. It is Sebastian, not de Vries, who discovers the synthesis, who argues that the Divine Ground is also, potentially, a common ground. The viewpoints of Eustace and Veronica have been rejected but those of de Vries, Rontini, and

Sebastian's father have contributed to, and perhaps been super-seded by, Sebastian's own. Sebastian's 'Hypothesis' is to make possible for others what Rontini personified at his death: the bridging of the gap between the temporal and the permanent. On his deathbed Rontini was a shell full of eternity (xxx).

III

Unfortunately, Sebastian's 'Hypothesis', whether one sympathizes with it or not, is insufficient to allay Huxley's increasing distrust of the creative process. The Huxley who wrote *Point Counter Point* and responded to the philosophy of Rampion-Lawrence often felt art was an impediment to living the full life (though Lawrence never thought so). By *Time Must Have a Stop*, Huxley has switched some of his allegiances and presented new solutions to some of his old problems. But the standing of art has not improved. The early novels may have satirized art and artists for failing to provide society with new standards, but art is now no substitute for acquired knowledge and its efficacy even as a prelude to that knowledge is now reduced to a minimum. In *The Doors of Perception*, Huxley insisted that 'in the final stage of egolessness', 'an "obscure knowledge" that All is in all – that All is actually each' emerges. If this is so, and if, as Huxley further noted, the 'final stage' is 'as near, I take it, as a finite mind can come to "perceiving everything that is happening everywhere in the universe",'[17] then it is pointless to go on striving for simultaneity of scene and event as Quarles recommended and Huxley the novelist attempted. As Rontini tells Sebastian, 'if one gets better and knows more, one will be tempted to stop writing, because the all-absorbing labour of composition is an obstacle in the way of further knowledge' (xxvi). In the 'Epilogue', one learns that Sebastian has not written a play in five years, that is, not since Rontini's death. The notes he is making on Bruno's thought seem likely to be his final creative effort.

The case of Huxley the novelist is similar, even if it is doubtful he ever personally enjoyed genuine mystical experiences. *Time Must Have a Stop* is virtually his last real novel. *The Genius and the Goddess* can be described as Sebastian's story over again but without the 'Epilogue' and without Rontini, a final and unsatisfactory attempt to eliminate from the story of the mystic hero's development as much of the undramatic material as possible. *Ape and Essence* disguises itself as a film script in order to incorporate a Narrator's commentary and make full descriptions of scene and setting unnecessary.

In *Island*, the long-developing merger of Huxley the novelist and Huxley the essayist is virtually complete.

But although Huxley becomes less and less a novelist from *Eyeless in Gaza* onwards, he takes many of the novelist's techniques with him into his non-fiction. Maine de Biran in *Themes and Variations* (1950), Father Joseph of *Grey Eminence* (1941) and Urban Grandier in *The Devils of Loudun* (1952) – all historical personages – are presented with something of the novelist's feeling for setting and character development. Were it not for the long essay chapters they include, *Grey Eminence* and *The Devils of Loudun* could pass for excellent historical novels. The religious atmosphere of seventeenth-century France that emerges from these books is not readily found in any history of the period. The account of Grandier's torture and death at the stake would have to be included in any selection of Huxley's finest writing. Yet *The Devils of Loudun*, with its mixture of essays and of sequences that would suit a novel, does not seem to have in it the potential for a new form to replace the discussion-novel-of-ideas.

Nevertheless, all three protagonists just mentioned belong at least partially to the list of Huxley's fictional heroes. Perhaps the existence of historical examples of the type of man the Huxley of the 1950s wished to present made the creation of fictional heroes less pressing.

Maine de Biran, Father Joseph, and Urban Grandier form an interesting trio. The first appears to have been debarred from true mysticism by shortcomings of temperament. Father Joseph, by contrast, had all the qualifications but succumbed to the nationalism and power politics of his day. He is one of Huxley's historical villains (he comes third, behind his superior, who is the famous Richelieu, and Hitler). For Father Joseph became a split-man by his own actions. Apparently quite capable of union with the Divine Ground, he squandered half his time promoting French nationalism (i.e. the Thirty Years War) until his ability to meditate himself into the presence of his God dwindled and finally vanished. Grandier, again by contrast, was of the three the most unlikely candidate for mysticism, yet he had some degree of mystical knowledge virtually thrust upon him. In the early novels, characters are startled out of their egotism by the discovery of other people and their viewpoints, but in the later works, even in the non-fiction, the same effect is produced by a sudden awareness of God. The three non-fictional heroes are thus similar but different. They permit Huxley to present three different types or variations of mysticism.

Although most of Huxley's later essays do not lose their appeal when re-read, as some of the later novels do, it is Huxley's fiction that will determine his place in English literature. And it is the use of counterpoint, the interplay of satire and structural technique, that marks *Point Counter Point* and *Eyeless in Gaza* as the peak of Huxley's career. The revival of counterpoint in *Time Must Have a Stop* makes it the most successful of Huxley's later novels. In all three, the art of seeing, considered not only as a technical concern but as a question of moral or spiritual vision, is of primary importance. In the other novels just discussed (*After Many a Summer Dies the Swan* and *The Genius and the Goddess*), as well as in the non-fiction (for example, *The Devils of Loudun*), the question of sight is also an issue, but Huxley is less successful in fusing thematic and technical concerns. It is on the three novels in which counterpoint plays a significant role – along with Huxley's first three satiric novels – that one must place the responsibility of earning Huxley a place not of incontestable prominence but still of considerable distinction in any record of the twentieth-century novel.

CHAPTER VII

Utopian Counterpoint and the Compensatory Dream

Counterpoint, as a technical and structural device within a particular
novel, virtually disappears from Huxley's fiction after *Point Counter
Point* and *Eyeless in Gaza*. But his three utopias – *Brave New World*
(1932), *Ape and Essence* (1949), and *Island* (1962) – can best be
examined as a series of intentional variations on the same themes:
in short, as utopian counterpoint. Just as Huxley's first three novels
form a natural trilogy each member of which deals with the same
concerns in different ways, his three utopias, though scattered over a
thirty-year period, are really part of one life-long endeavour. They
offer three different presentiments of the future.

   Ape and Essence, the novel that stands between the two more
important utopias, is Huxley's version of the sort of twenty-second
century that will result from a neglect of contemporary problems.
Even the novel's arch-villain, the Arch-Vicar, is aware that the society
over which he presides missed its great opportunity to evolve satis-
factorily. Although *Brave New World* is also clearly the product of a
continuation of trends Huxley saw with alarm in the 30s, the novel
deals primarily with a civilization that has faced up to what Huxley
considers the problems of the modern world but it has done so by
answering all the right questions wrongly. By contrast, in *Island*,
the Vedantist's utopia, Huxley offers his own version of the future.
The Palanese have not missed the opportunity the society of *Ape
and Essence* neglected nor have they settled for the erroneous
responses of Mustapha Mond and his fellow World Controllers.

   By outlining two different ways of going forward in *Brave New
World* and *Island*, and warning against one method of going backward
in *Ape and Essence*, Huxley fulfils Quarles' prescription for the good
novelist: 'A novelist modulates by reduplicating situations and
characters' (XXII). *Brave New World* was conceived as a single work,
but Huxley, as he added a second and then a third glance into the
future, may have begun to see all three novels as part of one larger
volume or concern. He created the second two as different aspects of
the first. In *Ape and Essence*, he remedied an oversight he himself
detected in *Brave New World*; and in *Island*, having found his own

175

answers to the problems posed by the future, he rewrote *Brave New World* almost point by point. As in *Point Counter Point*, Huxley's goal, like that of Quarles, is 'Multiplicity of eyes and multiplicity of aspects seen' (XIV). He views the future first scientifically, in *Brave New World*, then as a historian in *Ape and Essence*, and finally as a combination of social planner and Vedantic philosopher in *Island*. By writing both positive and negative utopias, he attempts to dramatize in concrete form the advantages of what his essays recommend and the consequences of any continuation of the tendencies they satirize.

I

That Huxley should have written even one utopia is, from one point of view, very surprising. His early novels often seemed concerned mainly with exploding outworn ideas and revealing the mutual contradictoriness of modern alternatives. Readers of *Brave New World* invariably point to Mr. Scogan's comments in *Crome Yellow* as an indication of Huxley's perennial concern with the future. Indeed, Scogan, a gritty rationalist, could sue the author of *Brave New World*, for it contains little that he did not foresee. Scogan may, in fact, be a caricature of H. G. Wells, and it is thus intentionally ironic that his view of the future contrasts with his prehistoric appearance as a bird-lizard with an incisive beaked nose, dry and scaly skin, and the hands of a crocodile (III). Scogan predicts that, in the future, population will be obtained and controlled through bottle-breeding and the use of incubators. The family system, he continues, 'will disappear' (V) and Eros will be pursued without fear of consequences. At times he waxes lyrical over the prospect of 'the Rational State' wherein each child, properly classified by mind and temperament, will be duly 'labelled and docketed' for the education that will best enable him and his species 'to perform those functions which human beings of his variety are capable of performing' (XXII). Even the one prediction Scogan is less specific about is relevant. He complains that 'For us', virtual prisoners of society and its impositions, 'a complete holiday is out of the question' (XXV). He may not envision soma itself, but he is aware of his Rational State's need for it.

However, despite what Scogan says in his capacity as a twentieth-century extension of the nineteenth-century progress-oriented reformer, Huxley's early prose is full of utopian disclaimers in which he greets the idea of writing a utopia with contempt. In one of his earliest remarks about utopian writers, Huxley condemns them, as he condemns most of his own characters, for escapism and eccentricity, for an egoistic inability to accept reality as they find it: 'Outward reality disgusts them; the compensatory dream is the universe in which they live. The subject of their meditations is not man, but a monster of rationality and virtue – of one kind of rationality and virtue at that, their own.'[1] *Brave New World* is a 'monster of rationality' in which the rational is raised to an irrational power until, for example, the goal of sanitation reform in the nineteenth century, namely cleanliness, replaces godliness. Unfortunately, Huxley's comment about monsters of rationality also applies, eventually, to his own *Island*.

What Huxley's anti-utopian remarks in the late 1920s boil down to, then, is a hatred of the utopian speculations he was reading, or had read by 1930. Most of these, taking their cue from H. G. Wells, and ultimately from Bacon's *New Atlantis* (1627), were scientific. Those who foresee a utopian future, Huxley wrote, 'invoke not the god from the machine, but the machine itself'.[2] Huxley's spoofing of the Wellsian notion that people in utopia should take turns doing high-brow and low-brow tasks: 'While Jones plays the piano, Smith spreads the manure'[3] was just a preliminary for the full-fledged satire of *Brave New World*.

Thus although in one sense Huxley's novels and non-fiction prose prior to 1932 seemed to indicate that he would never stoop to utopian themes, in another they made *Brave New World* inevitable. One of the chief reasons why Huxley wrote the novel, it is tempting to conclude, was to discredit, if not discourage, the sort of utopian writing he was familiar with. The urge to write a literary satire on existing works went hand in hand with the desire to challenge, by means of a correcting, less optimistic vision of his own, the picture of the future that science was enthusiastically offering. In his prose essays, Huxley was thus composing *Brave New World* for years before starting the novel itself. In essays from *Music at Night*, such as 'Liberty and the Promised Land', 'History and the Past', 'Wanted a New Pleasure', and throughout *Proper Studies*, Huxley was indulging in distopian prose, from which the anti-utopian or distopian novel and eventually the positive utopia spring almost inevitably. The difference between the satirist and the writer of utopias is somewhat minimal to begin with, since the second, like the first, intends to expose the difference between what he beholds and what he would prefer to see. Once the anti-utopian novel is written, its counterpart already exists by implication. As Huxley became increasingly convinced that he had found the true path, he employed the medium of a positive utopia to explore a future of his own conceiving. Eventually, Huxley, too, disclosed his compensatory dream.

Even the anti-utopian non-fiction prose just mentioned, however, is hardly free of moments when Huxley is possibly not ridiculing scientific utopias, when he seems, instead, intrigued by their possibility – an attitude which often makes the reader suspect that *Brave New World* is not the total satire some critics claim. The question of 'eugenic reform' always has a fascination for Huxley. He entertains it in *Music at Night* as a means of raising the critical point beyond which increases in prosperity, leisure, and education now give diminishing returns. He even speaks, with apparent tolerance, of a new caste system based on differences in native ability and of an educational process that supplies an individual with just so much instruction as his position calls for.[4] He worries, in *Proper Studies*, about the threat to the world's IQ that the more rapidly reproducing inferior classes constitute. And when, in an essay catalogued above as distopian prose, he predicts that society 'will learn to breed babies in bottles', or talks, albeit somewhat critically, of theatres wherein 'egalitarians' will enjoy talkies, tasties, smellies, and feelies,[5] he almost seems to become Scogan.

Huxley is even more eloquent than Scogan on the possibilities of a holiday-inducing drug when he writes that: 'If we could sniff or swallow something that would, for five or six hours each day, abolish our solitude as individuals . . . earth would become paradise.'[6] What Scogan wanted was an escape hatch, but what Huxley wants is a means of breaking down the individual's isolation within his own ego. The difference between the two positions, however, is not so clear as to make pointing it out unnecessary. The drug called soma in *Brave New World* is not inherently unsatisfactory, but rather is an inadequate surrogate for something Huxley would accept in a more proper form.

And yet *Brave New World* is not utopia but distopia, even if the problems its society has confronted are the same ones the Palanese of *Island* must face. The difference between *Island* and *Brave New World* is that the Palanese have correctly solved the problems Mustapha Mond and his fellow World Controllers have mismanaged.

This will become clearer subsequently in a discussion of the ways in which *Island* is Huxley's corrective for *Brave New World*. What has escaped notice and what is possibly the surest way of discrediting the society of *Brave New World* is the fact that, judged on its own terms, it is manifestly a failure. All the old problems exist in new forms and the new society's use of language is one long and recurrent illustration of how life has not gained in meaning but become instead absolutely meaningless.

To begin with, despite the complicated mechanical processes at work in *Brave New World,* the manner in which each individual is artificially born on a sort of Fordian assembly line and trained for one job only, human errors persist. These are not only still made, but take infinitely longer to be discovered. Lenina, musing about the Savage, who has only recently arrived from a reservation outside the brave new world, forgets to give a bottle-baby its sleeping sickness injection and twenty-two years later an Alpha-Plus administrator becomes the first trypanosomiasis fatality in over half a century (XIII). Though it requires nearly a quarter of a century to happen, people still die from birth defects. Similarly, Bernard Marx's eccentric love of solitude and his fondness for walks in the Lake District are attributed to an overdose of 'Alcohol in his blood-surrogate' (VI). One might add that all babies born in *Brave New World* have what Huxley would consider birth defects: each is conditioned to do the same task over and over again and is thus as one-pointed or one-sided from birth as any typical eccentric in the four Huxley novels that precede *Brave New World*.

The problem of mental-physical imbalance has not been completely solved either. It exists in *Brave New World* just as it did for the imbalanced heroes of Huxley's previous novels. The ideal of proportion, a state of body-mind equilibrium recommended throughout *Antic Hay*, is still unattained: 'A mental excess had produced in Helmholtz Watson effects very similar to those which, in Bernard Marx, were the result of a physical defect' (IV). Both men, the anti-hero, Bernard, and the slogan-writer, Helmholtz, are misfits in a society that claims to have found the proper place for everyone. When the Savage arrives, the number of misfits increases to three. Even Lenina, who in so many ways is the product of her upbringing and who proves as disillusioning an experience for Bernard and the Savage as Barbara was for Chelifer in *Those Barren Leaves*, is not perfectly conditioned. She asks Bernard at one point if he still desires to spend a week with her. He blushes and she is 'astonished' by such a response, 'but at the same time touched by this strange tribute to her power' (IV). Cracks in everyone's conditioning are woefully apparent. The Epsilon-Minus Semi-Moron who operates a lift is startled 'from a dark annihilating stupor' by the 'warm glory of afternoon sunlight' as his elevator reaches the roof of the Central London Hatchery (IV).

Despite the complete mechanization of the birth process and the acceleration achieved by the Bokanovsky Process coupled with Podsnap's technique, it still takes 267 days, or three days less than nine months, to produce a child (I). The Bombay Green Rocket may do 'Twelve hundred and fifty kilometres an hour', as the Station Master boasts it can, but it is no substitute for the human imagination. 'Ariel', the Savage points out, 'could put a girdle round the earth in forty minutes' (XI). Even the womb complex survives in a new and curious form. In the Westminster Abbey Cabaret, the Sexophonists sing: 'Bottle of mine, it's you I've always wanted!/ Bottle of mine, why was I ever decanted?' (V).

The society of *Brave New World* still resorts to escapism, just as the typical Huxley character always inhabits a self-enclosed private world of his own. By means of soma, one can now take a holiday from reality almost at will. Even within a society supposed to be the realization of the compensatory dream, a means for additional compensation must be maintained. Nor have the inadequacies of organized religion been eliminated. Instead, the tops are sawed off all crosses to make T's, and the masses make 'the sign of the T' on their stomachs, presumably in deference to Ford's model-T car and the scientific know-how that feeds them (II). The new is consistently similar, even inferior, to the old. Thus although old taboos have been destroyed, the same youths who say 'ovary' and 'sperm' without hesitation snigger at new artificial obscenities such as 'parent' or 'mother' (II). The twentieth-century may have foolishly banned *The Rainbow* and *Ulysses*, but Mond's world has its own peculiar 'pornography', namely *The Imitation of Christ* and *The Varieties of Religious Experience* (XVII).

The result in *Brave New World* of society's admiration for scientific advances and of its worship of progress – two attitudes Huxley cannot share – is a condition in which neither is any longer allowable. But the consequences of progress have produced something very similar to the sort of society that existed in the mid-nineteenth century. The best society, contends Mustapha Mond, is like the iceberg: eight-ninths below the water line and one-ninth above (xvi). What the people of *Brave New World* have accomplished by the most exacting scientific controls, the Victorians achieved through *laissez-faire*. Admittedly, the eight-ninths now below the water line are neither desperately poor nor thoroughly diseased, yet they can hardly be called conscious of their comfort. The class system has been replaced by something worse, namely a caste system with Alphas on top and moronic Epsilons at the bottom.

Formerly, Mustapha Mond claims, 'exclusiveness, a narrow channelling of impulse and energy' was everywhere the rule, but now 'every one belongs to every one else' (iii). Unfortunately, Mond's statement, though cast in general and universal terms, has an exclusive, narrow meaning. It means that promiscuity is now possible for everyone. In terms of jobs, education, and emotional life, the 'narrow channelling' practised by *Brave New World* is unprecedented. Diversity has been completely eliminated and the individual, previously an unpredictable quantity, now remains 'constant throughout a whole lifetime' (iii). The one-pointedness for which Huxley always satirizes his egocentric characters is now built into them from birth.

Worst of all, language has virtually lost its meaning and few speakers in this model world of scientifically engineered precision realize how unscientific and imprecise their words really are. Many of the characters have Marxist names (Lenina, Bernard Marx, Polly Trotsky) and Benito Hoover's name is an oxymoronic combination of capitalism and Fascism, but none of them have any notion of Russian history or of what genuine Communism is. Helmholtz Watson's name, a curious amalgam of Hermann Ludwig von Helmholtz (1821–1894), the German scientist, and Sir William Watson (1858–1935), an English poet, seems to imply that science and art are now united, but innocuously so, in the job of furnishing slogans for the state. In fact, the famous names of these characters form a pointed contrast to a World State that is simply one of Henry Ford's Detroit plants magnified many times. Polish, French, and German are now classified among the dead languages (ii), and that is also where the Savage's pure Shakespearian English belongs (vii), especially the allusion he (seriously) and the novel's title (ironically) make to Miranda's speech in *The Tempest* (v, i, 181–184).

What happens to the meaning of *normality* when Mr. Foster

explains he wants to give the Epsilon embryo 'the normality of dogs and cows' (I)? Does Foster realize what he is saying when he remarks that on the morning of the 267th day, in the Decanting Room, the bottle baby achieves 'Independent existence – so called' (I)? The once powerful theological term 'predestination' now means little more than suiting people to an 'unescapable social destiny' (I). When Lenina describes her Malthusian belt, itself a preventive or substitution device, as 'real morocco-surrogate' (III), one realizes how confused the relation between things and words has become. Can individuals who have not blood but 'blood surrogate' in their veins be termed human at all? The fact that women must take a 'Pregnancy Substitute' (III) to satisfy maternal urges underlines the extent to which *Brave New World*, in words and objects, is a world of facsimiles behind which certain genuine human feelings faintly persist.

From chapter to chapter the destruction of the meaning of words proceeds apace. Foster explains that childhood has been abolished because the years between an Epsilon's birth and the time he is fit for work constitute a 'superfluous and wasted immaturity' (I). Yet the Epsilon's so-called maturity is scarcely that of a five-year-old. Surely this is no great improvement on the treatment of children in nineteenth- century England. It would be too painful to point out the real meaning of each word in 'Community, Identity, Stability', the motto of *Brave New World*. And the same holds true for *group* in the scientific term 'Bokanovsky Group'. How meaningless the Savage's condemnation of the promiscuous Lenina – 'Whore!' he shouted. 'Whore! Impudent strumpet!' (XIII) – has become in a society where chastity is non-existent as a word or a concept.

In short, there is an overwhelming discrepancy between the reality of *Brave New World* and the picture it has formed of itself by means of its language. So much of the language used in *Brave New World* is not really stable, but is, like society and the formerly diverse individual, artificial, stagnant, virtually dead. Like the egoist-poet Denis in *Crome Yellow*, the society of *Brave New World* chooses words over things and makes an object an illustration of the word whether it is so or not.

In his 'Forward' (1947) to a re-printing of *Brave New World*, Huxley calls science 'Procrustes in modern dress' and laments the fact that mankind will be made to fit the bed science provides for it. Linguistically, this process is already far advanced. If the brave new world cannot insert a square peg into a round hole it will redefine roundness until a perfect fit results. Huxley is fully aware of the dangers inherent in any misuse of language, of the manifold ways in which a loss or perversion of the meaning of words furthers the designs of any centralized power, whether it is as inhumanly benevolent as Mustapha Mond or as blatantly militaristic as Col. Dipa of Rendang in *Island*. In *Words and Their Meanings* (1940), 'Words and Behaviour' in *The Olive Tree* (1937), and in *Brave New World Revisited* (1958), Huxley insists on the precise use of language as a safeguard against societies such as that of *Brave New World*. It comes as no surprise that the Palanese children of *Island* are given 'systematic and carefully graduated training in perception and the proper use of language' (XIII).

It is this awareness of the relation between the perversion of language and the rise of a centralized authority that possibly constitutes Huxley's main contribution to distopian literature. In George Orwell's *1984* (1949), O'Brien and his group, the Party, have at their disposal a whole new language (Newspeak). Eventually it will guarantee their stay in power. The eleventh edition of the Newspeak Dictionary will make thought contrary to the Party's purposes an impossibility.[7] Even so marginal a utopian work as Anthony Burgess' *The Clockwork Orange* (1963) seems implicitly to realize that to control a person's life and thought one need only manipulate his language. (The crudeness, the monosyllabic quality of much of the language used by Burgess' characters, may be the key to their bestial conduct.) Thus Mustapha Mond confiscates the work of an author who, like Huxley, both debunks the ideal of happiness as a sovereign good and talks, like Mr. Propter, of a 'goal . . . outside the present human sphere,' of an 'enlargement of knowledge' (XII). Thus Helmholtz Watson lacks the words and experiences for the serious literature he desires to write (XII).

Art, science, truth, and beauty may indeed be irreconcilable with comfort and happiness, as Mustapha Mond maintains (XVI), but one suspects this is because comfort and happiness have been assigned rather original meanings. Only in *Brave New World* could Mond argue that the religious sentiment is unnecessary because the population is death-conditioned and the concept of death has lost its meaning. The moral sense has been replaced by continued prosperity and sanctioned self-indulgence. Mond consciously typifies his society's linguistic practices when he explains to the Savage that God now 'manifests himself as an absence' (XVII).

II

Brave New World has much in common with the whole range of utopian literature, some of which Huxley appears to have had at his fingertips as he wrote. One is tempted to point out that utopian literature, like mysticism, is virtually a tradition in which an author can immerse himself and find innumerable guidelines, such as Samuel Butler's *Erewhon*, which Huxley edited in 1934. A good deal of the success of *Brave New World* and of the weakness of *Island* becomes clearer in light of the utopian tradition.

One of the ways in which Huxley's first utopia resembles its predecessors is in its use of a device that can be called the familiar-unfamiliar. The novel opens *in medias res* and showers the reader with a series of unexplained details. So much of the appeal of any utopian work depends on its initial sense of mystery and the reader's correspondent demand for an explanation. It is essential to learn what exactly Alphas, Betas, Deltas, and Epsilons are. Central London sounds familiar enough, but the Central London Hatchery and Conditioning Centre (I) is at first an unknown quantity, an even more intriguing enigma than 'the famous British Museum massacre' (III). Huxley suddenly introduces the reader into a new world, and it is not until the momentum with which puzzling details are presented slows down that one becomes an informed visitor and is ready for an explanation of how the society one lives in has become the society one is reading about.

Frequently the new and puzzling items have a partially familiar aspect: Big Henry (V) or *The Fordian Science Monitor* (XVIII). Interest is thus generated by the presentation of things already known but seen now in new combinations or an unfamiliar light. In William Morris' *News From Nowhere* (1897), for example, the Houses of Parliament are still recognizable to Mr. Guest but their use as a storage place for manure is startling (V). The picture of post-World-War-III California, with its ghost town of Los Angeles, thrusts the reader of *Ape and Essence* into a world he feels he partially knows but is totally unaccustomed to seeing in this fashion.

Like most previous utopias, *Brave New World* does its share of prophesying. It makes predictions about the future, and, as a lengthy analysis of *Brave New World Revisited* would show, is often close to the mark.[8] Its second sight in describing the future importance of drugs (a factor in the novel's continued popularity) is paralleled by the nonchalance with which it permits its characters to use a machine that has now become the familiar helicopter.[9] The personages in Edward Bellamy's *Looking Backward* (1888) employ something very similar to the modern credit card (IX). And Bellamy's phrase 'from the cradle to the grave' (IX), as a summary of the extent to which his utopian government supervises its people's needs, clearly anticipates the Welfare State. As Professor Burris notes in XX of B. F. Skinner's *Walden Two* (1948), Samuel Butler in *Erewhon* (1872) 'accurately . . . predicted the modern change in attitude toward criminal and moral lapses'. In *We* (1924), a distopia by the Russian, Eugene Zamiatin, that influenced Wells, Orwell, and Huxley, everyone has a number for a name and interplanetary rockets as well as much of modern Russia's political machinery are plausibly described.

Thus utopias are not only about the future but written for the future as well, either to represent a perennial and unattainable ideal or as a description of a state of affairs that is, for better or worse, to be realized gradually in succeeding years. When first read, they are both familiar and unfamiliar. With respect to some of their aspects one is in a totally new world, but other items are both old and new. However, it is the familiar that should increase – whether in the positive, practical utopia of Bellamy or the nightmarish distopia of Orwell – as the gap between the foreseen utopia and the actual world narrows. There are literally hundreds of utopias that are no longer readable, except as literary history, because little of what they envisioned ever came to pass. Part of the persuasiveness of any good positive, utopia and much of the horror in any distopia stem from the reader's conviction that he already lives in the initial stages of the society the utopian author describes and that he may live to witness the complete identification of fiction and reality. The truly great utopias maintain this power to convince long after they are written, even if the predictions they make are not yet accomplished and may never be. Francis Bacon's vision of a world dominated by science has come true in numerous respects, though neither Huxley nor Orwell are pleased. Thomas More's *Utopia* is scarcely closer to realization today than it was in 1516, but the Europe he found fault with has not totally changed and certain facets of his ideal state still retain the power to excite the imagination.

Both More and Plato, the latter in his *Republic* (380–370 B.C.), seem to have been interested in exhibiting what they themselves saw as a probably permanent gap between the ideal society and those in which men would always live. More modern utopias, following Bacon rather than More, appear to be written in the belief they represent, for better or worse, the world of the author's grandchildren. This is certainly true of Bellamy, Wells, Huxley, and Orwell, though not perhaps of Butler. The difference between some sections of Bellamy or Orwell and a factual article by John R. Pierce about events almost imminent is often minimal.[10]

Plato and More were classical even as they wrote. They were describing what they saw as a perennially ideal but unattainable state rather than offering a blueprint for the immediate or even distant future. More's *Utopia* and Bacon's *New Atlantis* were seen already existing in some unfrequented corner of the globe that was virtually synonymous with their creators' imaginations or with some vanished golden age. In Bacon, the ideal seems to be a combination of the unfallen past and a progressive future. Since Bacon, however, utopias seem to have become more and more practical until the golden age or its opposite is in the immediate future. In Orwell, the gap between composition and realization has narrowed from the century and a half of *Ape and Essence* to a mere thirty-five years, although what readers will make of *1984* in the years 1985 and following remains to be seen.

Unlike *Island* – in fact, unlike most of utopian literature in English with the exception of *1984* – *Brave New World*, and *Ape and Essence* to a lesser degree, do not have the almost inevitable breaking point where most of the novelty vanishes to be replaced by a tedious essay. Once Guest learns where he is and what century it is, the rest of Morris' book belongs to garrulous Old Hammond. In *Island*, after the initial strangeness of Pala wears off, the book becomes a series of essays spoken in the direction of Will Farnaby by a number of characters who know Huxley's views. Orwell does have to permit his hero, Winston, to read Goldstein's book so the reader will understand how the Party rose to power, but the book device is quite dissimilar from the rest of *1984*, whereas Will's conversations with the MacPhails and his perusal of *Notes on What's What* are almost identical. Although it is preoccupied with the perennial utopian concerns (centralization versus decentralization, reform of the family, experiments in breeding and in education), *Brave New World* escapes many of the traditional weaknesses of utopian writings. So too with *Ape and Essence*, even if it cannot match the former for its extravagant sense of humour and occasionally hyperbolic style. Both works contain a sufficiently interesting plot to keep them in motion after the novelty of their respective milieus begins to fade.

What *Brave New World* actually involves is a doubling of the device by which initial strangeness is usually secured. Throughout the opening chapters, it is the reader who plays the part of Morris' Mr. Guest or Bellamy's Mr. West. It is the reader who, like Swift's Gulliver, has landed in a strange world. After ten chapters, the device is used all over again as the Savage from a New Mexican reservation lands in London. The reader must then compare his own reactions to the new world with John's. In addition, the introduction of a second visitor or stranger, the reader being the first, provides Huxley with the opportunity of using the Wellsian scientific future, represented by London, and the Lawrencian primitive past, as personified by the Savage, to discredit each other. This reaches its climax in the confrontation scene between John and Mustapha Mond in which both speakers' viewpoints are exposed as incomplete and the speakers themselves become parallel lines (XVII), like Denis and Mary in *Crome Yellow* (XXIV). The world Mond argues for is in need of the beauty poetry can provide, while John's world overlooks the advantages science offers.

The extent to which *Brave New World* satirizes previous utopias, particularly the Wellsian utopia, demands an essay in itself. There is a sense in which Wells exhibits the nineteenth century in what he considers its ultimate and ideal form while Huxley presents the same century and its goals (controlled evolution, happiness) carried to an alarmingly successful and essentially insane conclusion. Wells' Samurai from *A Modern Utopia* (1905) become Huxley's World Controllers. Wells' prediction of the increased role of the machine, his concern with controlled breeding, his classification of inhabitants by temperament and mental ability – all of these are satirized in Huxley's distopia. In fact, Wells' *The First Men in the Moon* (1901) may be the chief target and inspiration behind *Brave New World*. The Selenite community of ant-like creatures Bedford and Cavor stumble on and that Cavor describes at length (XXIII-XXIV) is virtually identical with the London Huxley creates in *Brave New World*, except that Cavor is ambiguously pro and con in his reactions to the Selenites in a way that Huxley, in satirizing Wells, chooses to ignore.

Largely because it is a distopia aimed at discrediting the utopian musings of Wells and Lawrence, *Brave New World* escapes the 'pervading smugness of tone' that Northrop Frye correctly finds in most self-satisfied utopian planners,[11] and that he would no doubt detect in *Island*. If one reads a speech of Morris' Old Hammond (or of Bellamy's Dr. Leete) along with one from Huxley's Dr. MacPhail, all three spokesmen turn out to be certain they live in the best of possible worlds, but all three cannot be correct. Most positive utopias fail to prove, though most assume, that a changed social environment means better people. One generally feels, however, that the writer is incredibly naive, that it was human nature that miraculously changed first and society afterwards. Neither Morris, Bellamy, nor the Huxley of *Island* can convince one differently.

Despite supposedly humanistic aims, the utopian author often appears to have insurmountable prejudices. His utopia permits him to assume the privileges of a god and recreate the world in his own image. Morris' prejudices are writ large in *News From Nowhere*, in which the perfect society is his own medieval dream come true and everyone is transformed into a practising craftsman. By turning his own workshop into the pattern for an entire world, Morris personifies the egotism and wish-fulfilment inherent in most positive utopian conceptions, Huxley's *Island* of mystics included.

The gravest weakness of almost all utopias, however, is their unattractiveness as possible places to live. Few are open-ended enough to allow for additional change. Bellamy's seems so perfect yet so dull. Morris' is terribly provincial and incurious. Wells' *A Modern Utopia* (1905) insists there is 'no limit to the invasion of life by the machine', but his ideal society, like Plato's, has an oppressive air of assured stability. It is this stagnant quality that Mustapha Mond's society represents at its worst and that O'Brien's Party in *1984*, by different means, is trying to achieve. Of all the positive utopias written over the past century, *Island* is one of the few in which life preserves some variety and excitement. How to be stable without becoming stagnant is a problem no positive utopia has ever perfectly solved. Much of the excitement in *Island* may in fact be due simply to Pala's tenuous existence as an ideal spot in an otherwise non-utopian world.

What this brief and by no means inclusive section on Huxley in relation to other utopians has tried to suggest is that Huxley was aware of his place in a long line of utopian writers. He borrowed from, openly imitated, and at times severely satirized his predecessors. Also, his distopias, because they are by nature negative and because they are seriously concerned with plot, avoid the failings common to most positive utopias, including Huxley's own *Island*. The distopia appears to be the generically superior literary form. That Huxley eventually attempted the positive form of utopian composition, a form in which the weaknesses catalogued above are virtually inherent, is a tribute more to the strength of his convictions than to his literary sagacity. Nevertheless, the positive utopia catered to the ever-present essayist in Huxley. It was the logical outcome for a novelist concerned with ideas but who became, from *Eyeless in Gaza* onwards, less interested in dramatizing or personifying them. The world we are creating, Orwell writes in *1984*, 'is the exact opposite of the stupid hedonistic Utopias that the old reformers imagined'. But once this new sort of world is exposed, the allure of the positive utopias of the past, for Huxley if not for Orwell, becomes harder to resist.

III

Though one reviewer called *Ape and Essence* a 'merciless allegory', Huxley saw it as a partial redressing of a cruel oversight in *Brave New World*. In his 1947 'Forward' to *Brave New World*, Huxley complained that the Savage retreats into despair because he is given a choice between two undesirables: an insane modern utopia and an unappetizing reservation life. Huxley has either forgotten, or chooses to disregard, the isolated community to which Helmholtz Watson and Bernard Marx are deported. It is, however, under Mustapha Mond's jurisdiction and the Savage would never have been offered the chance to go there. 'If I were now to rewrite the book,' Huxley said in 1947, 'I would offer the Savage a third alternative. Between the utopian and the primitive horns of his dilemma would lie the possibility of sanity – a possibility already actualized, to some extent, in a community of exiles and refugees from the Brave New World, living within the borders of the Reservation.' This community, with its decentralized economics and sane use of science, would be primarily concerned with 'man's Final End'. Huxley is describing what he will eventually develop into the Pala of *Island*. But he also has in mind, in 1947, the community of 'Hots' Alfred Poole and Loola flee to at the end of *Ape and Essence* (1949), a novel that includes the all-important trap door of justifiable escape.

To understand *Ape and Essence* thoroughly and pinpoint its role in Huxley's utopian trilogy, one must first grasp Huxley's idea of commendable evolution as described by both Mr. Propter in *After Many a Summer Dies the Swan* and Sebastian Barnack in *Time Must Have a Stop*. Pete Boone asks: 'Where ought we to fight for good?' And Propter replies: 'On the level below the human and on the level above. On the animal level and on the level . . . of eternity' (Part I, IX). It is the middle plateau of time, personality, and craving that is irredeemably evil. Sebastian offers an additional explanation. In the 'Epilogue' (XXX), he defines life as a progression 'from animal eternity into time, into the strictly human world of memory and anticipation; and from time, if one chooses to go on, into the world of spiritual eternity, into the Divine Ground.' *Brave New World* and *Island* chronicle the attempts of two different societies to progress from the world of time, memory, and anticipation. Where *Island* seeks 'the world of spiritual eternity', *Brave New World* dwells in the eternal now of a life-style that has abolished the past (memory) and ignores the future (anticipation). History, in the words of Our Ford, is bunk (III). 'Was and will make me ill, I take a gramme and only am,' Lenina recites (VI).

By contrast with his other two utopias, *Ape and Essence* is a story of retrogression and recovery. In it Huxley reconsiders his predictions for the future so as to allow for the possibility of a devastating war and a reversion to 'animal eternity'. Where *Brave New World* and *Island* deal with steps forward, *Ape and Essence* is thus a step backward. Like the Fifth Earl of Hauberk in *After Many a Summer Dies the Swan*, the inhabitants of post-World-War-III America have fallen from the world of time to become more simian than human. As Propter would have realized, if men descend to the animal level, they must regain the human before attempting to climb onto the level of eternity. Dr. Alfred Poole and the simple-minded Loola become the potential Adam and Eve of a new race once they escape from the ape-like society of twenty-second-century California to go in search of a more complete way of life. Because they fall truly in love, Alfred and Loola can live on the 'animal level' in a different and more promising way than those they flee from. What they discover on this 'animal' or physical level awakens Poole to the higher possibilities. It is on the animal level that he begins to fight for good.

Ape and Essence is written from a sort of historical viewpoint. In one sequence Huxley presents the New Zealand Rediscovery Expedition landing on what it believes to be a totally uninhabited America. It is February 20, 2108. New Zealanders have not travelled anywhere for over a century due to the radioactive condition of the rest of the world. This puts the destruction one may call World War III in the late twentieth or early twenty-first century. Because of its geographic isolation, New Zealand is the only country that survived the war intact. In a second sequence, Huxley flashes back to battle scenes from World War III and to the meretricious culture of a pre-war America the reader is supposed to recognize as the present. These two sequences are handled in alternating sections which unfortunately fail as effective counterpoint. The World War III scenes seem too heavily satiric and allegoric ('Church and State/Greed and Hate!/ Two Baboon Persons in One Supreme Gorilla'), while the frequent images of 'an almost unruffled sea' and an imperturbable blue sky are blatant symbols of an ignored timelessness or eternity. Ostensibly, *Ape and Essence* pretends to be a film script by a certain William Tallis. Huxley stumbles on the script by accident (it falls off a truck taking papers to the incinerator) and he prints it 'as I found it'. But the core of the novel depends on a comparison of the way the world was destroyed with the way it is being re-discovered.

These two alternating processes are depressingly similar. For one thing, the old America was destroyed by science and is being re-discovered by scientists. Dr. Poole's nickname, 'Stagnant', thus seems to stand not only for his lacklustre emotional life but also for science's contribution to a historical process that is cyclical rather than pro-gressive. The battlefield scenes from World War III show two armies of baboons engaged in combat, each army with a captive Einstein on a leash. The two Einsteins are the last to die and the Narrator, whose voice breaks into the script at frequent intervals, pronounces 'the death by suicide of twentieth-century science'.[12] When Dr. Poole of the Rediscovery Expedition is captured by the race of baboon-like humans who survived the holocaust in America, their chief is overjoyed. He asks Poole if New Zealand has trains, engines, and modern scientific conveniences. When Poole replies affirmatively, the Chief exclaims: 'Then you can help us to get it all going again.' Even Poole's objection that he is only a biologist who studies plant life fails to dampen the Chief's enthusiasm. 'War plants?' he asks hopefully.

After Poole is forcibly conducted to this primitive society's main base, the device of the familiar-unfamiliar takes over. Los Angeles has become a ghost town, and the main occupation of the surviving Americans is scavenging in graveyards for clothes there are no longer any factories to produce. Books are transported from the nearby Public Library to provide fuel for bakery ovens.

From the Arch-Vicar, a high-ranking member of the society's eunuch priesthood, Poole learns that the causes of World War III were all the things the reader will remember Huxley castigating in his essays of the 1930s and 40s. *Ape and Essence*, though written later, is less futuristic than *Brave New World* and more Orwellian. Throughout *Ape and Essence*, Huxley operates from the premise that an Orwellian vision of the future may be more reliable than his own, and he tries to envision what will happen to his own positive concerns in an Orwellian world. Before Mustapha Mond's society came into being, struggles such as the 'famous British Museum massacre' took place. Pre-war America was in a similarly restive state, only the war that followed there had more destructive consequences. Huxley realizes that overpopulation, for example, may lead to World War III before it will occasion controlled breeding, although it may eventually cause the latter also. Before World War III, as *Ape and Essence* makes clear, there were in fact too many people for too little food.[13]

Also responsible for World War III were the false utopian ideals represented by Progress (the theory that utopia lies ahead and ideal ends justify abominable means) and Nationalism (the theory that the state one lives in is utopia and the only true deity).[14] Here the echoes of essays in *An Encyclopedia of Pacifism* and in *Ends and Means* are unmistakable. 'As I read history,' says the Arch-Vicar, 'it's like this. Man putting himself against Nature, the Ego against the Order of Things. Belial... against the Other One.' Thus egotism, Huxley's perennial enemy, also played a significant part. In fact, the ego has been objectified by the surviving Americans as the Devil himself and worshipped accordingly. The priests wear horns instead of mitres and 'May you never be impaled on His Horns' becomes a form of well-wishing.

Undercutting the simian antics of all Poole meets are the Narrator's recurring lines: 'But man, proud man,/Drest in a little brief authority –/Most ignorant of what he is most assured. His glassy essence – like an angry ape,/Plays such fantastic tricks before high heaven/As make the angels weep.' The lines, originally spoken by Isabella in *Measure for Measure* (II, ii, 117–122), clearly emphasize the choices as retrogression or devolution as opposed to recognition in man of an inherent spiritual principle ('glassy essence'), which Sebastian

Barnack of *Time Must Have a Stop* would call the Atman.

Nowhere does the choice the society of *Ape and Essence* has made become so evident as in the yearly ritual that includes Belial Eve and Belial Day. These occasions comprise the annual mating season, a brief orgiastic respite from an otherwise total sexual repression. Where *Brave New World* sanctioned promiscuity, *Ape and Essence* enforces continence for most of the year. All women conceive at about the same time and most children are born during one period some nine months later. Purification Day, on which all babies born with deformities due to radioactivity are systematically destroyed, is made possible by a controlled breeding period not unlike what Plato recommends in his *Republic* (v) and by the almost simultaneous births that result. For the Belial Day ceremonies, the women discard the 'NO' patches sewn onto their breasts and buttocks. In effect, humans now have the same breeding habits as animals, 'sex has become seasonal', and, as the Narrator remarks, the 'female's chemical compulsion to mate has abolished courtship, chivalry, tenderness, love itself'.

Fortunately, Dr. Poole, a bachelor at thirty-eight, arrives in time for the annual orgy. Unfortunately, he is the typical Huxley male (such as Rivers in *The Genius and the Goddess* or Jeremy Pordage in *After Many a Summer Dies the Swan*), a man who was bullied by his mother and is still intimidated by his own desires. He 'has spent half a lifetime surreptitiously burning'. He has never been able to bring himself to do what the eighteen-year-old Loola and her society must force themselves to stop. Neither he nor she, as representatives of their respective societies, can manage physical and emotional relationships. Neither the unlimited intercourse of *Brave New World*, an extreme extension of the new sexual freedom of the 1920s, nor the total repression of *Ape and Essence*, a novel whose society is as anti-love as that of *1984*, can produce the balance of body and mind sought by Philip and Elinor Quarles in *Point Counter Point*. In the course of the annual orgy, however, Alfred Poole and Loola discover in each other something akin to old-fashioned love. This is, however, an odd event, even in a distopia, from which to date one's hopes for a better humanity and it is here the novel's major weakness lies. Out of this ludicrous couple Huxley must create the future of the human race. He must transform Alfred Poole from Denis Stone of *Crome Yellow* into Anthony Beavis of *Eyeless in Gaza*.

Although the transformation does take place, it is hardly credible.

Loola's vapid 'Alfie, I believe I shall never want to say Yes to anyone except you' is followed by the Narrator's overwritten reflection:

> And so, by the dialectic of sentiment, these two have rediscovered for themselves that synthesis of the chemical and the personal, to which we give the names of monogamy and romantic love. In her case it was the hormone that excluded the person; in his, the person that could not come to terms with the hormone. But now there is the beginning of a larger wholeness.[15]

Loola escapes the sheer animalism of the mating season and Alfred becomes more human as a result of having behaved like an animal. A sort of balance is restored by the pair and in each of its members. The larger wholeness, the re-ascent to the human level and the possibilities beyond it, becomes the main concern in the scant thirty pages of the novel that remain.

But the novel itself lacks wholeness. Huxley's attempt to blend farce and high seriousness seldom succeeds. Each element works individually as long as one does not think of the other. The scene in which Alfred, several days after the orgy, when constraint is again the rule, cautiously advances towards Loola and the scavengers 'from behind the tomb of Rudolf Valentino' is quite successful. So too with Poole's epiphanic realization, as though he were Anthony Beavis or Sebastian Barnack, of the supernatural reality underlying appearances.[16] But it is impossible to believe these two events involve the same man. Admittedly, in one of his earliest appearances, Poole's intelligence was said to be 'potential, his attractiveness no more than latent', but Shelleyan and mystical tendencies were hardly apparent.

Nevertheless, it is with Shelley and his semi-mystical poetry that Huxley, through Poole's search for the 'larger wholeness', makes his peace in *Ape and Essence*. In *Those Barren Leaves*, Chelifer classified Shelley's poetry as escapism (Part 2, 1) and in *Point Counter Point*, apparently with Huxley's approval, Rampion defined Shelley as a poet filled with 'a bloodless kind of slime' (x). Yet when Poole wishes to dissuade Loola from her allegiance to the restrictive sexual customs practised by the society of *Ape and Essence*, he begins to quote from the volume of Shelley he rescued from the bakery oven in much the same fashion that Huxley salvaged Tallis' script from the incinerator. Thirty-four years earlier, in *Point Counter Point*,

Burlap, and not the hero, would be behaving in this manner. 'We shall become the same, we shall be one/Spirit within two frames, oh! Wherefore two?' Poole asks, quoting *Epipsychidion*. He realizes that making love like human beings 'mightn't always and everywhere be the right thing. But here and now it is – definitely.'[17]

It is a limited ideal, Huxley feels, though it is superior to that held by the rest of society in *Ape and Essence*. Beyond it, perhaps because of it, Poole already perceives something higher. The Narrator perceives it too and asks: 'is there already the beginning of an understanding that beyond *Epipsychidion* there is *Adonais* and beyond *Adonais*, the wordless doctrine of the Pure in Heart?' Presumably so, since the novel concludes with Poole quoting the next to last stanza (54) of *Adonais* in which, for Huxley, the 'Light whose smile kindles the Universe' is 'The fire for which all thirst' or, in other words, the mystic's Divine Ground.

As the novel ends, Loola and Poole are on their way to join an isolated community of 'Hots' near Fresno, a group of individuals too combustible to conform to society's strictures on sex. The Arch-Vicar previously described this settlement to Poole. It is the 'community of exiles' the Savage had no chance to seek. And though it seems preoccupied with sex and may never have heard of 'man's Final End', Poole is now potentially capable of explaining it to them. Soon enough the 'Hots' may find themselves transformed into the Vedanta Society of Southern California.[18]

One recalls that *Ape and Essence* began with a meeting of two script-writers, one of whom is presumably Huxley himself, on the day of Gandhi's assassination. It ends with the emergence, in Tallis' film script, of a new religious leader, thus confirming the incipient mystic Alfred Poole's own statement that the 'Order of Things' always reasserts itself, even if it requires centuries. The description Huxley gives in the opening pages of the novel of Gandhi's Indians 'governing themselves, village by village, and worshipping the Brahman who is also Atman' is perhaps meant as a forecast of the future in store for the 'Hots'. Oddly enough, Gandhi was labelled a reactionary, whereas, according to Sebastian Barnack's outline of life as a progression into the world of spiritual eternity, he was spiritually in the forefront of evolutionary development. Nevertheless, any implied comparison between Alfred Poole and Mahatma Gandhi only accentuates the former's failure to move convincingly from comic butt to mystic hero.

IV

Huxley's final work of fiction, *Island*, is not only a point by point reply to *Brave New World* but a successful replay of an opportunity bungled by society in *Ape and Essence*. The Arch-Vicar, pleased to be living in the worst of possible worlds, admits it almost became the best. If Eastern mysticism and Western science had only modified one another, says the Arch-Vicar, if Eastern art had refined Western energy while Western individualism tempered Eastern totalitarianism, 'it would have been the kingdom of heaven'.[19] Whereas the devil-worshipping Arch-Vicar 'shakes his head in pious horror' at the thought of such a utopia, Huxley attempts to bring it to life in *Island*.

Perhaps the central fact behind Pala's survival and success in a hostile world is the union of East and West it represents. It is thus, as Philip Quarles would be pleased to note, a blend of contrasting viewpoints out of which a total picture has resulted. The novel relates how Dr. Andrew MacPhail, stranded in India in the late nineteenth century, was hastily summoned to Pala to treat its Raja for an apparently incurable tumour (VII). Drawing on the revolutionary 'animal magnetism' techniques of a certain Professor Elliotson, MacPhail effects an impossible cure and stays on as a sort of prime minister. The Scottish doctor and the Palanese king, 'the Calvanist-turned atheist and the pious Mahayana Buddust', represent Western knowledge and Eastern religion. They are a pair 'of complementary temperaments', Huxley writes, and they soon teach one another 'to make the best of both worlds – the Oriental and the European, the ancient and the modern'. Unlike Denis and Mary in *Crome Yellow* or Lord Edward and Webley in *Point Counter Point*, the doctor and the Raja are not parallel lines each of which ignores the other's viewpoint. Neither finds his outlook, whether scientific or religious, completely sufficient. Instead, the pair bring about what Huxley considers the perfect synthesis. They accomplish a fusion that the Arch-Vicar would deplore but which every Vedantist believes is the key to a utopian future.

To the West Swami Vivekananda and the Ramakrishna Order of Vedanta preached the need for spiritual experience. To the East they recommended social improvements and Western know-how.[20] For the Vedantist, the perennial philosophy of Vedanta is 'a potential bridge between science and religion' because its notion of a higher form of consciousness, called God or Brahman, underlying the world's diversity, is 'largely in accord with the latest theories of astronomy and atomic physics'.[21] Pala is the Vedantist's paradise, a working out in fiction of what Huxley and his mystic-oriented co-religionists feel is the best possible programme for tomorrow. Modern Pala, as a society, holds to the perennial philosophy. Where William Morris presented a nation of medieval craftsmen, Huxley offers an island of mystics. The society composed entirely of Alphas that Mustapha Mond of *Brave New World* says failed miserably (XVI), here succeeds. The Palanese are of many different capacities intellectually, but they are all Alphas spiritually; and not even the sham mystics, such as the Rani or the industrialist, Joe Aldehyde, can offset their attractiveness.

Mysticism and utopian thought are less far apart than one might suppose. Where the latter wishes to build the best possible civilization in this world, the former insists that one can have a taste of eternal life while still in the temporal-physical order. Both seek to transform the present into their respective ideas of what constitutes its most elevated state. From Huxley's earlier point of view, however, the writer of the Wells or Bellamy caliber is entertaining a 'compensatory dream', an unrealizable and unnecessary ideal, whereas the Huxley of *Island* is neither dreaming nor contradicting his earlier self. The myna birds that cover Pala and keep repeating 'Attention', 'here and now', or 'Compassion', are continual reminders that one must seek the ultimate reality of union with the Divine Ground. Ultimate reality, which countless mystics claim to have experienced, cannot be synonymous, Huxley would no doubt contend, with compensatory dream.

What *Island* represents is Huxley's heroic attempt to reconcile science, sex, and religion, three items that have always been at odds in all of his fiction, especially the previous utopias. *Brave New World* was built by the first and the happiness of its inhabitants depended on an unlimited supply of the second, but religion was essentially absent. *Ape and Essence* contained a society that was destroyed by science and that had, as a result, perverse forms of religion and sex. Perhaps it is more correct to say Huxley, in *Island*, is endeavouring to create a religious society wherein both science and sex – towards each of which he has certain antipathies – will have an undisputed place. His method of integrating these three elements is to make both science and sex somewhat religious. Thus Dr. MacPhail, the direct descendant of Dr. Andrew, personifies the two strains that originally went into the making of Pala and is a physician-scientist as well as a virtual guru to the visiting Will Farnaby. And the Palanese practice *maithuna* (VI) or 'the yoga of love', in which the goal is as much spiritual as physical, a combination of mystical awareness and sensual satisfaction.[22]

What is less easy to detect (but no less relevant) is that Huxley has also made religion somewhat scientific and sensual. In *The Mystics of the Church*, Evelyn Underhill once defined mysticism as 'the science of the Love of God' and Vedanta unabashedly insists mysticism is a sort of experiment wherein, if one follows the teaching of past mystics, one can approach by determinable stages to a knowledge of the Infinite. Indeed, the moksha-medicine that Will takes (a commendable replacement for the escapist drug, soma, in *Brave New World*) gives him what Huxley himself, in *Heaven and Hell*, claims to have had: a scientifically-induced spiritual experience that Huxley believes to be genuine, even if the more traditional-minded students of mysticism would object. The Palanese call this drug the 'reality revealer', the 'truth-and-beauty-pill' (IX). The scientific validity and indestructability of this mystic experience is asserted by Will in an almost Gradgrindian manner: 'the fact remained and would remain always . . . the fact that the ground of all being could be totally manifest . . . the fact that there was a light and that this light was also compassion' (XV).

The ultimate scientific sanction, however, is Huxley and Sebastian Barnack's notion that mystic awareness is the eventual goal of the evolutionary process, that one moves from animal eternity to time to spiritual eternity. The Vedanta-oriented essays of Christopher Isherwood and Swami Prabhavananda overflow with similar assurances, as do those of Gerald Heard. Heard insists that 'the end of evolution is not the creation of bigger and more complicated societies and more elaborate economic structures but the attainment of a higher and intenser form of consciousness'.[23] Sexually, the union with the Divine Ground is celebrated by mystics such as Jacob Boehme and St. John of the Cross as a fusion more intense and liberating than any purely physical experience. It results, Huxley contends, in a loss of self and a simultaneous accession of being that are incomparably greater than any two lovers, even the Birkin and Ursula of *Women in Love*, whom Huxley once admired, can attain.

Huxley's utopian trilogy also involves three different attempts by society to cope with Huxley's (and the Vedantist's) primary enemy: the ego. Mustapha Mond's society sanctioned a false escape from the narrowness of egotism by encouraging unlimited fornication and soma holidays. Only in a physical sense does everyone belong to everyone else. The society that bravely survives in *Ape and Essence* spurred on its own downfall by opposing the ego to the Order of Things. Only *Island*, as a society of mystics, has found the way to transcend the ego, to discover, as did Anthony Beavis in *Eyeless in Gaza*, the Atman in each individual. More so than any other utopia, Pala claims to be a bridge between this world and the next, to be, almost literally, heaven on earth.

Even more important to Huxley than the fusion of science, sex, and religion, however, is the attempt in *Island* to rewrite *Brave New World*, to redress the picture of the future he previously offered with one that is positive and Vedantic. Viewed from the vantage point of *Island*, in which many of the questions Huxley raised in 1932 are revived and updated, *Brave New World* is seen as a society that confronted the right problems but with the wrong answers. *Island* is also an effort to consolidate ideas previously expressed in numerous essays, such as those in *Ends and Means* (1937), *The Perennial Philosophy* (1945), *Tomorrow and Tomorrow and Tomorrow* (1956), and *Brave New World Revisited* (1958). Huxley is bent on showing how all of his previous recommendations, both social and moral, coalesce into a viable whole. *Island* is truly the summation of most of Huxley's writing since *Brave New World*.

There is scarcely an event, attitude, or programme in *Brave New World* that does not find what Huxley considers its more commendable counterpart in *Island*. The needs and trends from which *Brave New World* resulted must be reconciled with Vedanta or Huxley's own life and thought will be split and disconnected. Thus where the Director of Hatcheries and Conditioning uses hypnopaedia (sleep-teaching) (II), a Palanese educator, Mrs. Narayan, implements a system that teaches short cuts to memorizing: 'One starts by learning how to experience twenty seconds as ten minutes, a minute as half an hour' (XIII). The children are taught a method of speed-learning instead of being brain-washed in their sleep. The method is as much spiritual as educational since it gives the practitioner a means of escaping briefly from time and space limitations, a taste, as it were, of the eternal.

Nowhere in Pala is specialization or narrowness condoned in any form. A major rule of Palanese education is 'Never give children a chance of imagining that anything exists in isolation', teach them 'Balance, give and take, no excesses' because 'it's the rule in nature' (XIII). Every course the children take 'is punctuated by periodical bridge-building sessions' (XIII) that Paul de Vries of *Time Must Have a Stop* would envy. Quarles wished to present reality from all the 'various aspects – emotional, scientific, economic, religious, metaphysical' (XXII); and every subject in Palanese schools is considered 'as a fact of aesthetic or spiritual experience as well as in terms of science or history or economics'. What Quarles recommends in *Point Counter Point*, the Palanese practice. For them, a confrontation between the scientist, Lord Edward, and the politician, Webley, could not result in mutually impenetrable viewpoints.

Where the Deltas and Epsilons of *Brave New World* are animated Pavlovian experiments trained to do one job only, the Palanese are thoroughly familiar with Jung's theories about psychological types and with the Sheldonian classifications Huxley admires.[24] Pala provides the way of devotion for extroverts, the way of self-knowledge for introverts, and the way of disinterested action for muscular, athletic individuals (XIII). Children are divided into groups by temperament and then into a given group, such as that of introverts, some extroverts and muscle-men are introduced. Tolerance is encouraged. *Brave New World*, by contrast, was the logical outcome, engineered by science, of the society seen in all of Huxley's early novels: a society of egoists each of whom could only tolerate his own one-pointed preoccupation and lived in a private world. *Island* is thus an attempt to abolish the targets Huxley has satirized throughout his novels. The Palanese oppose their openness to the many forms of narrowness and exclusiveness Mustapha Mond's society thrived on. Even as adults, the Palanese are forced to specialize as little as possible and then only in the jobs (not job) best suited to their talents. Though he laughed at the idea when it appeared in Wells, Huxley has the Palanese exchange jobs repeatedly, moving, as in Vijaya Bhattacharya's case, from a scientific lab to a position chopping wood.

A complete list of parallel situations in *Brave New World* and *Island* would cover several pages. The Solidarity Service in *Brave New World* (v), for example, and the Purification Day ceremonies of

Ape and Essence are unsatisfactory variations of the ritual in which young Palanese get their first taste of the moksha-medicine (x). Where the infantile adults of *Brave New World* play Centrifugal Bumble-puppy and the children indulge in rudimentary sexual games, Palanese youngsters receive a sound sexual training. The rather adult infants of Pala also play such informative but possibly boring games as Psychological Bridge and Evolutionary Snakes and Ladders (xiii).

The scene in *Brave New World* wherein Linda, the Savage's mother, dies from soma addiction in the midst of indifferent, death-conditioned youngsters is balanced by the death of Dr. MacPhail's wife in *Island*. The Palanese are also death-conditioned, but for them this means being prepared to 'go on practising the art of living even while they're dying' (xiv). Like the deceased Eustace Barnack in *Time Must Have a Stop*, the dying Lakshmi is conscious of the presence of a light. She, however, does not refuse to be absorbed into it. The entire death scene, including Susila MacPhail's advice to the dying woman, is almost a direct dramatization of the moment of death as described in the 'Tibetan Book of the Dead'.[25]

Huxley was not satirizing the society of *Brave New World* for tampering with the family, using drugs to expand consciousness, or for controlling the breeding process. Nor was he opposed to taking the utmost care in matching the individual with the position most suited to his capabilities. The Palanese do all these things, but in a manner Huxley can approve of because it is neither impersonally scientific nor inhumanly mechanical. It is all done by humane means in the light of what Huxley takes to be man's Final End, not to promote a stagnant hedonism such as that of Mustapha Mond's world. Vijaya and Shanta's youngest child, for example, is the product of artificial insemination and should have some of the characteristics of his real father, the painter Gobind Singh (xii). The artist has been dead for years, but his seed has been preserved by a process called, somewhat grotesquely, Deep Freeze. By similar experiments in eugenics, the practical Palanese plan to raise their average IQ to 115 within a century. Although science and the centralized government of brave new world society were hand in hand, it is the decentralized world of MacPhail, foreshadowed in 'Centralization and Decentralization' in *Ends and Means*, that seems to have co-ordinated science and unlimited progress.

Huxley was not totally unsympathetic to the unfavourable opinion that *Brave New World* had of motherhood and family life. His novels show he regards both as possible barriers to the child's development. Jeremy Pordage of *After Many a Summer Dies the Swan*, Rivers of *The Genius and the Goddess*, and even Mark Rampion in *Point Counter Point* suffered under domineering mothers. Murugan, the future Raja of Pala, is also the victim of possessive motherhood in the person of the Rani. Pala, however, has what Huxley considers a saner solution to the inadequacies of the family system in its Mutual Adoption Clubs, an arrangement not unlike the revision of the family Plato advocated in Book v of his *Republic*. Any child in difficulty at home (or causing difficulty) can temporarily move or be moved into any of the other nineteen families in the club his family belongs to (VII). This prevents parental tyranny and discourages the formation of strong family ties on anything but a wide, social basis. Mustapha Mond talked of older societies as being exclusive and narrow, but the Palanese family system, like all of Pala, is, in Susila MacPhail's words, 'not exclusive . . . but inclusive.'

Thus in many respects the ends of *Brave New World* society and those of Pala are similar, but the all-important means are invariably different. Both societies have heard Malthus' warnings, but Pala does not respond by severing all connection between sex and pro-creation. Throughout *Island* Huxley attempts to reconsider the trends he uncovered in *Brave New World* and come up with answers to them that he and his fellow Vedantists will be able to live with.

Huxley's first two utopias are therefore extensions of previous visions. *Brave New World* is the society of mutually intolerant egotists in Huxley's first four novels pushed to its logical extreme. The world of *Ape and Essence* is an extension of the simian existence of Jo Stoyte and the Fifth Earl in *After Many a Summer Dies the Swan*. Yet *Island* is not really a universalization of the wisdom attained by Anthony Beavis in *Eyeless in Gaza*. Although Huxley's first utopia deals with England and the second with America, the third is literally nowhere. It is much more imaginary and it is not world-wide. Huxley could comfortably predict the destruction of Europe and America, but at the end of his life, could only foresee social and spiritual salvation for small, isolated communities. Outside these communities, surrounding them, the worlds of Mustapha Mond and the Arch-Vicar still exist. As Bahu, Rendang's ambassador, realizes, Pala can stay alive only as long as it remains deliberately out of touch with the rest of the contaminated world (v). Huxley's essays, such as 'Ozymandias, the Utopia that Failed' in *Tomorrow and Tomorrow and Tomorrow*, reveal his preoccupation with small, marginal groups (monasteries, Quaker settlements) and indicate that *Island* is possibly the only literary utopia partially based on what its author learned from actual utopian experiments past and present. But where many previous utopias, when not world-wide, felt certain they could exercise a beneficial influence, Pala regards the rest of the world as an encroaching insane asylum.

Only to readers familiar with Huxley's two previous utopias and with his perennial concerns will his final, Herculean attempt at resolution and synthesis be fully apparent. But although Pala is the only one of Huxley's utopias, and possibly the only positive literary utopia, that one would choose to live in, *Island*, considered as a work of literature, is scarcely successful. It resolves the problems faced by Huxley's previous utopian societies but it contains, as literature, nearly all the flaws of positive utopias mentioned earlier in the discussion of affirmative and negative utopias. The book is a novel only by courtesy of definition. It brings Huxley's life-long struggle with the dramatic requirements of the novel, even if one amends this to discussion-novel-of-ideas, to an unsuccessful conclusion. Its plot, wherein Will gradually discovers Pala's value and is in the midst of his first mystical experience at the moment Col. Dipa of Rendang stages his military coup, is the book's weakest aspect. This is the only novel of ideas Huxley wrote in which the plot gets in the way of ideas that are sufficiently interesting in themselves and that suffer from indifferent dramatization.

It is hard to believe in the efficacy of Pala's system when the plot of the novel shows the Palanese failing to convert (or at least neutralize) Murugan, their future Raja. The young man remains an unshaken egoist (v), fails to respond to sex education, is a latent homosexual and the victim of his mother's sham spiritualism. He becomes an unintentional symbol of human nature's ability to become perverse despite the influence of the most ideal environment. In a society of non-attached people, his favourite reading is a Sears, Roebuck and Co. catalogue (IX). He insists he will 'get this place modernized' (v) as soon as he is old enough to rule. He reminds one of a Sebastian Barnack who will never grow up.

No genuinely religious society, however utopian and pacifist, would tolerate the Rani's plans to lease Pala's hitherto unworked oil concessions to the caricature of a capitalist that Huxley calls Joe Aldehyde. Murugan's mother, the Rani, fully intends to ruin a utopia to finance her so-called 'Crusade of the Spirit', a movement that is supposed to 'save Humanity from self-destruction' (v). In a society of fully developed mystics, she recalls Mr. Barbacue-Smith of *Crome Yellow* with his *Pipe-Lines to the Infinite*. It is impossible to believe the Rani can be as blind as Huxley makes her or that her society is willing to let her persist in her blindness.

With the aid of Col. Dipa of nearby Rendang, Murugan illegally assumes power before his eighteenth birthday. His and his mother's dream of a Westernized, materialistic country seems about to come true. The Palanese, as pacifists, offer no resistance and Dr. MacPhail is summarily shot. While it is abundantly clear that each of Huxley's last two utopias is written with its predecessor in mind, it is not certain that Pala is to be the final variation. The goals of Col. Dipa and the desires of Murugan seem likely to produce Mustapha Mond's world all over again if they do not produce the Arch-Vicar's first. Murugan advocates 'an intensive programme of industrialization' to make insecticides, for 'If you can make insecticides, you can make nerve gas' (v). One recollects that the two rival armies of baboons in *Ape and Essence* destroyed each other with a type of gas called 'plague-fog'.

If one recalls the smugness of certain Palanese – such as eighteen-year-old Nurse Apu discussing the spiritual quality of orgasms (vi) – the destruction of Pala becomes less difficult to bear. A society in which the ability to practice advanced psychology extends to all the inhabitants including the children cannot be consistently appealing. One is tempted to equate Pala, despite its spiritual maturity, with a magnified Boy Scout Camp, just as *Brave New World* was an enlarged assembly line. The unflagging attention each person pays to his own mental and spiritual development while prescribing for that of all around him seems almost neurotic. The formulas and injections given the bottle-babies in *Brave New World* are haphazard by comparison. Yet Pala does personify a life-style more complete than that found in most positive utopias prior to Huxley's, even if much of Pala's success is explained or simply asserted rather than depicted. As Col. Dipa's tanks roll in, the contrast between what is being destroyed and what will take its place does more than certain parts of the novel can to increase our admiration for Pala. The synthesis of East and West that Vedanta and Huxley both call for is ironically destroyed by the East's desire to become as imperialistic and materialistic as the modern West.

By destroying his own utopia, however, Huxley does not necessarily reveal himself as a cynical salvationist.[26] Usually, the utopia remains and the visitor is somehow forced to return to his own time (as in Morris). Here, Will Farnaby's own time overtakes both him and Pala simultaneously. But the myna birds come out again after the tanks have passed and resume their cries of 'Attention.' The pacifist, Vedantic Palanese will never become the standing army Murugan desires. Pala is no less real now than it was throughout the novel as a province of Huxley's mind. Its very fragility in the face of Dipa's assault is a sort of guarantee to Huxley that it is no charmed, compensatory fantasy but rather a realizable ideal. It is the type of society that the militaristic and materialistic world of Col. Dipa would regard as a genuine threat and which, regardless of its vulnerability, Huxley and Vedanta feel should be the goal for the future.

Despite Pala, however, *Brave New World* remains Huxley's most convincing picture of the future and his best blending of utopian concerns with novelistic format. *Brave New World* is also Huxley's most plausible excuse for writing *Island* as a corrective vision, even if many readers will regard the latter as his 'compensatory dream'.

Notes

PREFACE

1 Edwin Muir, 'Aldous Huxley: The Ultra-Modern Satirist', in Raymond Weaver, ed., *Aldous Huxley: A Collection of Critical and Biographical Studies* (New York, 1929), p. 22. Reprinted from *The Nation*, CXXII (February 10, 1926), 144–145.

2 James Sutherland, *English Satire* (Cambridge, 1962), p. 132. First printed in 1958.

3 An interesting phenomenon inasmuch as the intellectual or higher life is often Huxley's target.

4 Grant Overton, 'Aldous Huxley: The Twentieth Century Gothic', in *Cargoes for Crusoes* (New York, 1924), p. 106.

5 Julian Huxley, ed., *Aldous Huxley: A Memorial Volume* (New York, 1965), p. 17.

6 Robert Lovett and Helen Hughes, *The History of the Novel in England* (New York, 1932), p. 453.

7 The Van Dorens make their remarks in *A Collection of Critical and Biographical Studies*, p. 19. The Van Dorens' essay first appeared in their *American and British Literature since 1890* (New York, 1925), pp. 210–211.

8 Aldous Huxley, ed., *The Letters of D. H. Lawrence* (New York, 1932), p. 765.

9 See M. M. Kirkwood, 'The Thought of Aldous Huxley', *University of Toronto Quarterly*, VI (January, 1937), 189–198.

10 See William York Tindall, 'The Trouble with Aldous Huxley', *American Scholar*, XI (Autumn, 1942), 452–464.
 Tindall's charge that Huxley cannot resist a dominant personality is somewhat corroborated by chapters four and six of this book which treat respectively Huxley's relationships with D. H. Lawrence and Gerald Heard. However, that Huxley is only attracted to those whose position he himself has already approximated and that he always retains a mind of his own should also become apparent.

11 David Daiches, 'Novels of Aldous Huxley', *New Republic*, C (November 1, 1939), p. 365.

12 See R. C. Bald, 'Aldous Huxley as a Borrower', *College English*, XI (January, 1950), 183–187.

13 Huxley wrote the introduction for the Swami's translation of the Bhagavad-Gita and was associated with the Vedanta Society of Southern California.

14 See pp. 75–77 in chapter three below.

15 *Ape and Essence* (New York, 1962), p. 101. Originally published in 1949.

CHAPTER I

1 The title of Huxley's third novel comes from Wordsworth's 'The Tables Turned' and refers to the lives of the characters as well as to the books of

science and art wherein we murder to dissect. Huxley was fond of taking his titles from major poets and borrowed, among others, from Shakespeare, Tennyson, Marlowe, and Milton.

2 *Do What You Will* (London, 1929), p. 234.

3 *Music at Night* (London, 1931), p. 47.

4 Compare this with Keats' statement in a letter to John Hamilton Reynolds for February 3, 1818: 'How beautiful are the retired flowers! how they would lose their beauty were they to throng the highway crying out, "admire me I am a violet! dote on me I am a primrose!" '

5 There is also an oceanic bird called a 'shearwater' that flies close to the waves but never makes contact with them. Huxley is not adverse to tag names, especially esoteric ones (i.e. Mercaptan in *Antic Hay*). Nor can it be accidental that in *Crome Yellow* it is Ivor *Lombard* who successfully lays siege to Mary *Bracegirdle*.

6 Aldous Huxley, *The Olive Tree* (New York, 1937), p. 5. First published 1936.

7 See 'Vulgarity in Literature' in *Music at Night and Other Essays* (London, 1931).

8 Stephen Marcus, *Dickens From Pickwick to Dombey* (New York, 1965), p. 36.

9 Here Dickens and Huxley seem to be on the same side, though Huxley might argue that Podsnap's self-satisfaction, even if it is satirized, does not differ from the self-centredness of Dickens' other characters who are not satirized. Like Dickens, who is harder on egoistic eccentrics in his later novels, Huxley too treated them more and more harshly. Yet even in his early novels, Huxley's caricatures are more malicious than Dickens'.

10 Chelifer's statement recalls Keats' belief that if we all go our own ways intensely enough, we will all arrive at the same point (Letter to John Hamilton Reynolds, February 19, 1818). In Huxley, everyone does go his own way, and the result is parallel lines.

   Several of Huxley's young men recall Keats: Chelifer, of course, and also Sebastian Barnack of *Time Must Have a Stop*. In *Point Counter Point* (VI), Philip Quarles possesses a certain approximation of negative capability but is as much a failure as Gumbril Jr., who dreams, in *Antic Hay* (I), of being able to identify with others but never succeeds.

   Many of the major Romantic poets leave some impression on Huxley's novels. It is Shelley (as well as Keats) that Chelifer discusses (Part 2, I), Mark Rampion castigates in *Point Counter Point* (X), and Alfred Poole, in *Ape and Essence*, admires. When Calamy reappears as Anthony Beavis in *Eyeless in Gaza* (I), Beavis is also a re-incarnation of Chelifer for he initially shares Chelifer's dislike (Part 2, III–IV) for Wordsworth's feeling that one's life is a continuum that makes the child the father of the man. The story of Beavis is thus the transformation of Chelifer into another Calamy. Behind certain facets of Quarles' theory of the novel (XIX), one suspects the influence of Blake, whom Rampion calls the last complete man (IX).

11 A. C. Ward, *The Nineteen-Twenties* (London, 1930), p. 201.

12 Sean O'Faolain, 'The Fervent Twenties', *The Vanishing Hero* (New York, 1956), p. xxix.

NOTES

13 Frank Swinnerton, *The Georgian Scene* (New York, 1934), p. 332.

14 See Alan Pryce-Jones, 'The Frightening Pundits of Bloomsbury', *Listener* (March 1, 1951), pp. 345–347 and V. S. Pritchett, 'Private Voices and Public Life', *Listener* (March 8, 1951), p. 374.

15 Most of the information in this and the following paragraph comes from Chapter VIII of Holbrook Jackson's *The Eighteen Nineties* (New York, 1913).

16 *On the Margin* (London, 1948), p.25. First published in 1923.

17 *Texts and Pretexts* (New York, 1962), p. 52. First published in 1933.

18 *The Olive Tree*, p. 42.

19 Charles Rolo, in his Introduction to *The World of Aldous Huxley* (New York, 1947), p. xix, notes that Walter Bidlake is still a mama's boy, Webley is still playing soldier; and Lucy pulls the legs off flies (men), while Burlap bathes with Beatrice as though the two of them were still infants.

20 *The Letters of D. H. Lawrence*, p. 791.

21 Thus one implication of the novel's title is that many of the characters have stopped time by refusing to grow up. They remain spiritually retarded.

Also of interest, is Gerald Heard's comment in *Vedanta for Modern Man*, ed. by Christopher Isherwood (New York, (1962), p. 438: '. . . so old age cannot be old age, but simply an inability to die, unless it has achieved vision'. First published 1951.

22 *Ape and Essence* (New York, 1962), p. 119.

23 *Music at Night*, p. 90.

24 Rolo, p. xvii.

25 *The Letters of D. H. Lawrence*, p. 724.

26 A line from the poem 'Frascati's' in Huxley's volume of poems entitled *Leda* (1920).

CHAPTER II

1 *On the Margin*, p. 202.

2 *Ape and Essence*, p. 36.

3 See Henry Cole, ed., *The Works of Thomas Love Peacock* (London, 1875), I, xxxi.

4 *Do What You Will*, p. 11.

5 The split-men also seem at times to be different sides of Huxley. Quarles is, of course, a fairly direct portrait and Walter Bidlake is patterned on the Huxley who worked for Middleton Murray on the *Athenaeum*.

6 *Jesting Pilate* (New York, 1926), p. 174.

7 *Ibid.*, p. 241.

8 See *Proper Studies* (London, 1949), p. 197. First published 1927.

9 Frederick Hoffman, 'Aldous Huxley and the Novel of Ideas', in William Van O'Connor, ed., *Forms of Modern Fiction* (Bloomington, Indiana, 1959), p. 190.

10 *The Letters of D. H. Lawrence*, p. 766.

11 *Ends and Means* (New York, 1937), p. 14.

12 *Texts and Pretexts*, p. 40.

13 *Themes and Variations* (London, 1954), p. 52. First published in 1950.
14 This Sanskrit formula is more fully explained in *The Perennial Philosophy* (I). For Huxley's views on mysticism, see the essays in *The Perennial Philosophy*, 'Readings in Mysticism' in Christopher Isherwood, ed. *Vedanta for the Western World* (London, 1948), *Grey Eminence* (1941) (especially III), *The Devils of Loudun* (1952) (particularly the second section of III), and 'Variations on a Philosopher' in *Themes and Variations* (1950). Also consult, in the Isherwood volume, Gerald Heard's 'The Philosophia Perennis'.
15 *Ends and Means*, p. 7.
16 *Themes and Variations*, p. 114.
17 *Ape and Essence*, p. 6.
18 *Texts and Pretexts*, p. 59.
19 *Proper Studies*, p. 47.
20 *Music at Night*, pp. 12–13.
21 *The Genius and the Goddess* (New York, 1963), p. 58. First published in 1955.
22 *Ends and Means*, p. 277.
23 Robert Humphries, *Stream of Consciousness in the Modern Novel* (Berkeley and Los Angeles, 1965), pp. 5, 14.
24 See Virginia Woolf, 'Modern Fiction' in Mark Schorer, ed., *Modern British Fiction* (New York, 1961), p. 7. Reprinted from *The Common Reader* (1925).
25 Humphries, p. 51.
26 *Along the Road* (London, 1948), pp. 32–36. First published in 1925.
27 This Hypothesis is outlined in *The Perennial Philosophy*, p. vii, and again by Sebastian Barnack in *Time Must Have a Stop* (xxx).

CHAPTER III

1 In *Aldous Huxley: A Memorial Volume*, p. 30, T. S. Eliot informs us that Crome is patterned on the house of Lady Ottoline Morrell at Garsington. Some of Lady Ottoline's guests, Eliot claims, appear in *Crome Yellow*. The guest-list at Garsington often included Bertrand Russell, Lytton Strachey, D. H. and Frieda Lawrence, Katherine Mansfield, and John Middleton Murry. Priscilla Wimbush is Lady Ottoline, Mr. Scogan is either H. G. Wells or Norman Douglas, Mary is Dora Carrington, Gombauld is Mark Gertler, and Jenny is Dorothy Brett.
2 See *Ends and Means*, p. 44, where Huxley argues that international chaos results because egoistic nations plan their policies solely from their own point of view.
3 In *The Devils of Loudun* (New York, 1965), p. 102 (first published 1952), Huxley notes that 'other people can see through us just as easily as we can see through them. The discovery of this fact is apt to be exceedingly disconcerting'.
4 Not only does Myra resemble Brett and Margot, two *femmes fatales* of the 1920s, but she also contrasts satirically with E. M. Forster's Mrs. Wilcox and Mrs. Moore, two highly sensitive, mystical women, and with Mrs. Woolf's Clarissa Dalloway and Mr. Ramsay.

5 For similarities between Lypiatt and Haydon, compare Casmir with the Haydon who appears in Huxley's introduction to *The Autobiography and Memoirs of Benjamin Haydon* (New York, 1926). Reprinted in *The Olive Tree* as 'B. R. Haydon'. To compare Gumbril Sr. and Wren, see the essay written for Wren's bi-centenary in *On the Margin* (1923). Wren is praised as a master of 'proportion', a quality Huxley's characters lack.

6 Another barrier Gumbril erects against life – and it too is a sign of his inability to make connections – is the stream of unrelated facts he can set flowing any time. Philip Quarles also has this encyclopedic facility (VI), as does Uncle Spencer in the story named after him in *Little Mexican and Other Stories* (London, 1924). Here again Huxley has himself in mind. In *Along the Road*, p. 71, he professes his fondness for reading a volume of *Encyclopedia Britannica* while on his travels.

7 *Texts and Pretexts*, p. 296.

8 'Two or Three Graces' is really a long short story or a novella. It was published along with three other stories in New York and London as *Two or Three Graces* in 1926.

9 This entire chapter, 'Du Côté de Chez Todd', suggests Dickens has a purely emotional effect on his readers, never a practical or permanent one.

10 As frequently happens in Huxley, a subject treated in the novels also appears in the essays, or *vice versa*. For more on Huxley's criticism of Dickens, see 'Vulgarity in Literature' in *Music at Night and Other Essays* (London, 1931).

CHAPTER IV

1 *The Olive Tree*, p. 231. The essay on Lawrence in *The Olive Tree* is a reprint of Huxley's Introduction to his edition of Lawrence's letters.

2 See *The Letters of D. H. Lawrence* (New York, 1932), p. 765. Subsequent references to this volume are included in the text.

3 William York Tindall, *Forces in Modern British Literature: 1885–1956* (New York, 1956), p. 172.

4 Diana Trilling, ed. *The Selected Letters of D. H. Lawrence* (New York, 1958), p. xxxiii.

5 John Hawley Roberts, 'Huxley and Lawrence', *Virginia Quarterly Review*, XIII (Autumn, 1937), 546.

6 John Atkins, *Aldous Huxley: A Literary Study* (London, 1956), p. 133.

7 Edward Nehls, *D. H. Lawrence: A Composite Biography* (Madison, 1958), III, 182, 291.

8 Richard Aldington, *D. H. Lawrence: Portrait of a Genius But . . .* (New York, 1961), p. 321. Originally published 1950.

9 See Lawrence's letter to William Gerhardi (November 14, 1928), quoted in Nehls, III, 265.

10 Compare *Point Counter Point* (X, XVI, XXI, XXXIV) with *Women in Love* (VIII, XXIII, XXX), *Aaron's Rod* (IX, XX, XXI), and *Lady Chatterley's Lover* (VII).

11 Mark Spilka, *The Love Ethic of D. H. Lawrence* (Bloomington, Indiana, 1955), p. 10. See also Julian Moynahan on Gerald Crich in *The Deed of Life* (Princeton, 1963), p. 84.

12 This is the observation of David J. Gordon in *D. H. Lawrence as a Literary Critic* (New Haven, Connecticut, 1966), p. 43.

13 See, for example, *Twilight in Italy* (New York, 1962), p. 50. Originally published in 1915.

14 See Huxley's 'Tragedy and the Whole Truth' in *Music at Night* (1931) and Gordon's treatment of Lawrence's life-long quarrel with tragedy, pp. 75–95.

15 *Two or Three Graces*, p. 23. The novella gives its title to the entire volume of stories.

16 See 'The Farcical History of Richard Greenow' in *Limbo* (1920). This story is discussed in chapter one.

17 Gordon, p. 9.

18 *Ibid.*, p. 62.

19 *Ibid.*,

20 Quoted from E. and A. Brewster, *Reminiscences and Correspondence of D. H. Lawrence*, p. 166, by Father William Tiverton in *D. H. Lawrence and Human Existence* (London, 1951), p. 80.

21 The first printed record of this statement is in Lawrence's letter to Ernest Collings for January 17, 1913 (*Letters*, p. 96).

22 Tiverton's view is presumably based on statements such as those in 'Indians and an Englishman' in *Selected Essays* (London, 1950), p. 197. Yet one must also consult *Twilight in Italy* (New York, 1962), p. 56 and Lawrence's 'Introduction to His Paintings' in *Selected Essays*, pp. 307–308. Most of all, one had best consult the novels themselves. Incidentally, the frontispiece to Father Tiverton's book is Lawrence's sketch of himself as Pan (note the pointed ears). He sees himself with the same sort of 'undying Pan face' he gives Cipriano.

23 *Beyond the Mexique Bay* (New York, 1960), p. 259. First published in 1934.

24 *Do What You Will*, p. 72.

25 *The Olive Tree*, p. 232.

26 *Beyond the Mexique Bay*, p. 104.

27 *Ibid.*, p. 208.

28 *Ibid.*, p. 261.

29 *The Olive Tree*, p. 232.

30 *Ibid.*, p. 236.

31 *Ibid.*, p. 229.

32 For a fine treatment of Murry's strengths and absurdities, see F. A. Lea's *John Middleton Murry* (London, 1960).

33 *Beyond the Mexique Bay*, p. 208.

CHAPTER V

1 Knud Jeppesen, *Counterpoint: The Polyphonic Vocal Style of the Sixteenth Century*, trans. by Glen Haydon (Englewood Cliffs, New Jersey, 1965), p. xi. Originally published in 1931.

NOTES

2 Walter Piston, *Counterpoint* (New York, 1947), p. 9.

3 Arthur Tillman Merritt, *Sixteenth-Century Polyphony: A Basis for the Study of Counterpoint* (Cambridge, Mass., 1939), p. 124.

4 *Ibid.*, p. 3.

5 Jeppesen, p. 83.

6 *Literature and Science* (New York, 1963), p. 18.

7 'Shakespeare and Religion' (1964) in Julian Huxley, ed., *Aldous Huxley: A Memorial Volume* (New York, 1965), p. 174.

8 Swami Nikhilananda, 'The Meaning of God', in Christopher Isherwood, ed., *Vedanta for Modern Man* (New York, 1962), p. 114. First published in 1951.

9 Swami Saradananda, 'Work and Worship', *Vedanta for Modern Man*, p. 103.

10 *The Doors of Perception* (1954) and *Heaven and Hell* (1956) (New York, 1963), pp. 50–51.

11 That Huxley admired Gide's novel is evident from Lawrence's reply to a Huxley letter. Gide's book, Lawrence tells Huxley (July, 1927), is not real but done to shock. See *The Letters of D. H. Lawrence*, p. 686.

12 See the 'Journal', trans. by Justin O'Brien and appended to Gide's *The Counterfeiters* (New York, 1955), p. 400. Gide's novel was published in 1925 and the 'Journal' in 1927.

13 Herbert J. Muller, *Modern Fiction: A Study of Values* (New York, n.d.), p. 355. Originally published in 1937.

14 Gide's 'Journal', p. 383.

15 Consult Huxley's opinion of 'talkies' in 'Silence is Golden' from *Do What You Will* (London, 1929). One should also mention the 'feelies' in *Brave New World* (1932), XI. Remarks about the movies are scattered throughout Huxley's works. He later did several film scripts in California and cast *Ape and Essence* (1949) in the form of one.

16 'Shakespeare and Religion', p. 172.

17 *Literature and Science*, pp. 17–18.

18 *On the Margin*, p. 127.

19 See Huxley's Introduction to Morris Philipson's edition of several Huxley essays collected under the title *On Art and Artists* (New York, 1960), pp. 7–8.

CHAPTER VI

1 David Daiches, *The Novel and The Modern World* (Chicago, 1939), p. 210.

2 See *Samson Agonistes*, ll. 38–42.

3 *Ends and Means*, p. 242.

4 *Ibid.*, p. 312.

5 *The Doors of Perception* (1954) and *Heaven and Hell* (1956), p. 14.

6 David Knowles, *The English Mystical Tradition* (New York, 1961), p. 35.

7 'Vulgarity in Literature' in *Music at Night and Other Essays*, p. 286.

8 Christopher Isherwood, 'Hypothesis and Belief' in *Vedanta for the Western World*, p. 37.

9 See William James' comments on mysticism written in 1901–2 in *The Varieties of Religious Experience* (New York, 1960), p. 374: 'The keynote [of the mystical experience] is invariably a reconciliation. It is as if the opposite of the world, whose contradictoriness and conflict make all our difficulties and troubles, were melted into unity.'

10 Prabhavananda's prose in *Vedanta and the West* is simple and homiletic. Heard's essays are more polemical and suggest a sort of Protestant sermon. Huxley's cover all fields and display incredible erudition.

11 *The Genius and the Goddess* (New York, 1963), p. 114.

12 *Ibid.*, p. 5.

13 *Ibid.*, p. 151.

14 *Music at Night and Other Essays*, pp. 72–73, contains a few very similar statements by Huxley himself.

15 The worst example is the following description of Bruno: '. . . the little flame in his heart seemed to expand, as it were, and aspire, until it touched that other light beyond it and within; and for a moment it was still in the timeless intensity of a yearning that was also consummation' (x).

16 The whole question of presenting a saintly hero is interestingly discussed in Christopher Isherwood's 'The Problem of the Religious Novel' in *Vedanta for Modern Man*, pp. 272–276.

17 *The Doors of Perception* and *Heaven and Hell*, p. 26.

CHAPTER VII

1 *Proper Studies* (London, 1949), p. x. First published in 1927.

2 *Music at Night and Other Essays* (London, 1931), p. 122.

3 *Proper Studies*, p. 281.

4 *Ibid.*, p. 136: 'A perfect education is one which trains up every human being to fit the place he or she is to occupy in the social hierarchy, but without, in the process destroying his or her individuality.' It is the last clause that separates Huxley's position from that of *Brave New World*.

5 *Music at Night*, p. 123.

6 *Ibid.*, pp. 254–255.

7 Orwell goes Huxley one better by adding an Appendix in which 'The Principles of Newspeak' are explained. Consider also the slogans of Oceania: War is Peace, Freedom is Slavery; and the definition of orthodoxy as a state in which one need not think. The impact of *Brave New World* on *1984* is too extensive to treat in detail. See G. C. LeRoy, 'A. F. 632 to *1984*', *College English*, XII (December, 1950), 135–138.

8 *Brave New World Revisited* is probably the best re-assessment of *Brave New World* with regard to accuracy of prediction that has been made. There is no sense in repeating what Huxley has already done.

9 Helicopters, according to *Encyclopedia Britannica*, were being used experimentally in the early 1930s, though a dependable model was not developed and produced until 1939 in Germany.

10 See John R. Pierce, 'Communications Technology and the Future' in the invaluable 'Utopia' issue of *Daedalus* (Spring, 1965), pp. 506–517. The entire issue is of immense interest to all who are interested in the concept of utopia.

11 Northrop Frye, 'Varieties of Literary Utopias' in *Daedalus*, p. 324.

12 *Ape and Essence* (New York, 1962), p. 40.

13 See p. 92. Also consult 'The Double Crisis' (shortage of food and increase of population) in *Themes and Variations* (London, 1950) and Anthony Burgess' Malthusian distopia, *The Wanting Seed* (1962).

14 *Ape and Essence*, pp. 94–95.

15 *Ibid.*, p. 122.

16 *Ibid.*, p. 140.

17 *Ibid.*, p. 145.

18 The Vedanta Society of Southern California began publishing its magazine, *Vedanta and the West*, in 1938, approximately the time of Gerald Heard and Aldous Huxley's arrival in America. *Vedanta for the Western World* and *Vedanta for Modern Man* are anthologies from this magazine. Huxley's allegiance is first to the perennial philosophy – the belief that man's Atman is identical to, and can be fused with, God or Brahman – and then to oriental Vedanta as the religion which basically consists of this philosophy and which tolerates all other religions in which that philosophy is at all discernible.

19 *Ape and Essence*, pp. 137–138.

20 See Swami Prabhavananda, 'Sri Ramakrishna and the Religion of Tomorrow' in Christopher Isherwood, ed., *Vedanta for Modern Man*; and Gerald Heard, 'Vedanta as the Scientific Approach to Religion' and 'The Future of Mankind's Religion' in *Vedanta for the Western World*.

21 Isherwood's Introduction to *Vedanta for Modern Man*, p. 13. In 'Vedanta and Western History', p. 27, Heard speaks of 'the transcendent-immanent eternal life that physics has now deduced to be the nature of the universe.' Vedanta's position receives some indirect support from Teilhard de Chardin's *The Phenomenon of Man* (New York, 1959), for which Julian Huxley wrote the introduction. Heard may be the model for Miller, Propter, and Rontini.

22 Maithuna has several similarities to the male continence or *coitus reservatus* practised by the Oneida Community of John Humphrey Noyes. The Community's practice is referred to by name in *Island* (VI). See also Huxley's discussion of 'sexual salvation' in the Appendix of *Tomorrow and Tomorrow and Tomorrow* (New York, 1956).

23 *Vedanta for the Western World*, p. 31. This is also one of the central tenets in Heard's book: *Pain, Sex and Time: A New Outlook on Evolution and the Future of Man* (New York, 1939).

24 Although he attacks Wells for classifying people by mental ability and temperament, Huxley praises Jung's *Psychological Types* in *Proper Studies*, p. 42, and refers to Sheldon's two volumes (*The Varieties of Human Physique*

and *The Varieties of Temperament*) in, among other places, *The Perennial Philosophy* (VIII). In *Island* (XII), he uses some of Sheldon's terminology.

25 See Edward Conze, trans., *Buddhist Scriptures* (Baltimore, 1966), pp. 227–232. The passage from the scriptures is perhaps better than Huxley's dramatization of it.

26 That is the central thesis (applied to the whole Huxley canon) of Sisirkumar Ghose in *Aldous Huxley, A Cynical Salvationist* (London, 1962).

Selected Bibliography

Atkins, John. *Aldous Huxley: A Literary Study*. London, 1965. Revised edition, 1967.

Beach, Joseph W. 'Counterpoint: Aldous Huxley.' *The Twentieth-Century Novel: Studies in Technique*. New York, 1932. See pp. 458–469.

Burgum, Edwin B. 'Aldous Huxley and His Dying Swan.' *The Novel and the World's Dilemma*. New York, 1947. See pp. 140–156.

Clark, Ronald W. *The Huxleys*. New York, 1968.

Daiches, David. *The Novel and the Modern World*. Chicago, 1939.

Duval, Hanson R. *Aldous Huxley: A Bibliography*. New York, 1939.

Eschelbach, Clair and Joyce Lee Shober. *Aldous Huxley: A Bibliography 1916–1959*. Berkeley and Los Angeles, 1961.

Ghose, Sisirkumar. *Aldous Huxley: A Cynical Salvationist*. London, 1962.

Greenblatt, Stephen J. *Three Modern Satirists: Waugh, Orwell, and Huxley*. New Haven, 1965.

Hoffman, Frederick J. 'Aldous Huxley and the Novel of Ideas.' *Forms of Modern Fiction*. Edited by William Van O'Connor. Minneapolis, 1948. See pp. 189–200.

Huxley, Aldous. *The Collected Works of Aldous Huxley*. London, 1946–1951. 23 volumes. Incomplete.

Huxley, Julian, ed. *Aldous Huxley: A Memorial Volume*. Essays by Stephen Spender, T. S. Eliot, Leonard Woolf, Gerald Heard, Christopher Isherwood, and others. New York, 1965.

Huxley, Laura Archera. *This Timeless Moment: A Personal View of Aldous Huxley*. New York, 1968.

Jouguelet, Pierre. *Aldous Huxley*. Paris, 1948.

MacCarthy, Desmond. 'Aldous Huxley.' *Criticism*. London, 1932. See pp. 235–246.

Meckier, Jerome. 'Aldous Huxley: Satire and Structure.' *Wisconsin Studies in Contemporary Literature*, VII (Autumn, 1966), 284–294.

— 'Shakespeare and Aldous Huxley.' Forthcoming in *Shakespeare Quarterly*.

O'Faolain, Sean. 'Huxley and Waugh.' *The Vanishing Hero*. New York, 1956. See pp. 33–69.

Overton, Grant. 'The Twentieth Century Gothic of Aldous Huxley.' *Cargoes for Crusoes*. New York, 1924. See pp. 97–113.

Rogers, Winfield H. 'Aldous Huxley's Humanism.' *Sewanee Review*, XXXXIII (July–September, 1935), 262–272.

Schmerl, Rudolf B. 'The Two Future Worlds of Aldous Huxley.' *PMLA* LXVII (June 1962), 328–334.

Swinnerton, Frank. *The Georgian Scene*. New York, 1934.

Ward, A. C. *The Nineteen-Twenties*. London, 1930.

Watts, Harold. 'Introduction' to the Harpers Classics edition of *Point Counter Point*. New York, 1947.

Waugh, Evelyn, Angus Wilson, Francis Wyndham, John Wain, and Peter Quennell. 'A Critical Symposium on Aldous Huxley.' *London Magazine*, II (August 1955), 51–64.

Weaver, Raymond, ed. *Aldous Huxley: A Collection of Critical and Biographical Studies*. Essays by Weaver, Carl and Mark Van Doren, Edwin Muir, Joseph Wood Krutch, and others. New York, 1929.

Writers at Work: The 'Paris Review' Interviews (second series; New York, 1968). An interview with Huxley, recorded in 1963, occupies pp. 193–214.

Index

INDEX

INDEX

INDEX